Welfare Research

Do we ashis promote
dependence?

Welfare Research:
A Critical Review

Fiona Williams
Jennie Popay
Ann Oakley

First published in 1999 by UCL Press

UCL Press Limited
1 Gunpowder Square
London EC4A 3DE
UK

and

325 Chestnut Street
8th Floor
Philadelphia
PA 19106
USA

The name of University College London (UCL) is a registered trade mark used by
UCL Press with the consent of the owner.

British Library Cataloguing-in-Publication Data
A CIP catalogue record for this book is available from the British Library.

Library of Congress Cataloging-in-Publication Data are available

ISBN: 1-85728-269-8 HB
      1-85728-270-1 PB

Typeset by Graphicraft Limited, Hong Kong.
Printed by T. J. International, Padstow, UK.

Contents

CONTENTS

Acknowledgements

This book is the result of many hours of discussion and debate amongst the seven research teams involved in The Management of Personal Welfare Research Initiative (MPWI). The Initiative was jointly funded by the ESRC and the Rowntree Foundation between 1990 and 1995. Two of the book's editors, Jennie Popay and Ann Oakley, were co-ordinators of the MPWI. They developed the original proposal for this book and negotiated with publishers. Fiona Williams was commissioned to produce one of three literature reviews which were intended to stimulate intellectual debate across the projects in the Initiative. She subsequently became an active participant in the regular meetings of the Initiative and a co-editor of this volume.

The three literature reviews – on the treatment of gender, structural inequalities and measurement issues in welfare research respectively – formed a springboard for the ideas that bind this book together. These ideas were further developed at an International Seminar organized by the Initiative researchers in the Spring of 1993. In addition to this book on welfare research, the research conducted as part of the MPWI has contributed to a sister volume: *Men, Gender Divisions and Welfare*, edited by Jennie Popay, Jeff Hearn and Jeanette Edwards (Routledge 1998).

Many people have made this book possible. Our thanks go to the members of the MPWI Commissioning Group, and in particular to Janet Lewis, Margaret Edmonds and Alan Walker, who supported the funding necessary to sustain a participative co-ordination model for the MPWI and for the production of the literature reviews. Our publishers and contributors should also be thanked for their patience in the face of what may have appeared at times to be editorial inertia. This volume has taken some time to produce, partly because of the scale of commitments amongst our contributors; timetables have also been stretched as the editors have redrafted key parts of the text to keep up with a rapidly transforming public discourse and political context for welfare research, policy and practice.

ACKNOWLEDGEMENTS

Several of the chapters draw on data from the studies funded within the Initiative and our thanks go to the many respondents who made this research possible. The projects include: Responses to Contemporary Change in Britain's Mining Communities, Chas Critcher et al. (X206252004); The Negotiation of Coping: Disablement, Caring and Marriage, Gillian Parker et al. (L206252002); Social Support and the Health and Welfare of Vulnerable Children: A Consumer Study, Ann Oakley et al. (L206252005); Social Support and the Health and Welfare of Vulnerable Children: A Provider Study, Jennie Popay et al. (X206252006); Violence, Abuse and the Stress-Coping Process: Project 1, Women, Jalna Hanmer and Project 2, Men, Jeff Hearn (L206252003).

As with all books, there are also many people who have made a direct, yet invisible, contribution to the production process. These include the administrative staff of our various workplaces, with particular thanks to Carla Warburton for her endless fortitude chasing up and editing numerous drafts, and Gill Fernley, Nicola Doyle and Chris Saunders for various contributions without which the manuscript would not have been completed.

Fiona Williams, Jennie Popay and Ann Oakley

Notes on Contributors

Chas Critcher is Professor of Communications in the Communication, Media and Communities Research Centre at Sheffield Hallam University. He has been researching mining communities for more than a decade. He is the co-author, with David Waddington, of *Flashpoints: Studies in Public Disorder* (London: Routledge, 1989) and *Split At The Seams: Community, Continuity and Change after the 1984–5 Coal Dispute* (Buckingham: Open University Press, 1991) and co-edited with David Waddington *Regeneration of the Coalfield Areas: Anglo-German Perspectives* (London: Pinter, 1995). His other research interests include popular culture and the mass media. He is currently embarking on a study of moral panics about social problems.

Bella Dicks is Lecturer in the School of Comparative and Applied Social Science at the University of Wales, Cardiff, at the School of Social and Administrative Studies. She is currently completing a PhD on heritage and locality based in the Rhondda Valleys. Her current research project is examining the authorizing of ethnographic texts through multi-media. Her research interests focus on locality and the representation of class, community and industry. She has published articles relating to coalmining communities in Yorkshire and Wales.

Jeanette Edwards is Lecturer in Social Anthropology, and director of the MSc in medical social anthropology at the University of Keele. One of her research interests is in kinship, and in particular, cultural understandings of parenthood in late twentieth century Britain. She is co-author with Franklin, Hirsch, Price & Strathern of *Technologies of Procreation: Kinship in the Age of Assisted Conception* (Manchester: Manchester University Press, 1993) and author of several articles on relatedness and new reproductive technologies, and the views of community health and social service providers on the needs of women and their children.

Jalna Hanmer is Professor of Women's Studies and Director of the Research Centre on Violence, Abuse and Gender Relations at Leeds Metropolitan University.

She is currently researching a new approach to policing repeat victimization of women by known men. Her publications include *Well-Founded Fear* (co-authored with Sheila Saunders, London: Hutchinson, 1984); *Women, Violence and Crime Prevention: A Community Study in West Yorkshire* (co-authored with Sheila Saunders, Aldershot, London: Gower, 1993); *Women, Violence and Social Control* (co-edited with Mary Maynard; London: Macmillan, 1987); *Women, Policing and Male Violence: International Perspectives* (co-edited with Jill Radford and Elizabeth Stanko, London: Routledge, 1989) and *Women and Social Work: Towards a Women-Centred Practice* (co-authored with Daphne Statham, London: Macmillan, 1988).

Jeff Hearn is Professorial Research Fellow in the Faculty of Economic and Social Studies, based in the Department of Social Policy and Social Work, University of Manchester, and Visiting Professor in Sociology at Åbo Akademi University, Finland. His publications include *The Gender of Oppression* (Brighton: Wheatsheaf, 1987); *Men, Masculinities and Social Theory* (co-editor with David Morgan, London: Unwin Hyman, 1990), *Men in the Public Eye* (London: Routledge, 1992); *"Sex" at "Work"* (with Wendy Parkin, London: Prentice-Hall, 1995); *Violence and Gender Relations* (co-editor with Barbara Fawcett, Brid Featherstone and Christine Toft, London: Sage, 1996); *Men as Managers, Managers as Men* (co-editor with David Collinson, London: Sage, 1996). He has just completed *The Violences of Men* (Sage) on ESRC research on men's violence to known women, and is currently researching organizations and violence.

Geraldine Macdonald is Professor of Social Work and Applied Social Studies at the School for Policy Studies, University of Bristol. She is also Archie Cochrane Research Fellow at Green College, University of Oxford and Visiting Professor at the Centre for Evidence-based Social Services at the University of Exeter. Her research interests include the evaluation of the effects of social interventions, particularly social work and probation; decision-making in child protection, and ethical issues in social work research and practice. She has recent publications in each of these areas.

Ann Oakley is Professor of Sociology and Social Policy and Director of the Social Science Research Unit at the University of London Institute of Education; she is also Honorary Professor in Social Sciences in the Division of Public Health Medicine at the Institute of Child Health. She has been researching and writing in the fields of gender, the family and health for more than 30 years. Her current research interests include the evaluation of social interventions, the history of gender and methodology, and the scientific basis for screening and treatment in the field of women's health. Among her recent publications are *Social Support and Motherhood* (Oxford: Blackwell, 1992), *Essays on Women, Medicine and Health* (Edinburgh: Edinburgh University Press, 1993), *The Politics of the Welfare State* (co-edited with Susan A. Williams, 1994), *Man and Wife* (London: HarperCollins, 1996) and *Who's Afraid of Feminism?* (co-edited with Juliet Mitchell, 1997).

Jennie Popay is Professor of Sociology and Community Health at the University of Salford and Director of the Public Health Research and Resource Centre. She is also an Associate Director of Research and Development at the National Primary Care Research and Development Centre. She has published widely in the fields of sociology of health and social policy. Her particular research interests include gender and social class inequalities in health and the sociology of knowledge with particular reference to the relationship between lay and professional knowledge in the sphere of public health. Her recent publications include the edited collections *Dilemmas in Health Care* (with Basiro Davey, Buckingham: Open University Press, 1993) *Researching the People's Health* (with Gareth Williams, London: Routledge, 1994) and *Men, Gender Divisions and Welfare* (with Jeff Hearn and Jeanette Edwards, London: Routledge, 1998).

Julie Seymour is Lecturer in Social Research in the School of Social and Human Sciences at the University of Hull. The research reported on in her chapter with Gillian Parker was carried out while employed as Research Fellow at the Social Policy Research Unit at the University of York. Her research interests include the distribution of resources in households and the associated negotiations between household members with a particular emphasis on gender; disability and social exclusion and research methodology. Recent publications include *Joint Accounts: Methodology and Practice in Research Interviews with Couples* (with Gill Dix and Tony Eardley, York: University of York, 1995). She is currently writing a book on research methodology.

David Waddington is Reader in Communication in the Communication, Media and Communities Research Centre at Sheffield Hallam University. He has been researching mining communities for more than a decade. He is the co-author, with Chas Critcher, of *Flashpoints: Studies in Public Disorder* (London: Routledge, 1989) and *Split At The Seams: Community, Continuity and Change after the 1984–5 Coal Dispute* (Buckingham: Open University Press, 1991), and co-editor, with Chas Critcher, of *Regeneration of the Coalfield Areas: Anglo–German Perspectives* (London: Pinter, 1995). His work on public order includes *Contemporary Issues in Public Order* (London: Routledge, 1992) and *Policing and Public Order*, co-edited with Chas Critcher (Aldershot, Hants: Avebury, 1996).

Fiona Williams is Professor of Social Policy in the Department of Sociology and Social Policy, Director of ESRC Research Group for the Study of Care, Values and the Future of Welfare, and Deputy Director for the Centre of Interdisciplinary Gender Studies at the University of Leeds. She is best known for *Social Policy, A Critical Introduction, Issues of Race, Gender and Class* (Cambridge: Polity Press, 1989). She has also co-edited *Know Me As I Am: An Anthology of Prose, Poetry and Art from the Lives of People with Learning Difficulties* (London: Hodder & Stoughton, 1990) with Dorothy Atkinson, and *Community Care: A Reader* (2nd edition, London: Macmillan, 1997) with Joanna Bornat, Julia Johnson, Charmaine Pereira and David Pilgrim. Her other published work is on comparative social policy, feminism and postmodernism.

Part 1

The Context

Chapter 1

Changing Paradigms of Welfare

Fiona Williams, Jennie Popay and Ann Oakley

Introduction

This book attempts to contribute a new framework for social research in the welfare field. As such, it engages with new theories, new approaches and new methods, alongside a constructive critique of both the old and the new. It attempts to illustrate approaches to conceptualization and operationalization within policy-relevant research, to reflect and explore both "new" thinking in social theory and in welfare policy, as well as to maintain a connection with "old" concerns. Our concern is with welfare research – both theory and method – broadly defined as the wider landscape of policy and provision captured, in the past at least, by the notion of the "welfare state".

The "new" thinking with which the book is primarily concerned involves a shift away from seeing people as the passive beneficiaries of "welfare" provided through state interventions and professional expertise and from seeing them as fixed single social categories of "poor", "old", "single parent" or as one-dimensional, objective socio-economic classifications. Instead, new approaches emphasize the capacity of people to be creative, reflexive human beings, that is, to be active agents in shaping their lives, experiencing, acting upon and reconstituting the outcomes of welfare policies in variable ways. These new approaches point to the complex, multiple, subjective and objective social positionings that welfare subjects inhabit. Other aspects of new thinking include an emphasis on the need for sound evidence about the benefits to be expected from different forms of intervention – a call for evidence-based decision-making at all levels of health and welfare systems which embodies a demand for professionals to be more accountable.

This book does not uncritically accept the advances in theory and method that new approaches to health and welfare have revealed. Rather, we seek to highlight how, in pursuing this complex inquiry into the variability of individual agency within a discursively (rather than statistically) constituted social policy, we cannot afford to lose sight of "old" welfare research concerns with the broader patterns of inequality and the structural constraints limiting people's opportunities

2

and choices. As we enter the next century, with the economics of the western world in disarray and inequality within and between nations widening, this old agenda for welfare research retains its relevance (Hutton 1995; Wilkinson 1996). So a key issue addressed in the book is how far a new framework for welfare research can incorporate new approaches which emphasize individual agency without losing sight of the other approach which emphasizes structural constraints.

Before setting out in greater detail what a new more synthesized framework for social research in the health and welfare field might entail, it is necessary to understand the wider context of new developments in thinking about welfare and social divisions. There are four major dimensions to this changing context for welfare research: the organization and delivery of welfare; the forms and expressions of political solidarity; the relationship between welfare research and the policy process; and shifts in the focus of welfare research and theory *per se*.

The Context for Welfare Research

The Changing Organization and Delivery of Welfare Provision

At a general societal level, the major contextual shift for welfare research has been the break up of the post-war welfare settlement. This settlement was encapsulated in the classic Keynesian Welfare State – committed to full white male employment, mass educational opportunities and state-provided, professionally-delivered forms of quasi-universal protection from poverty, unemployment, ill-health and homelessness. Charles Webster has argued that the degree of consensus around the NHS and the welfare state following the 1940s legislation in the UK was much less than generally believed (Webster 1994). Whatever the situation, it is arguably the case that since the mid-1970s, in the UK and elsewhere, the key organizational characteristics of the welfare state – mass/universal state-provided, bureaucratically-run and professionally-delivered services – have been more explicitly and directly challenged. The challenges came not only from the constraints imposed by economic recession. They also came from neo-conservative critiques of the welfare state's efficiency, and from progressive critiques of its equity. These latter critiques were associated with new forms of political collectivity on the left – especially from social movements campaigning around inequalities of gender, race, disability and sexuality. Both the political left and right attacked the power of professionals and bureaucrats. The right attacked them for their inefficiency, non-accountability, monopolism, self-interest and their failure to acknowledge the diversity of individual choice. The left and the new social movements attacked them for their sexism and racism and for hierarchial forms of delivery, in which knowledge meant power and in which users had little say or control.

By the mid-1980s a new form of welfare regime was emerging in Britain, tightly controlled by the centralized state, but organizationally dispersed through the creation of the three Ms – markets, managers and mixed economies. This shift from a "bureaucratic/professional welfare regime" to a managerialist one is not unique to Britain, but has taken place in most Western industrialized welfare states. What is, perhaps, unique to Britain in the 1990s is the combination of, on the one hand, the legacies of new right political ideology and policy which have coloured this welfare regime in particular ways and, on the other, the grass-roots influence of commitment to more democratic forms of welfare. Drawing from both of these, yet emerging as a new form of centrism between left and right, is New Labour. Although they have retained managers and mixed economies, the principle of the *market* has been replaced by the principle of *work* in the welfare-to-work programme. Paid work represents a focus for reducing "welfare dependency" among young people and single mothers and for the integration of the "socially excluded underclass". It is also presented as central to the tying of responsibilities to rights. Paid work represents that which you put into society in order to get that which you take out. It is the basis for a moral, social and economic integration as well as the basis for social rights such as pensions. At the same time New Labour, through various measures, has acknowledged some social injustices and has made some moves towards a more culturally, morally and sexually open and diverse society. In this way it overlaps with the legacy of the new social movements and welfare user-movements. This means that the new right politics of "consumer sovereignty", "individual choice" and "diversity of needs" jostle with notions of "responsibilities with rights" from New Labour, and with notions of "user control", "welfare citizenship" and "diversity of social rights" from the user-movements. However, common across the political spectrum is a new emphasis upon welfare citizens/consumers as, first, agents of their welfare destiny – whether through the market, moral obligations or through local, democratic forms – and second, as articulating their differential welfare needs. This emphasis is one which the new research framework developed in this book seeks to acknowledge and explore.

Changing Political Support for Welfare

Alongside the changing organization and delivery of welfare provision there have been profound shifts in the forms of political support for welfare. The Keynesian Welfare State sought to address the needs of an organized male working class, on whose solidarity it depended for its political support. Two processes have undermined this interdependence. The first is the development – or at least recognition – of a more complex relationship between social divisions and welfare. This is especially apparent in the growing realization of the gains achieved by the middle class in certain areas of universal provision – health and education in particular. It is also evident that state welfare has been limited in the extent to which it has met the specific needs of women and minority ethnic groups.

The second process undermining the interdependence between the Welfare State and the organized working class has been the break-up of older forms of work organizations and the power of class solidarity upon which the Welfare State depended. Alongside this, as noted above, there has been a rise of new forms of solidarity around gender, race, disability and sexuality. The growth of these diversely constituted solidarities has been accompanied by a reduction in opportunities for the formation of consensual politics, as well as by a weakening of the traditional organizations, such as the trade unions, representing such politics (Edgell et al. 1995). These changes point to the need for a more complex understanding of the subjective and objective elements of social position and the relationship between these and welfare needs. They also highlight changing social conditions and expectations, especially around the patterns of male and female employment and unemployment, changing household structures, and the changing arenas for the articulation of new welfare claims. All of this suggests an approach to welfare research which is much more sensitive to the complex and dynamic structuring of people's health and welfare needs, their resources, their networks of support, their opportunities and their social relations.

The Changing Research/Policy Interface

The third crucial dimension of the changing context for welfare research is the relationship of the researcher to policy. In the 1960s, the heyday of the old welfare regime in the UK, social policy research and analysis was dominated by Fabian and social democratic academics, whose relationship to the Labour governments had been close and influential. For example, Michael Young (late Director of the Institute for Community Studies in London) made a major contribution to the 1945 Labour manifesto, and David Donnison and Richard Titmuss at the LSE had leading roles in the Supplementary Benefits Commission in the 1960s and 70s. The marshalling of facts, the documenting of social conditions and the presentation of rational argument often led directly to policy changes (Peter Townsend's *The Last Refuge* on old people in 1962; Brian Jackson and Dennis Marsden's *Education and the Working Class* also in 1962 and John Greve's *Homeless in London* in 1971 are examples of texts which influenced policy thinking). By the 1980s that relationship had become far more distant and less direct. With the New Labour administration which came into office in the UK in 1997, the relationship between researcher, civil servant and policy-maker is set to change again. To be influential, research findings have to negotiate the discursive balance of power held by different groups – politicians, the media (in particular), organizations representing business interests, professional groups, single-issue campaigns, social movements, international political organizations, and so on. The capacity to influence policy rests not so much on the incontrovertibility of one's research findings as on the capacity to engage with, and control, the movement of the dominant welfare discourses (Bartley 1990; Bryant 1995).

The Changing Focus of Welfare Research

Finally, as the wider social and political context for welfare has changed, so too has the focus of welfare research itself. Up until the mid-1980s most British social policy research – both empirical and theoretical – contextualized itself within the state, and, in particular, the nation-state. This research traditionally tended to neglect the voices and lived experiences of the recipients of welfare, documenting these primarily through statistical proxies such as level of income and indicators of deprivation. A number of processes have changed this. Importantly, the development of a mixed economy of welfare provision, along with a greater recognition given to the informal provision of welfare, especially by unpaid women as carers in the home, has meant that the informal, voluntary and commercial sectors of welfare have acquired much greater significance within research during the 1980s (although they were on the agenda of welfare "pluralists" from the 1970s).

Additionally, for a number of reasons, the boundaries of welfare research have moved beyond the nation state. First, researchers have recognized that the international dimensions of economic recession and social changes were having variable and comparable effects upon welfare states in different industrialized countries. Second, the re-drawing of national and political boundaries between eastern and western Europe and the developments in the European Union provided new administrative and political contexts for the study of the development of social policies. Third, analyses of economic, social and cultural globalization pointed to an increasingly interconnected international social order. Fourth, in a different direction, moves towards devolution may redraw again the administrative boundaries of policy formation and implementation. Where once the British Welfare State had represented a contrast to the US system, comparisons are being drawn, first between Thatcher and Reagan and most recently between Blair and Clinton, especially in the approach to the so-called "underclass".

Together these processes pushed mainstream welfare research in the UK and Europe in the direction of a rapid development of concepts, theory and method based upon comparative social policy. At the same time, however, though much less visible, there was a growing body of complex, finely-textured research attempting to untangle the dynamics of social relations involved in, for example, the provision of care – such as relationships between young mothers and health visitors. Work began to focus on the experiences and identities of welfare subjects and the psychological and sociological dynamics of processes of care and dependency (see Finch 1989; Graham 1983; Ungerson 1987), and provided an opportunity to unravel issues of agency and subjectivity.[1] This also resonated strongly with the larger American literature on coping, stress and social support which began to be seen by many to provide a source for the new paradigm for welfare research. However, as the chapters in this book show, this body of work on care and dependency is importantly different in its reliance on qualitative methods and the exploration of subjective meanings. Comparative work has, with exceptions (Duncan & Edwards 1997), remained relatively marginal to large-scale welfare research projects. The theoretical core of welfare disciplines in Europe took off to more expansive international contexts, but in ways that still privileged the social relations of class and the relationship between the state and the market over and above issues of gender, race, the family and the informal sector, and still neglected the voices of welfare recipients themselves.

6

By the 1990s, a conceptual gap had emerged in European welfare research between the largely production-centred analysis of welfare regimes (Esping-Andersen 1990) or of post-Fordist welfare states (see the essays in Burrows & Loader 1994), and the small-scale studies on kinship, care and communities, although the recent development of a feminist comparative social policy has begun to challenge some of these analyses (Lewis 1992; Sainsbury 1994; Williams 1995). The creative, reflexive, welfare subject thus found herself in something of a conceptual vacuum. The problem has therefore become, not only how to explore the nature of subjectivity and agency, and the complexity of social divisions, but also how to find the middle-range concepts which can tie these concerns to the structural contexts of widespread poverty, inequality, globalization and the international restructuring of welfare.

The Management of Personal Welfare: A New Paradigm Emerges

The ESRC/Rowntree Foundation Welfare Research Programme: 1991–1995

The changing context for welfare research in the UK and elsewhere was, predictably, to have an influence on the policy of research funding bodies. This influence is clearly apparent in the history of the Management of Personal Welfare Research Initiative, funded jointly by the Economic and Social Research Council (ESRC) and the Rowntree Foundation, a charitable funding body. This programme of research ran for four years from 1991 to 1995 and had a budget of around £450,000. The ESRC is the main UK agency (in addition to the core funding for universities, which also includes an element for research infrastructure) allocating public funds for research in the social and economic fields. Welfare research, largely but not exclusively the domain of social policy, is therefore within the Council's remit, and in the mid-1980s the Council's Social Affairs Committee held this brief.

In 1985, a sub-committee of the ESRC's Social Affairs Committee, chaired by Nicholas Deakin, advertised for an academic consultant to produce a proposal for a new programme of research in the welfare field. Following a competitive process, Michael Hill, then a Senior Lecturer at the University of Bristol, was appointed to undertake this task. Over a period of 12 months, from around March 1985, he consulted widely with the social policy/welfare research community in the UK, commissioned five detailed reviews of specific topics, organized three one-day seminars to debate these, and made a number of overseas visits. A final report was submitted to the sub-committee in June 1986. This was an attempt to set out a coherent yet pragmatic agenda for a new welfare research programme which addressed the themes that the research community had identified as being of central concern in the mid-1980s, without taking an identifiable political position. Six priority themes were identified in the report: the market for private care and regulation; voluntary organizations and informal care in the community; evaluation of social work; community resources and service delivery; social security and the labour market; and the private pension industry. There can be no questioning the continued relevance of these themes to debates about welfare policy and provision today. They also resonate well with the contours of the changing welfare research landscape described in the previous section, giving primacy to structural issues, but incorporating different sectors of the mixed economy of welfare and the notion of community resources for welfare (although they do not touch on more complex notions of social divisions and identities).

It is important to note that Hill's report was prepared in the midst of the "Thatcher revolution" and welfare, in its many forms, was a politically highly sensitive issue – and remains so today. The academic community, like any other sector of society, can be expected to reflect the political divisions around welfare that are apparent within the wider society and, in this context, it is to be expected that the proposal would have had a stormy passage through the Council's decision-making processes. It appears to have done so. It was agreed by the sub-committee, with whom Michael Hill had maintained close contact throughout the consultancy period, and then by the full Social Affairs Committee. However, even at this stage it appears to have hit opposition and it failed to be agreed by the Council – the final arbiter on funding for the ESRC's programmes.

Some of the ideas put forward in Hill's proposal have subsequently been taken up in other ESRC research initiatives, for example, the Contracting and Competitions programme. In the meantime, however, it appears that there was still support within the ESRC for a separate welfare research initiative, albeit that this was to take a very different form than that presaged in the Hill proposal. In 1988, Michael Titterton, then at Glasgow University, was commissioned by the ESRC to produce a review paper drawing particularly on the largely American literature focusing on what has become known as the "personal management of welfare" – that is, research into the individual experience of life-events, stress, coping and social support and the impact on health and welfare outcomes. According to Titterton (1996) the commissioning of this review "was born out of a sense of frustration with the prevailing models dominating welfare research and a desire to promote a new way of thinking about people's needs and responses to them". The review paper, which was subsequently published (Titterton 1992) was debated at a specially convened seminar in York in the summer of 1989 and later formed the basis for the new ESRC/Rowntree research programme entitled The Management of Personal Welfare launched in 1991.

This was a small research initiative, by ESRC standards, and consisted of seven projects (one of which was funded by the Rowntree Foundation, who also provided support towards the co-ordination work across the Initiative). The seven projects included two linked projects looking at the needs of vulnerable children living in poor material circumstances from the perspective of service providers and mothers; two linked projects exploring women's experience of violence and the perspectives of men who have been violent to known women; a study of the negotiation of coping in marital relationships where one of the partners had a chronic illness/disability; research on parents' experience of caring for a disabled child; and a study of responses to contemporary labour market changes in mining communities.

All of the projects were designed to address the initiative's four central objectives: how do people under stress find the kinds of help they need to cope with the problems they face; what kinds of support can individuals turn to for help; how do informal sources of support interact with statutory and voluntary support services; and how are people best enabled to find their way through situations of social stress and personal difficulties? From the beginning, however, there was a shared concern among the research teams involved that, although these questions were of considerable salience to welfare research and policy, the "management of personal welfare" paradigm, which had so powerfully shaped the initiative, may not on its own provide an adequate conceptual and theoretical basis on which to seek the answers the programme posed. This book and another recent volume (Popay et al. 1998) arose out of the discussions and work undertaken across the research Initiative over a three-year period during which the research teams sought to identify a framework which might be better fitted for the task with which we were faced. There was, as we note in the next section, much that was sound in the critique of the old paradigm of welfare research, but much, too, that was lacking in the new paradigm.

New and Old Paradigms of Welfare

In his background paper that so strongly shaped the ESRC's Management of Personal Welfare Research programme, Titterton (1989; 1992) argues that the old paradigm of welfare concentrates on the structural determinants of people's needs and problems (poverty, housing, health, educational inequalities, etc.) and on the forms of provision necessary to meet these needs and problems. As such, the old paradigm, he suggests, worked with:

> a somewhat monolithic, indeed unidimensional, view of human agency: uniform needs and uniform responses are often simply ascribed to individuals within the vulnerable groupings with which the study of social welfare typically concerns itself. They share a common neglect of the differentiated nature of vulnerability and risk among individuals and the role of creative human agency in responding differentially to well-being across the life-span (1992: 2).

In other words, as we noted earlier, individuals and their needs were understood passively within categories of researchers', providers' or policy-makers' own making (socio-economic groups, children at risk, disabled, old, etc.). Insofar as individuals' own needs and strategies were studied, such studies tended towards a pathological view of poverty, ill-health and so on. Although the individual pathology type of explanation was rejected by many within welfare research, it had not been replaced with an alternative understanding of the needs and

9

problems facing individuals and the strategies they adopt to meet or overcome these. More particularly, Titterton suggests, what is needed is an understanding of the individual as a creative, reflexive agent, who helps to create, but is also constrained by, the social forces and conditions in which she or he exists. As proposed by Titterton, a new paradigm for welfare and research must consist of three elements. First, it should attempt to understand people's "differential vulnerability" to threats to their welfare and well-being in terms of the complexity of social, material and personal factors (the last factor drawing, for example, on life events). Second, it should examine the differential coping strategies (the "mediating structures") that people use when faced with such threats (from information seeking and problem solving to the use of social support) and explore how these, too, are shaped by differential access to material, social and personal resources. The third element in the new paradigm should expand the study of welfare outcomes to include those people who survive and see through the threats to their welfare – the "invulnerables" – and not focus simply on those people who cannot, or do not, cope, some of whom turn to health and social welfare agencies for help. The new paradigm for welfare research was therefore seen by Titterton to break with the old paradigm in three distinct ways by

- providing an analytical framework for understanding the dialectical relationship between personal history and the social and material world;
- expanding the study of "mediating structures" beyond formal welfare provision to include people's own psychological and social strategies;
- expanding the focus of study to include the resilience and resistance of the "invulnerables".

Following on from this, Titterton suggested that welfare research should look to the wealth of (largely American) literature on stress, risk, life events, coping and social support to provide the material to build the new paradigm.

The argument for a new paradigm of welfare is an important one. An attempt to elaborate an holistic theory of welfare which could take account of individual human action and relate this to social structure and vice versa would be an important step for the many disciplines involved in research in the health and welfare field. So, too, would an approach which could acknowledge the diversity of individual history, needs and behaviour, yet relate this diversity to general patterns of social difference and differentiation. In addition, an analysis of policy-making and provision, which took as its starting point people's own definitions, meanings and experiences of needs and risks and their preferred ways of dealing with these, would place welfare provision more firmly within a user-led approach. However, as we shall argue in this book, Titterton, and others since, have over-estimated the extent to which a new paradigm for welfare research can be readily constructed from the literature on stress, life events, coping and social support. At a general level, as we will show, this literature fails to provide a material context for individual agency and to a large extent therefore cannot explain and indeed largely fails to illuminate, the crucial relationship between identity, agency and structure.

The argument articulated by Titterton also raises the crucial question of the extent to which two separate paradigms – the old and the new – can be readily identified. To what extent is it reasonable to argue that the old paradigm has failed to address issues central to the new "personal welfare" paradigm?

Old and New Paradigms: A Helpful Dichotomy?

Titterton characterizes the old paradigm as working with a limited view of human agency. People feature insofar as they present problems, and these problems exist by virtue of structural factors – poverty, homelessness, etc. – or by virtue of people belonging to a professionally-defined category in need of help – "problem family", "at risk", etc. The problem with this characterization of the old paradigm is that it exaggerates and simplifies the development of welfare theory and assumes a too rigid break between research traditions. In doing so it ignores areas of work which, though rooted in the old paradigm and its emphasis on structural inequality, nevertheless reach out towards new personal and collective conceptualizations of welfare.

Certainly it is true that most mainstream welfare research of the 1960s and 1970s focused on the structural determinants of people's problems and that social inequalities were viewed deterministically and unidimensionally, in terms of social class. With the possible exception of Titmuss' work on altruism (Oakley & Ashton 1997; Titmuss 1971) the notion of human agency was, by and large, ignored. However, this is not the whole story. The development of a "political economy of welfare" introduced the notion of agency into theories of welfare through the notion of collective action – or class struggle. In this framework, the development of welfare provision was understood as the result of both capitalism's attempts to meet its own needs for accumulation, social reproduction and legitimation and the working-class's attempts to struggle for provision and support to buffer and improve its own social conditions. In this scenario, the human agent is seen as operating collectively through and on behalf of its individual members (Gough 1979).

Subsequent commentators on the political economy framework have criticized its unidimensional, class-deterministic approach to both agency and structure. It has been pointed out that other dimensions of power and inequality – especially those of gender and race – run through welfare provision, as well as through the collective actions of people's efforts to improve ways of meeting their own needs (Williams 1989). Such critiques emerged from attempts begun in the early 1970s by groups of feminists, black and anti-racist activists to challenge sexism and racism in welfare provision, and, importantly, to provide alternative, often separate, forms of welfare. Thus, for example, women's refuges, women's health groups and Saturday schools for black children were developed, both as responses to the problems and needs faced by women and/or black people and also as challenges to existing forms of welfare provision. These also challenged the hierarchial social relations of welfare – the provider/user split – in a number of ways; first,

11

by demystifying areas of professional knowledge (especially in health); second, by involving users as welfare providers; third, by insisting on the capacity of lay people to redefine their problems or risks in their own terms; and fourth, by asserting a relationship between an individual's problems (the personal) and social inequalities (the political).

Since the 1970s, there have been three further developments which suggest that a rigid division between the old and new paradigm of welfare research and practice is misleading. First, some of the new social movements have, as we have already noted, generally been marked by a move away from the "politics of liberation" towards the more person-centred "politics of identity".

These movements emphasize and celebrate diversity and difference over and above the search for universal strategies of liberation. Second, within and along-side the new social movements, there have developed movements whose key concerns are about welfare provision – the disability movement, for example, and groups like People First, the organization of people with learning difficulties and Survivors Speak Out, for users of mental health services. The major concern of these groups to articulate the perspectives of the recipients of welfare provi-sion – whose voices have traditionally either not been heard or have been ignored – provides more clues to the relationship between identity and need. The third development, which is rather different in origin, is a growing emphasis on the evaluation of forms of health and welfare intervention. Whereas the first two developments demand greater conceptual sophistication and an interrogation of the relationship between the user and provider of welfare, the third shift re-positions the role of the researcher in relation to welfare practice. It is also about the relationship between users and providers – once users become informed about literature and/or interested in evidence of effectiveness, the power balance changes.

The Evidence Base for Welfare Provision

The traditional field of health and welfare research and provision has demon-strated a growing acceptance that all health and welfare interventions must be based on solid evidence of effectiveness. In the past, many health and welfare interventions have been derived from "faith" about what will work rather than from demonstrable evidence about real improvements in people's lives. But faith as a form of professional certainty can damage as well as benefit. There is certainly evidence from soundly-designed evaluations that well-intended social welfare interventions may have deleterious effects (McCord 1981).

The model here is the critique of medicine as guided more by habit than by science: "Sick pay price as doctors put faith in hunches" as one media headline put it (Observer, 5 Feb 1995). Since 1993 in the UK a move towards evidence and away from faith as the basis of medical decision-making has been a central plank in the NHS Research and Development strategy. Much of this effort is now co-ordinated under the umbrella of the Cochrane Collaboration, an inter-national effort aimed at preparing and disseminating systematic reviews of the effectiveness of health care (Cochrane Collaboration 1997). It is central to the Cochrane philosophy that randomized controlled trials (RCTs) offer the best evaluation strategy for minimizing bias when attempting to decide what works, or what works best. The merits of the RCT as the "gold standard" evaluation design continue to be debated. However, it has been shown that when welfare and other social interventions are evaluated using methods other than well-designed RCTs, the conclusions reached about effectiveness can be misleading (Oakley & Fullerton 1996).

There is thus a growing reaction within health and welfare fields against the double standard which prefers uncontrolled experimentation (what social workers, doctors, etc. normally do because they believe it works) to controlled experimentation (subjecting those hunches to the test of an RCT). There is also increasing respect for the view that fields such as social welfare should not escape the ethical requirement applied to medicine – that professionals be able to support their claims to do more good than harm (Alderson 1996; Chalmers 1986; Oakley & Roberts 1996; Skrabanek 1990).

In neither old nor new paradigms of welfare research, however, are data about effectiveness well integrated with other types of data about the processes involved in providing and using welfare. While the evaluation design of the RCT can readily incorporate experiential data, few RCTs to date have been conducted in this way (see Oakley 1992a). Progress in this field tends to be impeded by an ideological resistance to experimental studies among certain professional and social groups (Oakley 1998a and b), and by the historical construction of *qualitative* and *quantitative* methods as somehow generically opposed (Oakley forthcoming). The area within medicine where the experiences of users has received most attention is the pregnancy and childbirth field (Oliver 1995). There is clearly much scope for linking welfare recipients' assessments of appropriateness and effectiveness to other measures of outcome.

The Elements of a New Framework for Welfare Research

Together, these different developments since the 1970s have created a new welfare agenda which has begun (albeit sometimes in a limited and problematic way) to link the old paradigm of welfare research with its focus on structural inequality to the new paradigm which prioritizes individual differences and personal resources. In particular, six new areas for enquiry have opened up. First, the notion of the social relations of power and inequality has been expanded beyond those of class to incorporate relations of gender, race, disability, sexuality and age; and the complex ways in which these intermesh has been recognized. Secondly, the social relations of welfare production – the relationship between users and providers, and strategies of user-empowerment – have been highlighted. Thirdly, gender divisions in the informal sector of care have been revealed and constitute the substance of a growing body of work. Fourthly, the importance of people's own experiences, definitions and meanings of the problems and risks in their lives has been asserted, and these are increasingly accepted as essential data in welfare research. Fifthly, new forms of personal coping strategies and the effectiveness of welfare provision, based on political perceptions of personal problems/risks, have been generated. Lastly, the notion of people simply as victims of inequalities has been transformed by the emphasis upon a positive reappraisal of identity (e.g. as survivor rather than victim). In some cases, this identity forms the basis of forms of social support and strategies for meeting welfare threats – for example in the development of social support in the gay and lesbian communities for people with AIDS or diagnosed as HIV positive; in the Independent Living Movement for disabled people; or the development of self-advocacy for people with learning difficulties. In addition, new methodological issues and opportunities exist for the interweaving of qualitative research with more quantitative. forms of evaluation.

Of course, these developments cannot alone solve the problems which must be resolved if a new framework for welfare research is to be developed which incorporates the best of the old and the new in social science. For a start, in much welfare research it remains the case that the notions of individual agency and subjectivity are not generally well-developed. However, work in these areas can be studied for its capacity to develop notions of identity and of difference and their relationship to structure, particularly to questions of power and inequality. This is especially important, given, as we shall show, the tendency to underexplanation of these areas in research work on stress, social support and coping – that is, within the literature which has been recommended by some as the building material for the new paradigm.

The Plan of the Book

This chapter has outlined the context and background to current research in the welfare field in general and to the ESRC/Rowntree Foundation MPWI. We have pointed to the need for a new framework for welfare research and set out some of the requirements of this framework. These involve an understanding of individuals as complex and multiply positioned, engaging with and acting upon the diverse policy landscapes that they inhabit and, through this, reconstituting the outcomes of policy and the discourses through which policies are constructed and debated. At the same time, we need also to examine the ways in which the contours of those landscapes are negotiated by active welfare subjects and are constructed by forces of inequality and social division. We need also to understand the central role of research methodology within all of this. The remainder of this book addresses these issues in different ways. Part 2 focuses on the concepts which link research upon personal welfare to aspects of publicly provided welfare. Part 3 examines the role of quantitative and qualitative methods in welfare research; and Part 4 is concerned with different social relations pertinent to the provision and delivery of welfare.

The two chapters in Part 2 are concerned with the conceptual and theoretical basis for a new framework for welfare research. In Chapter 2 Fiona Williams considers in more detail the claim that the literature on life events, stress, coping strategies and social support may help us in our quest for this new framework. On the basis of a selective review of this literature, she explores the case for claiming that this body of work will enable us better to understand the relationship between personal history and the social and material world and, more specifically, will help to connect the study of formal welfare provision to that of individuals' own psychological and social coping strategies. She examines how, and to what extent, research in this field takes account of, and builds upon, existing understandings of social inequalities and social divisions, elaborating an important distinction between difference-focused and division-led research. From this she draws out possible mediating concepts which link old and new paradigms. Julie Seymour in Chapter 3 continues this exploration of the potential offered by the wide ranging literature on the personal management of welfare in a different but complementary way. She focuses in detail on the way in which five key concepts in this field – stress, life events, coping, social support and vulnerability – are variously constructed across academic disciplines and by welfare professionals and lay people. In so doing she seeks to illuminate ways in which understandings of the nature of, and relationships between these concepts are changing and to explore the implications of this for welfare research, policy and professional practice.

Chapters 4 and 5 in Part 3 move on to consider some of the methodological issues raised by the pursuit of a new welfare research framework, many of which are touched on only fleetingly in the first three chapters. In Chapter 4, Chas Critcher, David Waddington and Bella Dicks look at the role of qualitative methods in specific areas of welfare research. They are not concerned here with epistemological debates between different versions of positivism and interpretivism, or with theoretical or political debates about different approaches to research methods. Rather, they seek to identify what qualitative methods have to offer to the study of stress, social support and coping and to explore the ways in which these methods have been and might be implemented. Whereas, as Fiona Williams argues in Chapter 2, many of the theoretical assumptions underpinning this body of work can be criticized, there are also important implications of such critiques for methodological choices. The central argument of Chapter 4 is that, although there is enormous potential to be derived from complementary methodological approaches to welfare research, this will only be fulfilled if qualitative methods are granted equal status and legitimacy in the practice, as well as the principles, of welfare research.

Geraldine Macdonald shifts the focus to the notion of evidence in Chapter 5. In this chapter, she argues that social work is ethically bound to evaluate the effectiveness of what it does and she is concerned to explore some of the barriers which are operating to constrain the pursuit of evidence based practice through experimental research within this profession. Pointing to the widespread acceptance within medicine in recent years of the need for sound research evidence on the effectiveness of interventions, she suggests that social work must not continue to reject the crucial contribution that RCTs have to make to evaluative research within social work in particular and welfare provision more generally. Although the argument for greater use of RCTs is forcefully put, the author does not seek to devalue the contribution of other approaches to the evaluation of process and appropriateness within welfare practice. Rather, again, the call is for complementary methods of evaluation, but within the context of interventions which are tightly defined and controlled in order to test effectiveness.

In the fourth part of the book we provide case-studies of empirical research which engage with key aspects of the social relations of welfare. Chapter 6 focuses on gender relations and welfare research. In this chapter, Jalna Hanmer and Jeff Hearn use their recent research into women's and men's experience of violence against women by known men to begin to consider how a research framework might be developed which more adequately links the new focus on individual human agency to the older focus on social structures of power and control. It is also, however, more than a single case study, for the authors use their own and others' research within the ESRC/Rowntree Initiative to describe the complex and pervasive relationship between welfare and gender and to point to the centrality of gender inequalities in all welfare research. In Chapter 7, Jeanette Edwards, Ann Oakley and Jennie Popay draw on their research from within the Management of Personal Welfare programme to explore the complex and multiple intersections between the frames of reference underlying lay and professional perspectives on welfare needs and how these are most appropriately and effectively met.

While this introductory chapter has set the contextual background for the research, Chapter 8 looks to the future. In this Jennie Popay seeks first to pull together the many strands in the arguments developed in preceding chapters. Second, Fiona Williams begins to elicit and make explicit mediating concepts, which may help us develop a framework which links old issues of structure and inequality to new issues of voice and agency. In doing this, she also highlights different dimensions of theoretical adequacy for welfare research. Finally she offers a new framework for welfare research which incorporates these mediating concepts and dimensions of theoretical adequacy.

Note

1   It is also the case that this shift in focus upon subjectivity reflected a shift in the social sciences in general, towards poststructuralist theory. The influence of poststructuralist thinking and developments in social theory is raised in Chapter 8 (see also Leonard 1997 and Williams 1996).

Part 2

Concepts

Chapter 2

Exploring Links Between Old and New Paradigms: A Critical Review

Fiona Williams

Introduction

It was suggested in Chapter 1 that an emphasis upon users of welfare as creative, active human agents could constitute an important way forward for welfare research (a new paradigm). At the same time, we suggested that it was important not to let go of the older concerns about the influence of structural inequalities upon people's behaviour and needs (the old paradigm). In order to pursue this further, this chapter tests the claim that the literature on stress, coping strategies and social support may help us in the quest for a framework which enables us to understand the relationship between personal history and the social and material world and, more specifically, that connects the study of formal welfare provision to that of individuals' own psychological and social coping strategies. The chapter is based on a review of literature in the field of stress, coping strategies and social support.[1] It examines how, and to what extent, research in these areas takes account of issues of social inequality and social division. In other words, it examines how far research which may be located within the new paradigm is informed by central concepts from the old paradigm. It attempts to draw out from this mediating concepts which may help us link the old to the new, as well as any relevance this research might have for the formal provision of welfare.

The chapter starts with a brief overview of the main characteristics of the literature on stress, coping strategies and social support and some of the critiques that have been made of it. It then reviews the different ways in which social categories associated with structural inequalities – class, gender, race, disability, age and sexuality – have been incorporated and represented in this body of literature, either as unitary or multiple categories. Finally, an assessment is made of the potential contribution of this field of studies to a new framework for welfare research and practice which sees people as creative agents both enabled and constrained by the structural conditions in which they exist. The chapter then highlights those concepts emerging from the literature that may provide the conceptual links between the agency of individuals and the material and social conditions in which they live. These are then picked up again and discussed in more detail in the final chapter of the book.

Earlier Critiques of Research on Stress, Social Support and Coping

The research in the area of coping, stress and social support is large enough (drawn from at least five different disciplines) and old enough (dating from the early 1960s) to generate its own epistemology. It is not the aim to develop this here. Overviews of the work on social support and coping are provided by Qureshi (1990); Titterton (1989) and on network analysis by Bulmer (1987). There are also a number of other relevant reviews which look at both empirical and theoretical aspects of social support, stress and coping (see for example, Gottlieb 1981; ibid. 1988; Stewart 1989). Work on social support, stress, coping and health includes the classic reviews by Berkman (1984) and Schaefer et al. (1981), Wan's (1982) work on gerontological health and Dean's (1986) on pathways of influence. The relationship between social support/networks and health inequalities has received less attention, although, as Fox (1988) has argued, social network interaction is increasingly part of the jargon in the health inequalities debate. Dean et al. (1994) have addressed methodological issues that may help to explain inconsistencies in this literature. The relationship between social support, friendship and community networks has been examined in such reviews as those by Duck (1990), Gottlieb (1981), and Willmott (1986; 1987).

The literature review on which this chapter is based identified a number of general characteristics of the "new paradigm literature" which are worthy of note. First, the main characteristic of the area is the study of the relationships between psychological distress, stress, life events and social support. This has usually involved attempts to measure, categorize and map distress and stress, and to measure the significance of different types, sources, costs, benefits of and motivations for social support.

Second, the literature search for the review also suggested that while research in the area is drawn from a number of different disciplines, it is largely written up in the social psychology journals and dominated by research done in the US or Canada. In addition, and possibly as a consequence, much of the research was based on formal questionnaires and quantitative analysis, in spite of the influence of Brown and Harris's groundbreaking work on women and depression published in 1978 (Brown & Harris 1978) and their use of semi-structured interviews. This raises some significant methodological issues which are discussed in Chapter 5. Third, although research in the area might have taken into account social support, little mention was made of the influence of, or implications for, the development of social policies.

A final important general comment is that this field of research has been challenged for its emphasis on empirical work and neglect of theory and for its failure to integrate fully the meaning and effect of social divisions and inequalities, among other things, into its analyses. So, for example, Qureshi observes in her brief but salient overview of social support research how

> theory, or lack of it, is reflected in measurement, and that although a concept may appear to have a clear meaning in everyday language, the process of attempting to construct a method of measuring it reveals a wide range of possible meanings and interpretations which may have different relationships to other concepts (1990: 2).

A lack of theoretical exploration in this literature has also been noted in two significant critiques of the field. The first by Allan Young (Young 1980), criticizes the discourse on stress for "detaching knowledge, action and events from their social settings" (142) and reducing social processes to the psychological attributes of individuals. Even where social characteristics are taken on board – e.g. gender, ethnicity, years of education – it has been argued that they represent only a new mediating variable. Of Pearlin and Schooler's classic work on coping (1978) – which established that those most at risk to stress were those who had the least effective modes of coping (the least educated and women) – Young comments,

> The apparent complexity is achieved through the untheorized proliferation of sociological variables, by fragmenting and obscuring the social processes and forces which determine the distribution and virulence of stresses, strains and outcomes in society (Young 1980: 143).

A second critique, by Valerie Haines in 1988, is of social network analysis. She suggests that work in this field tends towards psychologism (i.e. it explains social phenomena in terms of the psychological processes of individuals). She proposes a theoretical framework which connects the relationship between the individual and society through Anthony Giddens's work on "structuration theory". This sees the individual as a reflexive agent who is both enabled and constrained by social structure and process. These suggestions, which indicate possible mediating concepts to link the old paradigm to the new, are discussed further in the final chapter of this book.

It is possible to discern some responsiveness in the field to these sorts of critiques. For example, whilst Pearlin and Schooler's 1978 work focuses centrally upon the different psychological approaches to coping, Pearlin's benchmark paper of 1989, "The sociological study of stress", gives much greater room to the explanatory potential of social processes:

> I wish to emphasise that interrelated levels of social structure – social stratifications, social institutions, interpersonal relationships – mould and structure the experiences of individuals (Pearlin 1989: 242).

In other words, coping is not just about who you are but what you do with the personal, social and material resources available to you. Pearlin emphasizes in particular the differential effect of gender on exposure to stress, outcomes and resources, and he brings in the importance of values in people's experiences and understanding. A parallel shift can be seen in the paper by Coyne and Downey in 1991, "Social factors and psychopathology". This asserts that research on social factors and psychopathology has reached a critical juncture which entails leaving behind the quantitative research based on the exploitation of the non-independence of measures and embracing the semi-structured interview and life-history approach in order to understand the dynamics and complexities between people's psychological distress, their lives and their social contexts (1991: 403).

Dimensions of Difference and Inequality

Of the 65 articles selected for the review underpinning this chapter, 40 were concerned with one or more of the six dimensions of difference/inequality used in the literature search: class, gender, race, disability, age and sexuality. The following discussion is structured in terms of these separate dimensions of differ-ence/inequality. In reality however, both in research literature and in life, these dimensions rarely operate in a singular way but in complex and multiple forms. Where a combination of categories or variables has been used (e.g. gender and class) these have been discussed in terms of the variable leading the research. Importantly there were few studies concerned with social class alone and for this reason, class is not considered as a separate dimension, but where appropriate brought into the discussion of research on the other dimensions.

The literature reviewed fell broadly into two types. The first, which is called here *difference-focused*, concerns itself with these dimensions of class, gender, race, disability, age and sexuality as differentiating variables in the research, rather than as social categories embedded in unequal social relations. By contrast, the other broad category, which we call *division-led* research, tends to be informed by theoretical understandings of these categories operating within unequal social relations of power. Thus, in this case, the social category of, for example, gender or race is linked to structural inequalities and carries its own analytic or explanat-ory potential.

Difference-Focused Research

Gender

Twenty-two of the 65 articles identified in the literature reviewed were about gender or gender in association with class, race or age. There appear to be two reasons for this interest in gender: the first is because, as a social group, women, especially working-class women, display or report more often the symptoms of psychological distress, especially depression, and have thereby come in for greater scrutiny in research focusing on stress and distress. However, many of the studies, although focusing on women and on the unequal gender distribution of distress and stress, are not necessarily about women as a social group, or about unequal gender (or class, or race) relations. In so far as meanings and experiences are uncovered, these are the meanings of depression, of stress, of support, rather than, or as well as, the meanings of being a woman, being working-class or being black, or any combination of these. An example of this kind of research is the work of Brown and Harris (1978). This is an important and well-known piece of research and the comments here are restricted to its treatments of gender and class inequalities and are drawn from the critique by Davies and Roche (1980). The points made by this critique have significance for much of the research in this area which focuses upon inequalities.

One of the important findings from Brown and Harris's work is that working-class women with children at home are four times as likely to develop depression as middle-class women. They found that the vulnerability of working-class women to stress was greater when there was no confiding relationship such as that with a boyfriend or spouse, as well as, to a lesser extent, having lost a mother before the age of 11, having three or more children under the age of 14 at home and not being in employment. These vulnerability factors were related to character-istics of low self-esteem, hopelessness, guilt and loss.

Davies and Roche's critique points out that although the findings of the research speak volumes about gender and class inequalities (housing, income, employment), gender and class are used as methodological tools or units rather than understood as sets of social relations of power and inequality. Thus, their choice of women as research subjects is determined by practical and pathological considerations (women are at home; they suffer from depression) rather than being informed by any explicit theory of the position of women in society. Similarly, their use of class is as a control mechanism, to hold class-related differences between women constant in order to examine differential coping strategies, rather than, for example, to find out ways that social and material inequalities themselves may affect a woman's experience of life events and her capacity to cope with them (see also Chapters 3 and 6). This means that Brown and Harris's discussion of self-esteem focuses on individual attributes and life histories rather than on (or as well as) self-esteem as a product of gender and class relations.

In sum, Davies and Roche suggest that what Brown and Harris do is "reduce the social to the individual" whereas the task is really to "relate the individual to the political and social" (Davies & Roche: 651) and that their study while "being all about women, cannot be about women at all" (ibid.: 648). One might add that while being all about class, the study was also not about class at all.

With hindsight, and in view of our concern to break down the disciplinary boundaries between the psychological and the sociological, we would suggest that this conclusion of Davies and Roche to the work of Brown and Harris and similar research may have the effect of merely reinstating the sociological. Our intention is to find a framework to encompass both the individual and the social. In spite of Davies and Roche's criticisms, Brown and Harris's work does at least two important things for the study of stress, coping and support and its relation to structural inequality. First, it alerts us to some important aspects of the social conditions of women's existence. Second it lays store by subjective accounts of past and daily experience elicited through semi-structured interviews, even though these focused on life events and responses to these, rather than (or as well as) experiences of gender and class inequalities. This second aspect finds little reflection in other literature on stress/social support.

Insight Without Understanding

This point – that "difference-focused" studies generate important insights but do not necessarily illuminate the complex relationship between social relations of power and inequality and daily life – emerges from other studies. For example, the study by Koeske and Koeske, "Buffering aspects of social support and social stress" (1990), looks at parental stress through a quantitative analysis of questionnaires from 125 mothers who had at least one child at home between nine months and 14 years. They found that parenting stress explained lower maternal esteem, lower parent satisfaction and higher symptomatology. Social support was extremely important in buffering stress, especially when this stress was linked to the mother's perception of their youngest child's development. They also found, that "education level seemed to operate as a stress buffer in much the same way as social support did" (ibid.: 448). This led them to conclude that more service provision which made possible the benefits to mothers from social support and education was desirable, as was further investigation into these resources. In this study it is clear that although the concept of stress is unpacked and given a thorough airing and straightening out, the meanings of motherhood, (i.e. the specific gender-related condition) and the components and associations of education are still left in the drawer.

Leonard Pearlin's work, mentioned earlier, also focuses on gender, although generally the importance of this work is the development of a dynamic notion of social support, that is, that social support is not always facilitative, that it carries costs and benefits, that perceived support may be more significant than actual support in withstanding stress and that there is a two-way relationship between life-events, stress and support. (This is discussed in the next chapter). Pearlin and his colleagues have a consistent focus on gender differences in stress, coping and support denoting a mixture of interest derived from women as a pathological group, as a different group and to some extent as an unequal group. However, Pearlin's work is more concerned with difference itself than how we might explain it, though he does posit in earlier work that both role constraints and socialization have some bearing on women's less effective coping mechanisms (Pearlin & Schooler 1978: 15). This work examines the ways in which people deal with stress and the efficacy of these. They identify different methods of coping with stress and point to those which are most effective in any given situation – for example, problems at work are best solved by distancing the individual from the problem; problems at home are best solved by remaining committed and engaged in interpersonal relations. However, they found that those most exposed to stressful situations – women and those with less education – had the least effective coping mechanisms. In a later article in 1989, Pearlin summarized his findings of the significance of gender in four points:

- gender influences the stressors to which people are exposed (Pearlin & Aneshensel 1986; Pearlin & Lieberman 1978);
- the effects of these stressors on outcomes may be conditioned by gender, e.g. woman face different strains at work because of their role at home;
- personal and social mediating resources are mobilized differently by gender (Pearlin & Schooler 1978);
- gender affects the way in which stress manifests itself (stereotypically, men get drunk, women get depressed).

By isolating gender in this way this research, as with a great deal of this type of work, also overgeneralizes women's (and men's) experiences. One might also ask how class, race, ethnicity, disability, sexuality, age and marital status cut across these observations and how far, given changes in the organization of work and in family life since the 1970s and 1980s when this research was carried out, these conclusions about women's coping strategies would still be borne out. The long essay by Beatrix Campbell of working-class men and women's responses to unemployment and growing poverty in British inner-cities in the early 1990s paints a picture of women developing co-operative coping strategies compared with men whose responses have often been destructive to themselves or the communities in which they live (Campbell 1993).[2]

A final example of difference focused research concerned in particular with working-class women is Parry's study of "Paid employment, life events, social support and mental health in working-class mothers" (Parry 1986). This set out to test Brown and Harris's finding that employment enhances the psychological well-being of working-class women. In a community survey (in Sheffield) Parry interviewed 193 working-class women under 45 with a child of four to seven years at home and examined the relationship between the effects of employment and stress, social support and having a pre-school child. She found that there was no overall buffering effect of employment: more significant to loss of well-being was the incidence of a stressful event in the previous year. Employment, in this situation, could reduce stress, but only when social support was also available. She also found that "mothers without paid employment were more self-deprecating . . . more responsive to moderate levels of life event stress" (1986: 205). She contrasts her findings about the effects on mothers with young children of not having paid employment with studies of the detrimental effects of unemployment on single women wage-earners and men. Her findings lead her to surmise upon women's commitment to child-rearing over and above their commitment to the labour market.

Race, Ethnicity and Class

The literature search threw up only four race-related pieces of work, all of these American and one in a specialist journal (*Journal of Black Studies*). This major omission is worrying for at least two reasons. First, recent discussions in the United States about the "underclass" often reproduce pathological, stereotyped assessments of poor communities and especially the support systems of single mothers, many of whom are black, without a great deal of empirical evidence. Although attempts to export the racialized version of the underclass thesis to Britain have been only partly successful, (see Murray 1990) nevertheless the demonization of single mothers has been a constant theme of both policy and rhetoric in Britain over many years and particularly in the early 90s. Secondly, the few studies that do exist seem to point to different dynamics and issues from those found in general studies of women. The omission also suggests that information and data on black people's lives is to be drawn from other areas – black studies and black feminist writing in particular.

Of the four studies concerned with race that emerged from the literature search, one was difference-focused and also included a concern with class or poverty. Edwina Uehava's study, "Dual exchange theory, social networks, and informal social support" (Uehava 1990), explains the way low-income black women mobilized social support in the event of job loss. However, the primary concern of this study is in demonstrating a particular aspect of dual exchange theory to do with generalized and restricted exchange – it is only secondarily about black women's lives. Nevertheless, unusually, given the previously cited studies on social support, she draws her data from an ethnographic study, using a two-stage design with varied length, unstructured interviews with 19 women and 29 of their network members. Her findings are extremely complex (variety and density of networks, etc.) but some interesting points emerge. For example, generalized studies on kin versus friendship support suggest that it is kin who primarily provide material support, especially money. In contrast, Uehava found that half her women turned to friends as well as kin for material support, and that was seen as acceptable behaviour. She also found that different normative guidelines operated: those based on social co-operation and those based on self-reliance. She divided the women up into four types: gift receivers, frequent borrowers, reluctant exchangers and self-helpers. The gift receivers had stronger and more intense ties with kin and non-kin, the self-helpers less. This continuum was also reflected in terms of optimism – the gift receivers being more hopeful about seeing through their crisis than the self-helpers. Overall, however, as with the other studies reviewed so far, Uehava's work fails to relate these patterns of support to the material circumstances in which these women lived or to their experience as black women of racism and sexism. The three other studies which considered the issue of race are discussed in the later section on division-led research (see also Chapter 8).

Age

Interestingly, the studies focusing on older people yield a variety of different approaches as well as more thorough investigation into the meaning of old age and some of the inequalities associated with it. However, only three of the studies discussed in this chapter emerged directly from the stress/social support/coping literature (Antonucci & Akiyama 1987; Olsen et al. 1991; Wenger 1984).

Despite the greater diversity in this field than in the new paradigm research on gender and race, for example, it is still possible to discern two different ways in which age – or more specifically old age – is approached in these studies. The first is as an aspect of the life course and might be described in the terminology used in this chapter as difference-focused. However, this does not give this approach full credit for its attempt, by setting old age within the life-course, to remove it (old age) from the boundaries of a social problem category and into the scope of normality. The concept of the life-course also provides an additional analytic category to cross with those of stress, social support and coping. The second approach uses age as an indicator of inequalities and power-lessness in terms of income, health, employment and social discrimination – studies which we have categorized as division-led and which are discussed in a later section.

An example of difference-focused research on age-related issues is the Danish study by Olsen, Iverson and Sabroe (1991), "Age and the operationalisation of social support". Here, the concept of age is taken as the life course measured in intervals of 16–29, 30–39, 40–59, 60+. The sample was 1500 male manual shipyard workers who answered questionnaires about social support and health. The aim of the study was to examine changes in the men's social support (wife, family and friends) and health and well-being and the relationship between these two variables. They found that the amount of support from wives increased with age, although this support only had a positive impact on health for the 30–49 year-olds. Men had more social support from family and friends when they were younger, and this had a positive impact on health for both younger and older men.

The question of the nature of spouse support is explored more deeply in an interesting study in the US by Antonucci and Akiyama (1987), "An examination of sex differences in social support among older men and women". Their data were taken from the 1980 "Supports of the elderly national survey" of 214 men and 166 women aged between 50–95. They found that the general differences between men and women's social support networks, where women have larger and more multi-faceted networks while men have smaller networks where one person, usually their wife, is crucial, become more marked in older age. At the same time, men's perceptions of, and satisfaction with, their support was differ-ent from women's. Men were more likely to report giving and receiving support to and from their spouse, as well as greater satisfaction. Women, on the other hand, were more likely to report that their support did not come from their spouse but from their children and friends. Men and women expressed different expectations, criteria and evaluations of supportive intimate relationships. Women, for example, had higher expectations of their support network than men, seeking more intimacy than they found, whereas men seek *and* find intimacy through their wives. Sex differences in caring for a spouse who was ill were minimal, though women offered greater reassurance and talking over of upsetting events. Disruption of key figures in the network left men more vulnerable than women.

There were differences in the way support buffered against stress. Men reported that this did happen, but for women it depended on the quality of the support, and upon the fact that they experienced higher costs for the support they received and were vulnerable if their own source of support was itself under stress. One interesting finding was that both men and women said they preferred providing to receiving support. The authors suggest that this is to do with perceptions of dependence and independence which are especially important for older people. Notwithstanding these interesting and important studies, there is again little exploration in this study of the wider material context of these people's lives or of the experience of growing old in a society which does not value old age, nor of the different ways these impact on different groups of older people.

Disability

Disability was a third dimension of differences included in the literature review. The literature review involved a wide definition of disability which covered both physical disability, including disability caused by illness in old age and learning disability. However, it threw up only two studies (Atkinson 1986; Quittner et al. 1990). This implies that much of the work on stress, coping and social support in this area is within the informal care literature, the specialist disability and social work journals and the social movement/equal opportunities literature. In the following discussion there are references to some studies from this wider literature.

Apart from being a relatively neglected aspect of divisions within the new-paradigm literature, work concerned with disability, here and to some extent more widely, has also tended to focus on *difference* without seeking to understand the relationship with aspects of social divisions. Another problem with this area of research is that the problems of stress, strain, dependency or lack of support faced by carers of disabled children or adults are often studied in isolation from the similar, sometimes greater problems experienced by those for whom they care.

The US research study by Quittner, Gluekauf and Jackson (1990), "Chronic parenting stress: Moderating versus mediating effects of social support", illustrates these points. They examined 96 mothers of deaf children and 118 matched controls. Their aim was to examine social support in conditions of chronic or enduring stress (as opposed to life event stress). They found that mothers of deaf children experienced higher levels of parenting stress than mothers of non-impaired children and they had smaller support networks with fewer sources of either family or friendship support. In fact, these mothers relied much more on health care professionals than family and friends to meet their emotional support needs. In a situation of ongoing stress (as opposed to acute stress) informal support did not seem to mitigate the impact of stress. Although an increase of support is perceived as helpful for acute periods of stress, an increase of support in the context of chronic stress may be seen as intrusive or indicating the carer's incompetence. Additionally network members may not feel competent in knowing what sort of support to provide. They also found that the mothers' perceptions of their own competence decreased: "Mothers coping with a distractible, moody child on an ongoing basis may view themselves as ineffective and their child as unrewarding" (ibid.: 1276).

A different approach to this question of stigma and self-perception comes from the specialist mental handicap literature which incorporates the views of disabled people. Jahoda, Markova and Cattermole's UK study, "Stigma and the self-concept of people with a mild mental handicap" (Jahoda et al. 1988) is based on a small sample of interviews with both mothers and their adult sons or daughters with a learning difficulty. Although all the people interviewed recognized the stigma attached to being "mentally handicapped", the majority of mothers (eight of twelve) viewed their children as being "essentially different" from non-handicapped people, whereas only a minority of people with learning difficulties did (three of twelve), the majority perceiving themselves as "essentially the same". What is interesting about this study is its implication, first, that the perceptions and experiences of those who are cared-for do not necessarily accord with their carers, and secondly, that these young people with learning difficulties were aware of their own agency.

Another British study focusing on agency is the social support study by Dorothy Atkinson, "Engaging competent others" (Atkinson 1986). This looks at the strategies developed by people with learning difficulties on leaving a long-stay institution. She found a variety of coping strategies, but that most people developed a social network and engaged "competent others" – informal friends or relatives who supplemented or supplanted the roles of formal service workers.

Sexuality

Apart from a research paper on social support for gay men experiencing AIDS-related grief (Lennon et al. 1990) the issue of sexuality in the field of stress, support and coping is notable for its absence. This reflects an uncritical assumption within the literature of the universality and desirability of heterosexual-family-network systems. The importance of work in this area is discussed in a later section of this chapter.

In an important way then, research which is difference-focused is concerned with "the personal" and can generate questions which are concerned with the meanings and experiences of people's lives, the strategies they use and how these may be related to other social divisions. But the unravelling of these processes is not informed by a notion of the dynamics of social power and inequality. It is these issues that division-led research tries to grapple with, as discussed in the next section.

Division-led Research

So far we have been discussing the nature and extent of research in the "new paradigm" tradition which, while focusing on one or more dimension of social divisions and inequalities fails to make a conceptual or theoretical connection between the experience of individuals and the workings and discursive practices of wider social structures. There is, however, literature on stress, coping and social support which might help us to understand better the relationship between identity, agency and structure. As in the previous section, however, much of this work is concerned with gender, and to a lesser extent class rather than other dimensions of difference – race, age, disability and sexuality are all neglected.

Gender

Pressure for division-led work on gender has come from feminist writers or those writers whose work is more consistently informed by a theoretical understanding of unequal social relations. Much of the American work in this area focuses on the relationship of stress and support to women's roles as mother, partner and paid worker. Some of it sets out to offer a feminist critique of previous work. Thus Baruch et al. (1987) start from the position that research on stress at work has focused on men with the result that it has generalized from men's experiences to women's and has overlooked the salient issues in women's lives with the result that where such issues have relevance to men, these too have been ignored. They also observe the lack of research on women in this area which looks at the inter-relationship of gender to class and race. In particular they challenge the androcentric assumption that home acts as a buffer for stress experienced in paid work, or that for women, paid employment impairs women's role at home through "role overload". Theirs is a useful review of research in this area, including their own on women's multiple role involvement and psychological distress and well-being. They make a number of general points:

- that family roles generate considerable stress for women, especially in relation to control (the less controllable/predictable a task the more stressful), though this is mediated by "high marital quality";
- in general paid employment is more beneficial to well-being than non-employment ("a job is to a woman as a wife is to a man"), but that this is more the case for women in higher status jobs and less the case for women in poor work conditions and/or difficult family situations;

- paid work can act as a buffer against the stress generated from being a wife or a mother, but quality in all these roles is crucial, especially partners taking a share of family work;
- whereas paid work can mitigate the effect of marital stress, parenthood exacerbates the effects of work-related stress;
- it is not so much the quantity of roles which women have which produces stress but the quality of experience in those roles and that some degree of autonomy and control is an important factor contributing towards quality of experience.

They conclude by suggesting that social policies aimed at increasing psychological well-being for women need to take account of employment discrimination and enhancement of conditions in women's paid work (like flexible hours and child care provision) and individual-oriented programs on the management of family stressors. Their work exemplifies two aspects of division-led work in the area of gender: (a) the attempt to relate more directly women's well-being to social conditions and inequalities and (b) the attempt to draw in explanations of individual behaviour which link the individual as a creative agent to social processes – in this case, control and autonomy or lack of it, rather than the psychologically-bounded notion of self-esteem, or lack of it. (In fact Pearlin, quoted earlier, uses the concept of "mastery" as an important component of coping mechanisms.)

The issue of *control/autonomy* is one of two concepts to emerge from the division-led research which provides us with a connection between psychological and sociological approaches to the questions of how people cope. The other is the use by certain social groups of an *identity* as the basis for generating social support. Before looking at work which identifies these concepts, I refer briefly to a debate within the literature on gender which in many ways reflects some of the gaps between psychological and sociological ideas. This is the debate on whether socialization or role constraint provides a better understanding of gender differences in coping strategies.

Socialization or Role Constraint?

Reviewing the literature on gender differences in coping and social roles, Rosario and her colleagues in the US (Rosario et al. 1988) noted a tension between those who found gender differences (for example, women tend to emotion-focused problem-solving; women provide and receive more emotional as opposed to instrumental support) and put these down to differential gender patterns of socialization, and those who explained such differences in terms of the different roles men and women occupy and the different opportunities and constraints to which they are exposed.

The authors suggest that those explanations based on socialization have a tendency to blame the victim and to focus on behaviour rather than stresses or resources: "socialisation affects who one is; role constraints affect what one does" (Rosario et al. 1988: 56). Their own research is on the stress–coping strategies used by men and women in similar social roles as therapists, child care workers and undergraduates. They found little difference in the coping strategies used by men and women in similar social roles faced with similar stresses. However, in terms of social support women had more support available to them, though whether this is because they sought, perceived or accepted more support, or had more offered is unclear. They suggest that for these women this availability of support actually advantages them over men. The conclusion drawn was that there was little support in their findings for socialization theories of gender differences in coping efforts and that studies of coping needed to be more grounded in the situation or context with which women and men cope. In terms of practice they suggested that efforts should go into altering the social roles which constrain or stress women rather than on teaching women alternative and effective coping strategies.

These arguments and conclusions are reflected in other structuralist studies, for example, Gwen Moore's (US) study, "Structural determinants of men's and women's personal networks" (1990), and another American study by Karyn Loscocco and Glenna Spitz, "Working conditions, social support and well-being of female and male factory workers" (1990).

On the other side of the debate are those studies which support the socialization theory. For example Flaherty and Richman's US study, "Gender differences in the perception and utilization of social support: theoretical perspectives and an empirical test" (1988), draws evidence from a questionnaire survey of 210 medical students to show that women show a greater sensitivity to the needs of themselves and others, leading to a greater capacity to provide support and a greater dependence upon social support for psychological well-being. This difference is related to both personality and gender differences in socialization.

Two points can be made about these studies within the context of continuing debate about socialization or role constraints as explanatory factors. The first is that, to some extent, the fact that the debate persists illustrates the paucity of conceptual tools and analyses to link these two areas: socialization and structural determinants. The second is that while these works provide a perspective on social conditions, and even though they are division-led, there is a remarkable absence of "voices" from the research. The research methods used – formal, often interviewer completed questionnaires, based on measurements of variables – allow little room for the experience and meanings of the questions under study to be developed or articulated by the respondents themselves (see Chapter 5).

Power and Control

A second key area developed by division-led studies in the area of gender is concerned with issues of power and control/autonomy. Three studies identified in the review attempted to examine the significance of these issues and their relation to power, control or autonomy and its relation to psychological/emotional well-being (Rosenfeld 1989; Ross and Mirowsky 1989; Turner and Noh 1983). Turner and Noh's "Class and psychological vulnerability among women: the significance of social support and personal control" which somewhat unusually is concerned primarily with class rather than gender, begins promisingly with the following comment: "Our assumption is that there is something about social class position that matters for emotional health and well-being" (1983: 2). They focus on two variables which may help us to understand this: social support and personal control. Their concept of personal control has three elements: (a) a personal element that derives from one's life history (b) one's conceptualization of the external world (fatalism/realism) and (c) one's attitude towards one's own competence or efficacy. They interviewed 312 white women in Ontario four weeks after their giving birth. However, the research says very little about women or about the sorts of gender inequalities which might give rise to feelings of loss of personal control or need for social support at this stage in their lives. Instead this group of women is selected because of their disposition to psychological stress rather than for the factors which may give rise to it. Nevertheless, they found that:

- psychological distress correlated with lower-class status;
- personal control and social support both play a part in producing this correlation, although they have different significance for different groups, for example, social support matters more to those under stress;
- the class/distress relationship can be explained when personal control and social support together are high, but on their own high social support or high personal control cannot explain the relationship.

A similar American study is Ross and Mirowsky's (1989) "Explaining patterns of depression: Control and problem-solving – or support and talking?". In this they attempt to explain the recurrent finding that high income, education and being male are associated with low levels of depression through two key social perceptions: a sense of controlling one's own life and the sense of having a supportive and understanding person to talk to in times of trouble. They reported six key findings.

- High income and high level of education correlated with a feeling of being in control of one's own life and this reduces depression because people in this position will be in a better position to act upon their depression. If either control or support is missing, one can substitute for the other in lowering vulnerability to depression.
- Someone who feels in control of their life does not depend on support for their well-being, and someone with a strong sense of support does not depend so much on feeling in control.
- People with low levels of education have less personal control and less social support.
- Women have less personal control than men because of the roles women occupy in the family and labour market.

- Women also have higher levels of support, but while support is useful in keeping depression at bay, actually talking about one's depression increases vulnerability to depression (see Antonucci and Akiyama 1987 discussed earlier).
- This negative support factor contributes less to producing depression amongst women than conditions of family and paid work.

The penultimate point, which suggests that talking to someone about depression can exacerbate depression because it induces feelings of lesser worth and dependency, is also borne out by reports from self-help groups that helping others, in a similar position, rather than just being helped, assists people to survive trauma and stress – see for example a journalist's report on the work of self-help groups for child abuse survivors (Plachta 1992).

The third piece of research is by Sarah Rosenfeld (1989), "The effects of women's employment: personal control and sex differences in mental health". On the basis that lack of power contributes to differential rates of anxious and depressive symptoms among married women compared with married men, Rosenfeld looked at the contribution paid employment can make to reducing this powerlessness for women. She suggests that the contradictory evidence for the impact of paid employment on women's emotional well-being (see for example, Baruch et al. 1978; Brown & Harris 1978; Parry 1986, all discussed earlier) is to be explained by looking at the relationship of the different aspects of women's lives in terms of the overall sense of high demands and lack of personal control. Her study shows that when either family demands or job demands are low, paid employment is beneficial to women in terms of emotional well-being. Women can benefit specifically from the income and independent status of paid work. However, for some women, especially those with high family demands, any potential benefit from work is cancelled out by a feeling of greater loss of control. In this work, Rosenfeld attempts to unpack some of the component parts of women's powerlessness, in terms of demands placed upon them, and lack of control as well as lack of power through economic dependency. She also spells out a perspective of women's power/subordination in society in which socialization, gender role training and the social conditions of adulthood all play a part in producing perceptions of, as well as actual, lower levels of control by women.

This study, like Ross and Mirowsky's, is based on formal questionnaires in which measures of power, control and demands are deduced from factual details, e.g. relative resources of husband and wife in terms of income level, number of children, or questions on how often family members make demands or answers of "agree/disagree" to instrumentally worded control questions. One third of Rosenfeld's and all of Ross and Mirowsky's data was based on telephone interviews through random digit dialling. This means that the *meanings* of power, control and autonomy are not elicited from respondents themselves. We therefore get no sense of the different factors contributing to women's lack of control or powerlessness. Is it the physical or financial demands of their children or the emotional demands of their partners or the sexual harassment by their bosses? What do women do or think about this? How do they explain it? What options

are open to them? And how does class, race, age, sexuality or disability reconstitute these experiences? These are some of the unanswered questions thrown up
by this area of research.

Questions of Identity

The issue of how people identify themselves and how that may affect the sources
of mutual support they seek is raised indirectly by a study by Ann D'Ercole,
"Single mothers: stress, coping and social support" (D'Ercole 1988). The aim of
this study of 83 single mothers in New York was to examine the significance of
income in the stress faced by single mothers and the positive ways in which
single mothers cope and the sort of support they call upon. She found that
financial strain was the most significant factor in stress and ability to cope with
other stresses. However, what is interesting are her findings on social support.
First of all, these women drew their support from a few people rather than a
large network; secondly, these were likely to be co-workers in a similar situation
rather than family or neighbours. The benefit of this support was seen in terms
of its being based on mutuality rather than obligation. There were variations in
people who utilized this kind of mutual support. The higher a woman's job
status or income the less able she felt to draw on her co-workers for support
because she might also be in competition with them. Also the costs of fathers'
involvement was seen by these women to outweigh the benefits. At the end of
the study D'Ercole, in acknowledging the limits of her study, says that these
were members of a "special population" of people "in need of company of
people in a similar situation" (ibid. 1988: 52). In fact, what she points to is the
importance to these women of their identity as single mothers.

Given the development in the significance of "identity politics", this issue of
identity offers possibilities to explore further coping strategies of resistance and
resilience. This is discussed further in Chapter 8.

Race

Though more limited, the literature review identified a number of important
division-led studies concerned with race. The basis of solidarity for the use of
non-kin as well as kin in systems of reciprocity is an issue brought out in
Michelene Malson's American study, "The social support system of black families" (1983). This is an extremely useful review of contemporary US literature
on black family social support systems. Malson identifies three theoretical positions on work on black families: (a) the culturally equivalent model which
assumes that black families' cultures are similar to white families'; (b) the cultural
deviant model which views any differences in black families as pathological and
(c) the cultural variant model which identifies those differences as strengths, not
weaknesses, or at least as "sensible adaptations to external stresses and forces"

(ibid. 1983: 38). Malson presents a range of interesting findings drawn from ethnographic work and social surveys. For example, in terms of comparison with white families, she points to evidence of higher interaction among kin for black families, to support from non-kin – especially, for black women – support from co-workers and from "fictive-kin" ("aunties", etc.). She suggests that one strongly held normative principle guiding such support is care of children: "Children represent the next generation on whom one can place the hopes for mobility and success not experienced by parents" (ibid. 1983: 44).

In addition, she suggests that the existence of racism makes such support necessary especially where existing institutions or professional services are seen as culturally inappropriate or insensitive. As further evidence she looks at two different explanations for the strength of support systems among black families. The first suggests that these exist because of economic deprivation; the second, because of a strong cultural belief in mutual aid. Drawing on research work on black middle-class families Malson argues that the endurance of strong support systems in these families suggests that the cultural thesis is correct. Another interesting difference is in the role of older people; she points out that it is more likely for older black women to go and live with their daughter's or son's family. Finally, she sounds a note of caution about an approach which emphasizes the strengths of black family support systems. First, there needs to be more empirical work done on the costs to people of providing such support and secondly, she argues that evidence of supportive systems can be used to defend cutbacks on services and resources to black communities. Within Britain work on race and welfare provision (which was to thrown up by the literature research) points to exactly these problems (Ahmad & Atkin 1996; Connelly 1988; Mama 1989b; Torkington 1991; Williams 1989). In addition, some black feminists have pointed to the mixed blessings of a strengthening of "community solidarity" for black women where the hierarchy within community organizations is dominated by men with traditionalist or fundamentalist ideas about women's place in the community (Southall Black Sisters 1990).

An empirical study by Brown and Gary (1987), "Stressful life events, social support networks and the physical and mental health of urban black adults", is interesting because it encompasses aspects of race, class and gender; it also differentiates between the impact of social support upon physical and mental health. The study involved analysis of structured questionnaires from 451 black adults. The authors note three things: the lack of research on the impact of stressful life events experienced by poor urban black people; the reluctance of black people to use formal health care resources; and empirical evidence that demonstrates the buffering effect of families, voluntary organizations and churches.

They found significant gender differences in the role of social support in buffering mental health. Support from nearby relatives had a mitigating effect on psychological disturbance for black women, but not for black men. Social support had little effect on the physical health of either black men or women, although religious activity by black women minimized the stress from poor physical health. As with other studies of this sort, qualitative studies into the meanings behind this data would provide a better picture of these race, gender and class differences. What might be particularly interesting, given Malson's emphasis on cultural solidarity, is an investigation into the way in which understanding of, and resistance to, oppression (such as racism) is mediated through culturally solidaristic beliefs (or normative guidelines) and social support systems. A British study, not on social support, but the construction of British African Caribbean female identity, by Heidi Mirza (Mirza 1992) highlights this particular dynamic when she suggests that the cultural construction of femininity among young African Caribbean women differs from that of their white peers in that it stresses the relative autonomy of male and female roles and the relative independence of African Caribbean women. This is because the historical and economic necessity for women to be able to support themselves has been carried into both the British context and the cultural definitions of feminity: "Ironically, the dynamic that has produced this equality between the sexes within the black social structure has been the external imposition of oppression and brutality" (ibid.: 164).

Age

In general, though still limited in volume, division-led research concerned with the well-being of older people is marked by a greater fusion of both the multiplicity of social divisions and an openness to qualitative work on the perceptions of older people themselves. An important Scottish study which looks at inequalities in old age, including access to social support, is by Taylor and Ford, "Inequalities in old age: an examination of age, sex and class differences in a sample of community elderly" (1983). This examines the distribution of personal resources – income and savings, social support, health and psychological functioning – between age cohorts (60–74 and 75+) sex groups and social classes from a sample of 619 people in Aberdeen. They found that all groups experience a loss of most resources over time, but there are marked age, class and sex variations. Young elderly, middle-class men rank most highly on all resources except social support; younger elderly working-class men also rank low on all resources and older middle-class women rank low on all but close friends. Middle-class advantages are slightly eroded by old age, but this is particularly marked for women.

This quantitative study provides a good basis for more qualitative work on meanings and experiences of old age for different groups. Two examples of this type of work are noted here. First, Jo Harrison's Australian study, "Women and ageing: experience and implications" (1983), which is based on 16 biographical accounts and focuses in particular on the way these women both reflect and reject stereotypical notions of older women. Second is Helen Evers' UK study, "Old women's self-perceptions of dependency and some implications for service provision" (1984) which is based on 50 life histories of women over 75 living in the Birmingham area. She identifies two patterns of self-perception: active and passive which have important implications for the way providers intervene and the sorts of services that are offered. She argues that:

Women's self-perceptions . . . do not seem entirely congruent with the usual notions of dependency applied by health professionals and other formal service providers. Only a qualitative survey could have revealed this. Prematurely conducted surveys may be in danger of inappropriately applying pre-existing categories to research populations (Evers 1984: 308–9).

Finally there is the British study by Clare Wenger, *The Supportive Network: Coping with Old Age* (1984). Again this is important in presenting a positive image of older people as "creative human agents" providing as well as receiving care, adapting to old age, but still part of existing class and gender differences. There is a gap in research on the social support networks of older black people and the implications of this for provision, although some work has been done here (Ahmad & Atkin 1996; Bhalla & Blakemore 1981; Blakemore & Boneham 1993).

Sexuality

As noted earlier, work concerned with the relationship between personal welfare, sexuality and dimensions of inequality is largely absent from the new paradigm literature. There are three reasons why this absence needs urgent attention. First, as mentioned earlier, gay men and lesbians may prefer to, or have to, find alternative sources to family support and methods of coping. Secondly, the widespread discrimination faced by gay men and lesbians, either closeted or out, suggests that this may create a particular form of stress for which people develop particular and different coping strategies (raising again the relevance of "identity"). Thirdly, in recent years sexual harassment for women, and sexual abuse of women and children, has been identified as a significant, ongoing and often invisible stressor in people's lives (see Chapter 5). (The issue of the significance of child sexual abuse in adults' lives is recognized in the paper by Coyne & Downey 1991 already cited). To examine different aspects of sexuality as an aspect of inequality (in terms of identity and as a form of oppression), it is necessary to turn to feminist literature, to literature focusing on the experiences and lives of gay men and lesbians (see Chapter 8).

The research by Lennon, Martin and Dean, "The influence of social support on AIDS-related grief reaction among gay men" (1990), illustrates a further aspect of the need for research – the risks of AIDS in the gay community. This is a US study by structured interview of 180 gay men who lost their lover/close friend to AIDS up to 1985. The aim was to examine the relationship between instrumental and emotional support and the experience of grief reaction. They found that most gay men who develop AIDS relied on their lover and/or on close friends through the illness. Access to both family and professional sources of care was limited, in spite of the intense care and support needs of those who became ill with AIDS. This means that the support network which was usually composed of gay men became particularly involved in meeting these needs for care. This in itself, they found, intensified the men's grief reactions, and made them vulnerable to prolonged and unresolved distress. In addition, where formal support was used this was usually from voluntary agencies which were staffed by gay men, who themselves may develop close bonds with the person they are assisting, and they, too, experience intense grief following death. Furthermore this grief experienced by lovers, friends or volunteers is intensified by two other stress factors – that they themselves may be vulnerable to AIDS and that others in the network may also develop the illness and die. The authors conclude that support itself is not enough, but that it is necessary to have support which is able to meet the demands that the situation presents.

Disability

It was noted in the previous section that the literature research threw up only two articles on disability and that it was necessary to go to the literature to emerge from the disability movement to find work which looks at disability and support. Interestingly, much of this work reconceptualizes the notion of support in terms of the goal of empowering disabled people, breaking down structural barriers and enabling people to live independent lives (Morris 1993). Similarly, the interrelating of disability to gender, race, class and sexuality has emerged from those concerned with the notions of oppression and inequality (see for example Morris 1991 on women and disability, and Morris 1992 for a trenchant critique of the informal care literature written from a disabled feminist perspective; see Baxter et al. 1990, and Williams 1992b for gender, race and learning difficulty, Ahmad and Atkin 1996 on aspects of race and community care, and Shakespeare et al. 1996 for sexuality and disability). If the problem of "agency" is one that bedevils the social support literature then this problem is compounded in the area of disability where only recently has the collective voice of this group begun to be listened to.

In this discussion of division-led research reference has been made to bodies of literature not covered by the search into literature on stress, coping and social support. One of the most important areas is that on informal care which deals with the process of supporting rather than the nature of social support (e.g. Finch 1989; Graham 1983; Ungerson 1987). This literature may well provide us with pointers to some of the conceptual gaps in the field of research discussed above. For example, it was suggested earlier that the socialization–social role constraint debate exposed the lack of conceptual tools to understand the relationship between individual action and social structure. I have also referred to the fact that we get little sense from these studies of people acting out their lives, finding some way through the maze of constraints and contradictions. Women, working-class women in particular, appear as either conditioned or constrained, and probably depressed, their happiness and stability conditional upon a particular constellation of apparently unrelated variables. Alternative representations and analytical frameworks exist in the feminist work on informal care (e.g. Finch 1989) and these will be discussed in Chapter 8.

Assessment and Conclusion

To conclude this review of the treatment of social differences and social divisions in the literature on stress, coping strategies and social support I examine two sets of questions relevant to the concerns of this book. First, how far have studies in the new paradigm literature moved on in the light of the critiques of them, referenced at the beginning of the chapter, by Young and by Davies and Roche in 1980. In particular, how far do they meet the criticisms:

- that dimensions of inequality are represented only in terms of methodological units or control variables;
- that structural inequalities remain untheorized, except insofar as they present interesting/pathological difference;
- that the interrelationship between agency and structure is represented by reducing "the social to the individual" – explaining social phenomena in terms of individual attributes?

Secondly, how far does the literature in this area provide a fruitful basis for bringing the exploration of agency into welfare research. In particular:

- how far can these studies provide the conceptual links between the two paradigms of welfare, between agency and structure;
- how far can they provide the basis for a better understanding of the role of, and relationship between, informal, formal and voluntary provision?

An overall response to these two sets of questions would be: only partly. Some of the studies do go beyond using gender, class, etc. simply as control variables, though many still use these dimensions of inequality as controls, or as a focus for particular pathologies, or unexplained forms of difference. Those division-led studies that do go further often situate their explanations of inequality in terms of either social conditions of paid work and/or family life, or in socialization processes. The tendency of both explanations, particularly within the scientifically and quantitatively-based literature, is that they overgeneralize people, particularly women, as victims-by-degree of the conditions of their existence, and not as *creative agents*. In addition, the tendency of the socialization approach, though it focuses on the individual, is that it can draw us back into a sort of psychologically essentialist explanation for differences. If concepts like self-esteem are to be useful for examining the social relations of power and inequality then they need conceptual links to hook them into different social processes. Two particular concepts which emerge as potentially useful here are issues of personal control as a dimension of power and inequality, and (implicitly) from some of the literature on race, on single mothers, and from disability and sexuality, the notion of identity.

To deal with the concept of identity first: in relation to major forms of subordination and inequality it is possible to see the creation of identity as an important mechanism for enhancing self-esteem, understanding and acting and resisting within the social world, and creating alternative normative guidelines for the generation of social support. This would not include only identities based on gender, race, etc., but also those such as survivor or self-advocate which emerge from self-help movements within welfare. Given the significance of identity politics and the process of what some sociologists have called "individualisation" (Beck & Beck-Gernsheim 1995; Giddens 1991) which were identified in Chapter 1, the question of how people see themselves and explain their place in the social world, and what is enabling or constraining for them, constitutes a possible frame for connecting the psychological to the sociological. However, it would be necessary to go outside of the stress/coping/support literature to follow this up – to the social work, social movement and empowerment literature (see Chapter 8).

There are a number of interesting leads within the literature on the issue of personal control and autonomy. Particularly interesting is the idea that while personal control and social support are important for well-being there is a possibility for substitutability between them. The meanings behind this finding and the implications for formal support would, too, be worth pursuing. Here again, concepts of empowerment and self-determination used within the radical social work and equal opportunities literature on gender, race, disability and sexuality might be useful.

Does the literature lead us towards a better understanding of the role that the formal and voluntary sectors could play? Only very implicitly. Most of the literature does not concern itself with practice or policy implications except at the very broadest of levels (more jobs, more child care, etc.) The idea explicit in the notion that the studies of social support should generate more appropriate interventions by social workers, health workers and others is largely missing from much of the literature. There is, however, a study by Miriam Stewart, "Social support: diverse theoretical perspectives" (1989), which identifies four different approaches to social support: attribution theory, where people attribute blame to an individual for a cause of a problem which then may determine the support they get; coping theory, whereby alternative methods for dealing with stress are examined; social exchange (or equity) theory, which looks at the basis of social support – reciprocity, exchange, etc.; and loneliness theory, which examines the need for affective support. Stewart examines the usefulness of each theory for health care. For example, she suggests that attribution theory can alert professionals to the extent to which individuals or their support systems seek to attribute self-blame or blame for a particular condition (AIDS, sexual abuse) and then to find alternative and more helpful support systems (e.g. mutual aid groups). However, issues of social inequalities or even of the differential power relationship between providers and users of health care are not explored.

One British study which looks at social support and social inequalities and which also brings support from practitioners into the picture is Ann Oakley and Lynda Rajan's "Social class and social support: the same or different?" (1991). In many ways this study meets or recognizes many of the objections which have been raised in the existing literature on stress/coping/social support. The research is placed within the theoretical understanding of class and gender social relations of power and inequality and within a context of social, economic and political change. It attempts to draw together literature and issues from three areas: from feminist class analysis, social support and from health care/policy. Furthermore, the authors are reflexive about their methodology in several important ways – for example, they ask how it is possible: "to do sociological work without reducing the people whose experiences are drawn on to the limiting status of objects of others' interpretations" (Oakley & Rajan 1991: 36).

More generally, what is also missing in the new paradigm literature is an understanding of welfare as a system which itself carries its own hierarchies and social relations of power and inequality. It is important to explore how these interweave with existing patterns of inequality and subordination, and also what people themselves make of formal support, how they reconstitute it, the role it can/could play in their lives, the costs/benefits to them, and how these meanings and experiences transcend or are underpinned by class/race/gender, etc. as well as by existing discourses of welfare.

The point about methodology raised in the quotation above from Oakley and Rajan (1991) also suggests that the methods required to study many of these issues would have to be different from the dominant methods found in the stress/social support/coping literature, with its emphasis on scientific, quantitative analysis and its lack of attention to limitations of formal information gathering. This is not to minimize the usefulness of the findings which these quantitative studies have generated. Rather it is to say that qualitative studies on the meanings behind these findings are necessary, especially in order to uncover subjective experiences of different interrelated social relations of power and inequality and to see the research subject as a creative human agent. These issues are discussed in more depth in Chapters 5 and 8.

Finally it has to be said that the diversity of inequalities represented in the literature is very limited, focusing mainly on class and gender. The omissions represent major gaps. There is also an uneasy and unworked out tension between *difference* as pathology (especially gender and class, but also disability), difference as academically fascinating, difference as part of a more diverse society, and difference as a manifestation of inequality. Any overall theoretical understanding of the interconnections between different forms of difference/inequality is also minimal. Furthermore the overemphasis of some areas – gender in particular – leads to overgeneralization. Thus findings of studies focusing on working-class women of unspecified race, sexual orientation or marital status, are implicitly extended to all working-class women. In addition, the emphasis on carers in much of the literature may obscure the experiences of people in need of care/ support. Conversely and importantly, much of the literature in the field which is dealing with inequalities calls out for different concepts and methods which allow us to see people as active human agents. Chapter 8 of this book examines other areas of research which may provide further possibilities for developing a conceptual framework for welfare research which links the creative welfare agent to social structure and social change.

Notes

1   The literature search for the review was commissioned by the co-ordinators of the Management of Personal Welfare Initiative on behalf of the ESRC and carried out in 1992. It was based upon a cross-referencing of keywords from the new paradigm – stress, coping strategies/behaviour, social support and life events – with keywords from the old paradigm – inequalities, poverty, disadvantage, income, social divisions, social structure and class. To these were added those indicators of inequality and social division which emerged as significant social relations of power and inequality from the social movements of the 1960s, 70s and 80s – gender, race, disability, age and sexuality (see Chapter 1). Three indexes were searched for literature from the previous ten years covering sociology and psychology and this yielded 113 items. The abstracts of these were scanned for relevance on the basis of first, their focus on one or more dimensions of social divisions/inequality and, secondly, for their being a key contribution to content, methodological or theoretical debate. They were then reduced to 67 which were reviewed. The review also references research not thrown up by these three searches, either because it emerged as a key referent in the subsequent literature or because, in the process of analysis of the literature, it was work known to the reviewer which acted as a significant counterpoint to the emerging analysis. The key question framing the review was – in what ways do structural issues inform the research in social support, stress and coping? After an initial reading, the literature was organized in three different ways : first, in terms of the structural issues that it dealt with (e.g. class, gender, unemployment, etc.); secondly, how it dealt with it/them; and, thirdly, whether it introduced concepts which mediated between individual and structural issues, or agency and structure. On the second question a number of themes emerged and these were consolidated into the organizing principles of the review and the literature was read a second time. It should be noted that in the last five years the technology and methodology of literature reviews has become much more sophisticated and that there are limits to the methods of this review. However given (as is the case for commissioned work) the constraints of time, the review provided a useful springboard for discussion and debate. My thanks to Sarah Tibbs who did the three original searches.

2   These issues of changing gender relations and their connections to welfare policy and provision are explored in greater detail in the sister book to this volume – Popay et al. 1998.

Chapter 3

Constructs from the New Paradigm: An Exploration of Diverse Meanings

Julie Seymour

Introduction

The previous chapter began to explore the extent to which the research literature on stress, coping and social support may help us in our quest for a new framework for welfare research and practice – a framework which enables us to better understand the relationship between personal history and the social and material world. More specifically, it would be a framework that connects the study and practice of formal welfare provision to an understanding of personal psychological and social coping strategies. In this chapter we continue this exploration of the potential offered by this wide ranging literature in a different but complementary way. We will focus in detail on the way in which five key concepts within this field – stress, life events, coping, social support and vulnerability – are variously constructed across academic disciplines and by welfare practitioners and lay people. In so doing we will attempt to identify and illuminate ways in which constructs of the nature of and relationship between these concepts are changing and explore the research, policy and practice implications of the similarities and differences in constructs across disciplines and between practitioners and lay people.

Three disciplines are considered: psychology, sociology and epidemiology. It is recognized however, that the boundaries around these disciplines cannot and should not be rigidly defined. In particular, some of the work identified here as sociology, for example, sits at the intersection between this discipline and social policy. Additionally, within each of these disciplines, important sub–disciplines with different theoretical perspectives and epistemological roots can be identified. There may well be as much diversity within disciplines in the areas we are discussing, as between. Notwithstanding these considerations, we will primarily use broad but somewhat crude disciplinary categories.

The Concepts

Given the differences in interpretation of the key concepts with which we are concerned in this chapter, it is neither possible nor appropriate to provide the reader with unequivocal definitions. However, it is possible to provide an initial map of the general terrain over which we will be travelling.

Stress

In 1966, Lazarus commented that stress, "defines a large, complex amorphous, interdisciplinary area of interest and study" (p. 27). Twenty-five years later, although the study of stress has resulted in a tremendous outpouring of literature (over 630 citations in 1991 alone), it continues to present difficulties as to how it should be defined or applied and indeed, whether it has any validity as a concept at all (Engel 1985).

At its most basic, there is some agreement as to what constitutes stress. Applied to living things, "stress refers to the response of the organism to a noxious or threatening condition" (Pearlin 1982: 369). Although biological/physiological studies refer to stress as a stimulus or a response to a stimulus, sociological/psychological studies have come to consider it as a process; an interaction between the environment and the individual (Folkman & Lazarus 1980; Pearlin 1982). Manifestations of stress have been identified at a number of levels. In the individual it can result variously in microbiological, psychological, behavioural and emotional changes. Pearlin also considers that stress can operate at individual, familial, community and societal levels (Pearlin 1982). In this context, he has argued that it is important to recognize the "multidimensionality of this phenomenon" and to work towards "understanding how its multiple manifestations are interconnected" (op. cit.: 369).

Life Events

Life events have been described as occurrences in people's lives which require some form of change and adaptation to take place (Brown & Harris 1978). They therefore may be perceived as stressful. They are considered to be distinct from ongoing difficulties or continuing social roles by their short duration (Titterton 1989). Certain life events may be predictable, such as marriage or leaving the parental home, while others will be unexpected, as in the case of sudden bereavement, disasters or physical attack by a stranger. Clearly, not all life events are unpleasant but the fact that they create change means that all may be categorized as a form of stressor. Wheaton (1983) has pointed out that life events are not equally stressful to all people and it is necessary to review the event in the context of the individual's life. Recent research has criticized previous studies as tending to view life events as static and discrete occurrences, neglecting their role in the life-course. Instead, Pearlin (1989: 244) has argued, such events should be viewed as a "marker or surrogate indicator" of a life-course in a particular social context. He suggests that few life events occur completely "out of the blue" and may represent a culmination of long-term chronic stressors.

Coping

Broadly speaking coping can be described as a reaction to a stressful environment. Again as with stress, it has a number of definitions; confusingly it may be viewed as a process or an outcome, a dependent or an independent variable. Edwards and Cooper warn of the frequent confounding of the concepts of stress, coping and well-being "where some stressful life events may also be construed as an inability to cope (for example, divorce) or a symptom of well-being (for example, personal illness)" (1988: 15). In addition, whether one is considered to be successfully coping with the situation clearly depends on the nature of the outcome required. This may vary; is it to be measured, for example, in terms of physical and mental health, economic circumstances or successful social relationships?

Monat and Lazarus (1977) have shown how assessments of coping are dependent on the values, perspectives, temporal scale and situation of those involved. For example, behaviours which are effective from a physiological point of view may produce further psychological and social problems, for example, the experience of chemotherapy. Alternatively, it has been argued that responses which may be considered appropriate in the short term may be damaging if carried out for a longer period of time, such as a process of denial when faced with the terminal illness of a child (Friedman et al. 1963). This variation in opinion as to what constitutes coping may be particularly evident between welfare practitioners and service users (Murgatroyd & Woolfe 1982; Parker & Seymour 1998).

Much of the literature on coping concentrates on the adjustment of the individual to various stressors such as: ill-health (Felton et al. 1984; Waltz et al. 1988), bereavement (Friedman et al. 1963) or abuse (Herbert et al. 1991; Johnson & Kenkel 1991). Other levels of analysis have recognized that situations facing individuals usually involve others and have therefore considered the coping processes employed by dyads and families (Seymour, in press). The latter, which is frequently considered as a single unit rather than a collective of individuals, is considered to have coping strategies which are distinct from and different to those adopted by individual family members (Stetz et al. 1986). Similarly, it has been suggested that occurrences which involve larger groups of people or communities (natural or man-made disasters, unemployment) may require coping strategies on a larger scale (Deitch 1984; Gallers et al. 1988). Breznitz & Goldberger (1982) considered that an interest in coping mechanisms is predicated on the assumption that, given the right tools, one can cope effectively with most sources of stress. The search for these tools or resources, as they have also been termed, has occupied considerable numbers of researchers and the notions of *social support* and *vulnerability* have become prominent.

Social Support

The concept of social support focuses on both the formal and informal social resources available to individuals when faced with stressful situations. It is important to distinguish, as Lazarus & Folkman (1984) did, between social networks and social support. A person's social network consists of the variety of people with whom they associate, from family to friends to work colleagues. Social support, on the other hand, consists of those people who actually offer tangible support, whether this be material, practical or emotional. Often social networks and social support are conflated, based on erroneous assumptions that the former will automatically provide the latter. Hence, assessments of available social support are "typically inferred from the social characteristics of a person's life rather than from the psychological effects of social relationships" (Lazarus & Folkman 1984: 296).

Vulnerability

Finally, recognition of the differential response to stressors by individuals has led to a suggestion that some people are more vulnerable than others. In the literature, this vulnerability has been argued to be due to personal factors which influence the way people appraise a problem and their subsequent coping responses, or to social and material factors which delimit exposure to stressors and shape available coping resources. It should perhaps be emphasized here that, for at least some researchers, the concept of vulnerability is more subtle than simply predicting that persons with particular personal or social characteristics will have the least favourable outcomes. Instead, vulnerability may be summed up in the phrase "a propensity to". Hence, Rutter (1987) showed that while risk mechanisms may lead directly to disorder, vulnerability will interact with risk variables, rather than have a direct effect on adjustment.

Difference and Commonality in Disciplinary Perspectives

Within the social sciences, the discourse of stress and coping has been most prominent within the discipline of psychology, later being incorporated into sociological/social policy and epidemiological studies. As a result, the terminology and definitions used by psychological studies have been largely transferred to these other disciplines. However, as will be shown, this shared terminology obscures a variety of interpretations and operationalizations of these concepts. Significant differences of emphasis and focus remain between the disciplines which have methodological and policy implications. In the discussion that follows, the different disciplinary perspectives are considered for each of the concepts in turn: stress, life events, coping, social support and vulnerability.

Psychology

The study of stress has been most prolific within psychology; consequently, this is where definitions are most specific. Initially, early studies of stress concentrated on laboratory experiments or unusual naturalistic settings (Levi 1965). Stress was viewed as occurring in atypical or extreme situations such as war, natural disasters or bereavement (Bettelheim 1943, Bowlby 1961). This has gradually been supplanted by an understanding of stress as a varied feature of everyday life, rather than the result of discrete and unusual events.

Three main approaches to the study of stress within the psychological literature have been identified: the psychoanalytic, the situational and the process approach (for a more detailed treatment see Beresford 1992). The process approach, developed by Lazarus and his colleagues over the past 15 years, is now considered the "dominant research approach to the relationship between social factors and psychopathology" (Coyne & Downey 1991: 402). As its name suggests, this approach defines stress as part of a process; that is, the ongoing interaction between an individual and her or his environment (Lazarus & Folkman 1984). Stress is seen as the product of the relationship between the stressor and the stressed. Central to this approach is the notion of "perceived environment", where importance is placed on the situation as assessed by the individual rather than the experimenter. Hence, the assessment of environment stimuli as stressful is seen to be subject to mediation by the individual's cognitive processes.

Over time the previous focus on unusual or extreme life events has given way to a focus on more chronic life stresses or the cumulative effect of acute stressors during the life course (Kanner et al. 1981). It has been suggested that the previous focus on acute rather than chronic stressors was due mainly to methodological expediency arising from the difficulties associated with longitudinal studies (Kessler et al. 1985). Experiments carried out in a laboratory setting, looking at the response to stress as a stimulus, have, to a great extent, been replaced by more naturalistic studies, largely as a result of the shift in focus of Lazarus and his colleagues during the late 1970s. Coyne and Downey (1991) suggested that, at this point, naturally occurring life events were viewed by researchers as "experiments provided by Nature" (ibid.: 411).

The current emphasis on the processual nature of stress has led to a recognition of the need to consider the interaction between individuals and their environment as occurring over a considerable length of time. For example, researchers are beginning to explore the notion that psychological states may not be a response to life events in temporal proximity but the long-term effects of events over the life-course, for example, adult responses to abuse as a child (Avison & Turner 1988; Bryer et al. 1987).

As with work on stress, that on life events began within psychology and remains a major focus within this discipline. There are, however, a number of different approaches to life events evident within this body of work. In a review of life-event research in 1983, for example, Thoits distinguished between work which looked at the effect of one particular event over time and studies which considered the cumulative effect of a number of events during the life-course; research which parallels that on chronic stress described above. The first type of research considered the degree of exposure to stressors and the temporal effect of such events as wars, disasters and relocation of communities (Bettelheim 1943; Wamboldt et al. 1991). The psychological effect of such events appeared to differ with the extent of undesirability, severity, time-clustering and uncontrollability of the specific stressor.

This focus on discrete life events was compared with studies which looked at the cumulative effect of a number of events. Perhaps the best known research of this nature was that carried out by Holmes and Rahe (1967) who constructed a Schedule of Recent Life Events (SRE). This consisted of those events most commonly occurring to individuals which were then rated for the level of readjustment required. Respondents marked off a checklist of events which had occurred to them and were then tested for psychological distress levels. This form of research has been criticized methodologically, particularly for the danger of telescoping (Funch & Marshall 1984; Paykel 1983).

A more important criticism of life event research is its failure to take into account the influence of everyday experiences as stressors (Kanner et al. 1981; Pearlin 1989). The former researchers found that minor events (the hassles and uplifts of everyday life) proved to have better predictive value for psychological symptoms than life event checklists. These findings led to considerable attempts to disaggregate the effects of acute stressors and chronic strains (Avison & Turner 1988; Stone et al. 1991), while Pearlin (1989) argued that it may be necessary to consider the interactive nature of all events in the life course. Certainly, by taking a life course focus, researchers are highlighting the long term effects of early childhood events such as child abuse (Quinton & Rutter 1988) or parental loss (Geyer 1991).

The focus within psychological research on the effects of life events through-out the life course is comparatively recent. Not only has research considered whether children are affected in the same way as adults (Segal 1988) but it has also reviewed the importance of experience in responding to stressful events. This latter research appears to have been inconclusive. While Eysenck (1983) stated that prior exposure aids adaptation, it was contrarily proposed by Post et al. (1986) that stress thresholds to depression are lowered with repetitive stressors, due to some biological sensitizing effect. The main factor appears to be the success or otherwise of coping responses to previous life events.

Coping has a very specific definition within the psychological literature. It is seen as the mechanism employed by individuals responding to a stressor. It is suggested that conditions such as anxiety, depression, psychological distress and somatic complaints may be manifestations of unsuccessful or inappropriate coping strategies. The most widely used definition of coping in psychology is that in Lazarus and Folkman's transactional model of stress and coping. For these authors, coping is "the process of managing demands (external or internal) that are appraised as taxing or exceeding the resources of the person" (1984: 283). They consider that coping must involve the mobilization of effort otherwise "coping would consist of almost everything we do"; this latter process they refer to as *adaptation* (op. cit.: 283).

Central to this view of coping are the concepts of *primary* and *secondary* appraisal. Primary appraisal is defined as a cognitive assessment of the situation as harmful, threatening, challenging or nurturing (McCrae 1984). Secondary appraisal as the assessment of personal options available for coping. McCrae considers that the type of stressor has a consistent and significant effect on the choice of coping mechanisms employed. The process of appraisal and coping is also presented as interactive, with the situation varying as one responds to the stressor and reappraises the situation. Forsythe and Compas (1987), examining the relationship between appraisal, coping and psychological symptoms, argue for "goodness of fit"; that is, that which is defined as an "accurate" appraisal, leads to "appropriate" coping mechanisms and aids psychological well-being.

Secondary appraisal is seen to depend on the event itself and the resources available to the individual (or group) concerned. These resources are conceptualized as both social (social networks, social support, financial resources and institutional factors) and personal (social skills, energy, beliefs such as locus of control, Lefcourt 1973; 1976, and commitment). It is argued that having appraised the resources available, individuals will "actively and consciously select and engage in particular coping behaviours" (Endler & Parker 1990: 844).

According to Folkman et al. (1986), coping behaviours can be categorized as either problem-focused, where efforts are directed at doing something constructive about the conditions of threat/harm, or emotion-focused, concerned with regulating the emotions arising from the situation. Examples of problem-focused behaviour might include active coping, planning, suppression of competing activities and seeking instrumental social support. In contrast, emotion-focused behaviour employs strategies such as enlisting emotional social support, positive reinterpretation, acceptance, denial and adoption of religious beliefs.

Other emotion-focused strategies, which Carver et al. (1989) considered less useful than those listed above, are venting emotions and behavioural and mental disengagement. In a study published in 1980, Folkman and Lazarus considered that workplace stressors led to a problem-focused approach while health issues usually resulted in an emotion-focused response. Gender differences occurred mostly because men mentioned more work-based situations leading the authors to suggest that "women and men do not differ in their use of emotion-focused coping within similar contexts of living but they do differ in the contexts in which their stressful encounters occur" (1980: 235). The research did find, however, that men tended to adopt problem-focused approaches when an emotion-focused acceptance might be considered to be more appropriate. The authors found no difference in the approach adopted with age. Overall they found that people are more varied than consistent in their coping patterns.

Coyne and Smith (1991) have recently suggested that this dichotomous taxonomy of coping behaviour should be expanded to include a third relationship-focused dimension which acknowledges that people do not only cope as individuals but as partners in relationships. The authors proposed two forms of relationship-focused behaviour, active engagement and protective buffering. This relationship-focused approach has been considered in-depth by Parker and Seymour in their study of the negotiation of coping with the onset of disablement by married and co-habiting couples. This research confirmed that there are distinct relationship-focused coping behaviours employed in response to the onset of disablement and that, in some instances, their adoption may increase levels of distress for individuals (Seymour 1994). This occurs where the use of relationship-focused behaviours conflicts with the needs of the individual but is continued as the relationship is given precedence over personal requirements. The project confirmed the finding of Coyne and Smith (1991), that the quality of the marital relationship prior to the onset of the stressor was a key factor in the subsequent adaptation of couples.

Psychological outcomes of coping behaviours are measured in a number of ways including: morale, somatic health and social functioning. The latter outcome is considered by Renne (1974), in a value-laden judgement, to include employability, marital satisfaction, community involvement and sociability, that is, social health. Lazarus and Folkman argue that outcomes should be viewed on the intra-individual level since "it is often more useful to know a given individual (or group) is doing well or badly in comparison with his or her own norm or ideal than it is to know that one individual or group is more or less effective in functioning as compared with others" (1984: 309).

As psychological work on coping behaviour developed, there was an increasing recognition of the importance of social resources in aiding the coping process. In this context, social support was formulated as a resource that acts as a buffer to deleterious life events (Antonovsky 1974; Kaplan et al. 1977). Early psychological studies of social support examined how much support appeared to be available to different groups and compared depressed patients with control groups, concluding that the former had fewer friends and were less satisfied with their marital relationships (Billings & Moos 1984; Leaf et al. 1984). As research developed, attention however, turned to the role of *perceived*, rather than *actual*, social support (Turner 1983). Similarly initial research on individuals facing stressful events, which unproblematically viewed kin and friends as a source of social support, has been supplanted recently by a focus on interpersonal dynamics. As the negative, as well as positive, aspects of close relationships have been examined, assumptions about the role of spouses, family and friends have been reviewed (Finkelhor et al. 1983). Attention was turned to the effect of lack of social support where it may have been expected to exist, for example in a marriage. Findings have suggested that the absence of an intimate relationship is less deleterious than having such a relationship in which social support is not available (Pagel et al. 1987). This led Coyne and Downey (1991) to suggest that the concept of social support needed to be turned on its head, arguing that the presence of social support means one is buffered from the negative effects of a poor relationship. Work in this area has highlighted the importance of not taking social variables such as marital status as a proxy for social support (Morgan et al. 1984).

While some research has highlighted the way in which a lack of social support might make people more vulnerable to negative health and welfare outcomes in the context of adverse life events, other psychological research has highlighted individual propensity as the central element of vulnerability. For example, Coyne and Downey (1991) have argued that studies of depression suggest a pre-existing vulnerability which may be caused by biological dysregulation (Goplerud & Depue 1985), negative self-concept (Hammen 1988) or personal coping strategies such as rumination (Nolen-Hoeksema 1987). They are critical however, of the non-dynamic nature of these studies, which fail to take into account changes in vulnerability over time. They cite Werner (1989), who has demonstrated that American men were more vulnerable than women in their first decade, less so in the second and again more so at the start of their third decade. This led Coyne and Downey to comment:

the vulnerabilities identified have generally been viewed as fixed attributes of the person that interact with contextual stressors to influence the onset of psychopathology. Such a view ignores how vulnerabilities to psychopathology originate, what circumstances maintain or modify them and what personal and social resources are available to confront stress (1991: 407).

Recent research carried out on children has attempted to combine these factors and has concluded that the vulnerability of individual children to stressful conditions is related to a range of factors including: the disposition of the child, the degree of family support and the availability of welfare services to support the family (Garmezy 1985). However, Farber and Egeland (1987) argue that so-called "invulnerable" children may not be exhibiting behavioural problems but may have low indices of emotional health. In addition, longitudinal studies of so-called "resilient" adults have reported that not all respondents were happy or satisfied with their lives (Werner 1989).

As already noted, psychology is, in a sense, the original site for the development of research on stress and coping. No surprisingly, therefore, the constructs reviewed above are prominent in many other disciplines. However, as we shall see, within the other two disciplinary domains we shall review – sociology and epidemiology – there are obvious and important differences alongside strong similarities.

Sociology

As discussed in the previous chapter, the 1980s saw a number of influential critiques of the psychological literature on stress and coping. One of these came from the American sociologist Pearlin, who, in an article published in 1982 called on researchers outside sociology to pay greater attention to the social context of people's lives, which he argued had been ignored by the concentration in psychological studies on the individual's adaptation process. He noted that much of the research into stress was concerned with the responses to, rather than the causes of, stressful experiences and suggested that this latter area was the appropriate focus of sociological research into stress. He also called for sociologists to recognize the "domains of the stress process" (i.e. stressors, mediators and outcomes) as legitimate foci for investigation (Pearlin 1982: 241). One major problem was that traditional areas of sociological study such as social disorganization, so-called deviant groups, dysfunction and conflict, although addressing the issue of stress, were not defined as such.

As also noted in the previous chapter, research in this field did respond to these criticisms and in an important review article in 1989, Pearlin argued that it was generally accepted that "the structural contexts of people's lives are not extraneous to the stress process but are fundamental to that process" (Pearlin 1989: 242). Many of the sociological studies reviewed by Pearlin, used the framework developed in the work on psychological "domains of the stress process" – stressors, stress mediators (coping resources and strategies) and stress outcomes (Pearlin 1989: 241) – but considered the context within which these domains occurred. However, Pearlin also highlighted the tendency, still apparent in sociological, psychological and epidemiological research, for social/structural factors to be treated as control variables and screened out as obfuscating the process being examined. In a similar light, and more recently, Coyne and Downey have warned that a focus on life events which does not take socio-economic variables into account "may distract us from the problematic and relatively intractable continuities in persons' lives". In addition, we must "be careful not to infer personal shortcomings, poor coping, or incompetency from what are actually effects of enduring features" (1991: 411).

As with psychology, sociological research on stress and coping has recognized the role of long-term chronic stressors and acknowledged that life events often do not occur without warning but are the result of gradually developing social circumstances (Avison & Turner 1988). Similarly, as is evident in the psychological literature, as stress research continues to elucidate the importance of interpersonal relations, sociological work has also recognized that life events rarely occur to individuals in isolation. McGuffin and Bebbington (1988) found, for example, that the relatives of people with depression had experienced more life events than those of the control population. This led Coyne and Downey to raise "the possibility that the tendency to experience adversity may be familial" (1991: 410).

Sociological studies of stress and coping which adopt a structural approach have been carried out at three levels. First, at the level of society as a whole and the manner in which it is stratified; whether by class (Hornung 1977; Jackson 1967), race and ethnicity (Ulbrich et al. 1989), gender (Barnett et al. 1987; Gore & Mangione 1983) or age (Meeks et al. 1989). Here the focus is on the manner in which the unequal distribution of resources, opportunities and self-regard manifest themselves in responses and outcomes. As already discussed in Chapter 2 few studies however, have taken a multi-faceted approach which considers the way in which these aspects of stratification interact for individuals. Secondly, there are studies of social institutions where roles may be problematic, for example occupational (Fletcher & Payne 1980; Kahn 1973; Payne & Firth 1987) or familial (Gove & Tudor 1973; McCubbin et al. 1980; Pearlin 1983; Sharpe 1984). Finally, some studies have concentrated on the area of interpersonal relationships which, when problematic and filled with conflict, can produce considerable stress, especially in the domestic sphere (Gelles 1974; Straus & Hotaling 1980).

Another, more interpretive, group of studies has considered the stress process by examining the social and cultural meanings that are attached to each stage of Lazarus and Folkman's (1984) model (Jacobson 1989; Slavin et al. 1991). Here, it is argued that it is not merely the presence of a stressor which is important but the meaning of this stressor to those under study. Similarly, certain coping responses may be culturally unacceptable. For example, Pouchaud (1977) discussed how information-seeking behaviour involved loss of face for the Cambodians in his study. Migrants may require several differing coping strategies to adapt to multi-cultural demands (Ben-Porath 1987). This work echoes the cognitive appraisal process discussed in psychological studies but stresses that such appraisal is to a large extent socially constructed. Slavin and colleagues (1991) also argued that cultural differences in the significance attached to status, age, gender and ethnicity will affect the resources considered available for coping, the mechanisms used to cope and the perceived efficacy of the outcome. Thus, they suggested the questions raised by one life-event – is the event a problem, who "owns" the problem, what is to be done, who will do it and is the outcome satisfactory – can generate immense variations in reply, both within and between cultures (Slavin et al. 1991). However, it should be noted, that the approach of Slavin et al. to subjective meaning does not constitute division-led research, to use the classifications introduced in Chapter 2. In relation to gender for example they noted: "the meaning a person's particular cultural group attaches to being a woman or a man is more relevant than is gender per se for understanding stress responses" (op. cit. p. 157). Also they considered that the manner in which fate is viewed in a culture will affect whether coping is viewed in terms of action or acceptance (1991: 161).

Several researchers have suggested that the role of cultural factors in shaping responses to stress may be overemphasized in sociological work. Anderson and colleagues for example, in their study of the coping responses of migrant Chinese and Anglo-Canadian women with diabetes, commented that "when the circumstances of women's lives are examined, styles of managing illness that could be attributed to ethnicity become recognisable as pragmatic ways of dealing with the harsh realities of material existence"(1991: 1). Citing the effects of low paid jobs on daytime clinic attendance they concluded that material resources may provide greater explanatory power than could be attributed to ethnicity. Similarly, Taylor et al. (1990) considered that ethnicity had been focused on at the expense of social class and economic factors when considering the behaviour of African-American families.

An interpretive approach to stressful events and the way people cope is particularly evident in the field of medical sociology – albeit marginal to the mainstream stress and coping literature. A number of writers have explored the interplay between ideology, meanings and experiences which influence how individuals respond to the stress of (particularly chronic) illness, both from the point of view of those who are undergoing such an experience and those who are caring for them, formally or informally (Bury 1982; Handy 1991; Karp 1996; Williams 1984). The work of Brown and Harris (1978) also emphasized subjective meanings though, as noted in Chapter 2, there have been severe critiques of this work. Despite the limitations, Brown and Harris's study (1978) of depression amongst working class women is one of the most influential sociological studies focusing on the role of life events in the stress process. It has highlighted important aspects of the relationship between life events and social conditions. The study found that working-class women were more prone to depression due to experiencing more severe life events. Additionally, it is suggested that loss events are more likely to result in depression, whereas events appraised as dangerous lead to states of anxiety.

Pearlin's own work is also a prominent stand in the sociological literature on stress and coping. As already discussed, in their early work Pearlin and Schooler (1978) compared the efficacy of coping responses and reviewed the importance of social and personal resources on the coping process. They argued that the most effective coping responses (defined in terms of stress levels measured by an adjective checklist) occurred when the issue concerned interpersonal relationships and the least effective took place in the workplace. They considered this mirrored the degree of control perceived as available to individuals in both situations, a finding later confirmed by Straw and Kendrick (1988). In examining the effect of social and personal resources, they found that social resources proved most important in coping with the demands of financial issues whereas psychological resources were more effective in the workplace.

Men were considered by Pearlin and Schooler as "more effective copers" than women when considering marriage roles; that is, they exhibited less stress in this area. However, this finding may relate to a later comment by the authors that "the most effective copers may be those who have the capacity to gather support from others without having to solicit it" (1978: 10). Overall, Pearlin and Schooler argue that while age appeared to have little impact on the efficacy of the coping strategy chosen, more effective modes are used by men, the educated and the affluent. This led them to conclude that the higher rate of depression found among women may in part arise "not only of their having to bear more severe hardships, but also of their being socialised in a way that less adequately equips them with effective coping patterns" (1978: 15). In addition, "the less educated and the poorer are more exposed to hardships and at the same time, less likely to have the means to fend off the stresses resulting from the hardships. Not only are life-problems distributed unequally among social groups and collectivities but it is apparent that the ability to deal with the problems is similarly unequal" (1978: 17). As already discussed in the previous chapter, these arguments neglect diversity among individuals within social groups and tend to pathologize individuals rather than focus on the social structures which limit the universal availability or effectiveness of certain forms of coping strategies and resources.

As noted in the previous chapter, the work of Pearlin and his colleagues is also significant for the development of a dynamic notion of social support – social support is not always facilitative, it carries costs and benefits. Perceived support may be more significant than actual support in understanding stress and there is a two-way relationship between life events, stress and support (Pearlin 1982, 1989; Pearlin & Schooler 1978; Pearlin et al. 1981). Sociological work on social support has, in general, explored the effect of social characteristics such as gender, class, age, sexuality or ethnicity on the availability of social support which may be direct (the amount of material goods that can be given) or indirect, through the operation of ideologies. For example, studies have shown how gender ideologies of care influence who it is deemed appropriate will give and receive emotional support (Dalley 1988; Graham 1982). As previously discussed, Pearlin's assessment of the most effective copers included those who received social support without having to seek it (Pearlin & Schooler 1978). Hence, men may have greater emotional support in the domestic sphere due to wives having the responsibility of maintaining domestic harmony (Oakley 1974). Conversely, women may be more able than men to receive such support from close friends and relatives (Chodorow 1978; Gilligan 1982). The importance of a supportive relationship with a spouse was shown by Brown and Harris's (1978) study of depression in women. Some researchers have, however, suggested that the issue may be compounded by so-called "selective mating", whereby women with a propensity to depression have partners who are unable to provide adequate social support (Brown et al. 1986; Merikangas 1982). Sociological studies have also been important in highlighting the interactions between material circumstances and an individual's ability to access support. For example, studies have shown that working-class women may be less able to mobilize support networks than middle-class women (Oakley & Rajan 1991) contrary to the conclusions of earlier community research (Young & Willmot 1957). On a purely pragmatic level, this is due to material circumstances, such as the availability of a telephone or access to a car (Oakley & Rajan 1991: 51).

In contrast to the psychological work which focuses on personal factors, sociological studies of vulnerability pivot around the possession of certain social characteristics. As noted earlier Titterton (1989) argues that in such research vulnerable people are, for example, "the poor", "single parents", "the elderly" or "young people". He suggests that this grouping reflects the pathological stance taken by social studies which have, in general, failed to focus on successful copers or "invulnerables" within such categories. In addition to neglecting such individuals within groups, there is a possibility that vulnerability will be assumed rather than proven. For example, in relation to vulnerability and age or stage in the life-cycle, Pearlin and Schooler (1978: 16) found that their results did "not support views of ageing as a process in which people inexorably become increasingly vulnerable and unable to cope effectively with life-strains". They found that elderly people used different strategies from those employed by younger people, but that these strategies were equally effective.

General studies of the role of social factors in creating differential vulnerability have been carried out by Kessler (1979) and Bebbington et al. (1991). More specific studies include race and socio-economic status (Ulbrich et al. 1989) and socio-economic status alone (McLeod & Kessler 1990). Oakley et al. (1990) studied pregnant women who may have been vulnerable to adverse health and social outcomes. Their sample was predicated on a previous obstetric history of low birthweight babies or perinatal mortality which is clearly correlated with low social class. This latter study is noteworthy for its use of a randomized controlled trial design, rarely used within sociological research (see Chapter 6).

Epidemiology

Epidemiological research is concerned with the aetiology (causes) of disease and death within populations. Within this field, studies of stress have looked at its relationship with both physical and mental health (Berkman 1985; Cobb 1976). Much work has concentrated on the distribution and preponderance among the population (both clinical and general) of stress-related diseases (Burnam et al. 1987; Jones 1986; Karno et al. 1987).

The focus here is on the relationship between the environment and health. Initially this was formulated as the physical/biological environment but later broadened to include the psychosocial and social environment (Marmot & Madge 1987). Epidemiological studies have tended to view stress as an independent variable; a factor which contributes to ill-health. The influence of stress is seen as unidirectional with the role of ill-health as a stressor being less studied. This differs from the model dominant within psychology and sociology which sees the stress process as transactional, that is, involving an interactive process in which the assessment of an outcome contributes to an individual's reappraisal of the original stressor (Lazarus & Folkman 1984).

Aneshensel et al. (1991) have highlighted significant differences between the sociomedical (epidemiological) and the sociological model of the stress process. The sociomedical model works backwards to antecedents: not, as Aneshensel et al. note, in research design, but in conceptual orientations toward social characteristics and stressors. In epidemiological studies illness, particularly psychiatric disorder, is viewed as atypical and the researchers are looking for some explanation for this outcome. Social characteristics are viewed as background or confounding factors. Aneshensel et al. have argued that this perspective may be sufficient for explaining the aetiology of specific disorders, but cannot be used "for identifying the mental health consequences of social organisation" because of the multi factorial nature of the processes involved (1991: 167). For Aneshensel and colleagues, the narrow epidemiological approach fails to acknowledge that the mode of expressing psychological reaction to stressful life events appears to vary with social factors such as gender (Aneshensel et al. 1981; Newmann 1986).

In comparison, they argue sociological studies view stress as an intervening variable in a process where health disorders are the inevitable consequence of particular patterns of social organization (Aneshensel et al. 1991: 167).

Epidemiological research into the effect of the social environment on health has included the areas of work and migration. Much work has been carried out on the relationship between paid employment and health, either the effect of occupational stressors (Karasek et al. 1982; Marmot et al. 1984) or of unemployment (Moser et al. 1986). The latter has been considered at both an individual and community level (Gore 1978; *Journal of Social Issues* 1988; Stern 1981). Recently, research has looked at the incidence of post traumatic stress disorder in the community rather than in the clinic (Davidson et al. 1991). Attempts to study the stress process across cultures have been made by looking at migrant workers (Beaglehole et al. 1977; Cassel 1975). However, as Marmot (1984) points out, this type of work is complex, requiring detailed knowledge of others' cultures and measures which are not culture-specific.

A major issue within epidemiology has been the relationship between the degree of stress and the resulting extent of ill-health. Epidemiologists have addressed the question as to whether more stress equals more ill-health. As Marmot and Madge (1987: 11) have argued, if this is not the case, then "the epidemiologist loses one of the main tools available to assess whether an association is likely to be causal".

In attempting to isolate causal mechanisms, the epidemiological study of stress may suffer from the conflation of social variables. For example, studies relating health to occupational stress must ensure that the stressors are related to the job rather than social class or lifestyle. Similarly, the processes through which ill-health comes about – whether the response is primarily physiological, psychological or behavioural – are not always clear (Marmot & Madge 1987).

Epidemiologists have also attempted to ascertain whether life events lead to physical or psychosomatic ill-health independently of prior health status. Research has found, for example, a strong relationship between independent life events and depression (Shrout et al. 1989), acute schizophrenia (Day et al. 1987) and schizophrenic relapse (Ventura et al. 1989). Of specific life events, it was found that a total of only 12 events explained 77 per cent of health statuses with aetiological significance, and considering that most people undergo a number of life events, it is perhaps not surprising that Davidson et al. (1991) found considerable levels of sub-clinical depression in the general population.

Epidemiological studies of coping behaviour within the population have looked at both physiological and psychosomatic outcomes of various coping strategies. Selye (1976) proposed a general adaptation syndrome which did not distinguish between the nature of the stressor experienced. Mason et al. (1976) argued however, that the type of stressor is important. As a result, a specificity model was proposed which linked certain stressors to certain coping behaviours and thus to specific physiological responses and health outcomes, such as ulcers (Cohen 1979). For example, Holroyd & Lazarus (1982) showed that appraisal of an event as either a threat or a challenge influenced the subsequent physiological response, in this case, cortisol levels. Epidemiological research, like that in other disciplines, hastened to focus on stress-related responses. In this context, Lazarus and Folkman have suggested that the physiological benefits of eustress (positive stress) have been insufficiently considered. They suggest that "substances in the brain could serve as a physiological analogue of palliative forms of cognitive coping" (1984: 315).

Other epidemiological research has looked at the long-term health effects of various coping styles. Comparisons of Type A behaviour (defined as behaviour characterized by competitiveness, time urgency and easily evoked hostility) and Type B (placid) behaviour have shown the former to result in physiological changes associated with an increased risk of heart disease (Haynes et al. 1980). Similarly, coping behaviours involving increased eating, drinking and smoking may have long-term health implications while denial has been linked to failure of medical intervention as shown by the Katz et al. (1970) study of responses to the discovery of lumps in the breast.

Much of the epidemiological literature has followed the buffering thesis of social support whereby its presence it is seen as acting in a preventative or ameliorative way on health outcomes (Berkman 1984; House et al. 1982). This has been shown in studies of topics as varied as complications in pregnancy (Nuckolls et al. 1972), psychological health (Ho et al. 1988) and mortality rates (Blazer 1982). Berkman (1984) proposed that social support can have positive effects on physical health due to the combination of practical help (advice, aids, services and economic assistance) and the psychological benefits of a feeling of belonging. The moderating effect of social support has also been considered in a more complex way when looking at the health outcomes of a stressful life event such as unemployment (Gore 1978). In such studies, the focus has been less on the direct health benefits of social support than on the way it may mediate or protect against poor health outcomes of stressors. More recently, Marmot and colleagues have been exploring the role of social support in understanding the finely stratified health experience evident in their longtitudinal study of a large sample of Whitehall civil servants (Marmot et al. 1984).

Epidemiologists are less likely than psychologists or sociologists to use the term vulnerability, favouring instead the concept of risk. This concept has now, however, taken on a sociological interpretation (Beck 1992). Individuals are seen as being at risk of disease, either in a passive way (by possessing certain social characteristics) or in a more active way by indulging in particular behaviours or lifestyles. Predisposing characteristics identified in research include: geographical location, including place of birth (Curtis 1987; Osmond et al. 1990), social class (Dowding and Barry 1990) and race (Donaldson and Clayton 1984). Studies of behaviour likely to increase propensity to illness have considered: smoking (Higenbottam et al. 1982), exercise (Chave et al. 1978) and the adoption of healthy regimes following earlier illness (West and Evans 1986). It has been suggested that the recognition of risk factors could be used to allocate prevent-ative measures, such as screening for breast cancer (Alexander et al. 1988). In recognition of the long-term aetiology of some variables, consideration has been given to the effect of childhood poverty (Burr and Sweetnam 1980) birthplace (Osmond et al. 1990), and in-utero conditions (Barker 1994) particularly on the risk of subsequent cardiovascular disease. Interestingly, risk factor epidemiology has been strongly criticized for failing to uncover the multicausal mechanisms inherent in the genesis of contemporary health problems (Dean 1993).

Methodological Issues

Within most disciplines, the methods used within a particular study will be influenced by the theoretical and epistemological underpinnings of the research. Within the disciplines considered here, however, it would probably be fair to say that the methods used for research in the stress-coping field have been predominantly quantitative, as we discuss in Chapter 4. The methods utilized have also changed over time – as theory and methods have developed. In psychology the focus has moved from laboratory experiments to field investigations. Community studies in the early 1960s took an approach similar to that of epidemiology in looking for social causes or correlates for psychopathological conditions (Gurin et al. 1960). Following this, the use of self-report checklists of life events and questionnaires became widespread. Such checklists were analysed statistically, often controlling for social variables. As Coyne and Downey (1991) commented, such treatment may obscure the often complex relationships between social factors and the stress process.

Self report checklists were also being used to determine coping behaviour, with individuals providing responses to actual or hypothesized events. In the latter case, questions were phrased so as to ask how a person would usually cope with a suggested event rather than how they actually coped with a real life event and, as such, they have proved to be poor predictors of behaviour. The most well-known of these checklists is the Ways of Coping Checklist (WCC) devised by Folkman and Lazarus, containing a 68 item checklist of acts or thoughts on ways to cope in a given encounter. These checklists can be collapsed into two scales, a problem-focused or emotion-focused strategy, although studies have found that 98 per cent of respondents used both types of approach, showing the behaviours were not exclusive (Folkman et al. 1986). Such checklists can also be used to attribute individual scores on a scale: for example, task-oriented, emotion-oriented and avoidance-oriented scales (Carver et al. 1989).

However, as data on personal and social factors was collected, there was more emphasis placed on understanding the circumstances of, and interpretations placed on, life events for individuals. To this end, as Coyne and Downey (op. cit. p. 403) noted semi-structured interviews began to be used to gain standardized information on history, social functioning and symptom status for diagnostic purposes using, for example, SADS (the Schedule for Affective Disorders and Schizophrenia) devised by Endicott and Spitzer (1978). This information was then examined by trained evaluators to make an assessment of the amount of stress an event would present to a particular respondent. With epidemiology, the widespread reliance on tightly structured standardized instruments is also being supplemented by somewhat less structured interview schedules. This is also a consequence of the concern that reports of health are highly subjective (Scheff 1966). The scale of studies has varied from small-scale clinical populations to community studies (Myers et al. 1984; Dew et al. 1987; Kessler et al. 1989).

Currently within psychology there is a move towards adopting a life course perspective, in recognition of the influence of factors which are not temporally proximinal. This reduces the effects of studying specific life events in isolation but can present problems of recall – particularly that of telescoping which results in a fall-off of reporting of events over time (Funch & Marshall 1984).

Large-scale survey research is also the dominant research design within sociological work in this field both in the USA, where the literature is greater, and in the UK. In the UK, Brown and Harris's work on depression in working-class women (1978) is particularly innovative in its use of subjective accounts obtained from women in largely unstructured interviews. The accounts were subsequently coded by highly trained analysts to produce quantifiable data – an approach discussed in some detail in the previous chapter. There are also a few examples of qualitative methods being used within both the USA and UK sociological literature, in studies seeking to understand the meaning of events in peoples lives (see Chapters 2 and 5). There is, however, an urgent need for more research on stress and coping in the interpretive tradition.

The Welfare Practitioner and Lay Discourses

From the perspective of welfare policy and practice, practitioners' perspectives on the key concepts considered here are important, as is the way in which these perspectives shape professional behaviour. As others have argued, the knowledge base for professional practice is both formal (acquired through professional training and accreditation) and informal (acquired through experience at paid work and in other domains of life). In an important sense then, professional welfare practitioners also have lay knowledge and the interaction between the different types of knowledge practitioners bring to their tasks should be an important focus for research. Additionally, the perspectives of lay people as users and/or potential users of welfare services can be expected to shape their views on the appropriateness of particular services and patterns of utilization. Finally, the relationship between the perspective of practitioners and lay people/users has important implications for the way people experience services.

Unfortunately, despite the obvious relevance of research into welfare practitioners and lay people's perspectives on stress and coping, relatively few studies have attempted to describe these perspectives or explore the way in which they influence service provision and use. Below, the limited research that has been undertaken is briefly reviewed.

Practioners' Discourses

There is a body of literature on the experience of stress amongst professionals in the welfare fields. Among others, investigations have taken place into the stressful nature of police work (Lord et al. 1991), psychiatric work (Handy 1991), social work (*Social Work Today* 13.6.91), management (Fletcher & Payne 1980) and professional work in general (Gadzella et al. 1990). This, to some extent, is a reflection of the development of stress research, which has focused for some time on the stressors relating to paid employment and only recently on interpersonal and domestic issues.

In the workplace, lack of resources and a poor physical environment have been shown to exacerbate situations of stress as do problems of management style and control (Murphy 1991). The existence of a "be tough" culture in the social work child protection team studied by Murphy meant that individuals felt they could not request or attend counselling as this would have been an admission that the reasons behind their stress were personal rather than organizational. Such a culture failed to take account of practitioners' non-work lives despite the effect occupational stress had on personal relationships and sleep patterns. Howe (1986) has also highlighted the importance of workplace practices and ideology in influencing the coping strategies workers adopted in response to a stressor.

Handy (1991) emphasized the importance of viewing practitioners in the context of the relationships they have with clients and considering the way in which this interacts with the structures and ideology of the profession in which they are working. By concentrating on these factors in the work of psychiatric nurses, Handy reinforced the transactional view of the stress process and the reciprocal nature of relationships between practitioners and their clients. Adaptation to a life event may have started long before help is sought from a formal agency. Indeed, the action of approaching an agency may be a later coping strategy. There is, for example, a considerable literature on the ways in which people manage the symptoms of an illness before consulting a doctor yet this selfcare can be neglected by practitioners (see Rogers and Elliott 1997). Practitioners (or researchers) may also focus upon a particular life event, such as bereavement or divorce, without putting it into the whole context of people's lives and thereby inadvertently pathologize particular service users. Segal (1988) for example, pointed out the problems of making assumptions as to the effects of specific events on children. Similarly, as the long-term effects of child abuse are further researched, the importance to practitioners of recognizing the occurrence of non-contemporaneous life events is becoming clearer (Bryer et al. 1987). However, it is possible that the episodic nature of welfare intervention may encourage a more short-term perspective.

The literature relating to coping and the response of welfare agencies appears to be divided first into how agencies decide whether a service user is coping or not coping and secondly, their responses to the particular coping strategies employed. Hence, coping is seen variously as an outcome or a process. For an event to be defined as a problem, it must first be perceived as such. Mitchell and

Hodson (1983) have considered the institutional response to domestic violence and highlighted the difficulties involved in obtaining aid for battered women (also Martin 1976; Walker 1979). Here the role of the agency as gatekeeper, both to resources and to other agencies through referrals, is emphasized. This and other literature on violence to women is discussed in detail in Chapter 4. Even if a stressful situation is acknowledged, the practitioner may consider that clients are coping if they are not actively requesting intervention. In their study of informal carers, Twigg et al. reported the following exchange:

> the social worker, however, explained that it was unlikely that she would receive respite as there were only three available places, and the carer reported her as saying: "If we do go to somebody and they appear to be managing . . . I'm afraid you just have to get on with it, because we've got so many people that just can't cope."
>
> The carer added: "They don't ask how you are coping, do they? They don't see you at the screaming habdab stage" (1990: 141).

Clearly allocation of scarce resources is based on assumptions of need and such decisions will have gender, class, age and ethnic dimensions (Mason 1989; Parker & Seymour 1998). There is a suggestion in the literature that people who are seen as making excessive demands on services are viewed as not coping. Research into childbirth has shown that mothers who are particularly vocal during their labour are so-labelled (Curtis 1991; Graham 1982) although this may be culturally defined.

The second strand of literature relating to welfare agencies and coping consists of the assessment of the appropriateness of the strategy adopted. Booth (1978) discussed how many of the coping styles adopted by parents of children with disabilities (such as normalization, protection or denial) conflict with the strategies and tactics preferred by professionals. For people with disabilities and those who care for them, the extent to which support groups should have a social, information-providing or political dimension is an area of dissent (Twigg & Atkin 1991). Similarly, Straus (1978) showed that police intervention in cases of domestic violence focused on preserving the family rather than providing women with protection from further assault. These conflicting perceptions between practitioner and service users can provide a source of stress in themselves. Using for example, one study from the Management of Personal Welfare Initiative, Beresford's research on caring for a severely disabled child (1994) showed that such conflict could negatively impact on parents' ability to cope. Practitioner judgements of coping strategies have been criticized by Murgatroyd and Woolfe who considered that the helper's aim should be to use the coping strategy that best suits those coping with the situation, since, for them, "whatever the strategy, it is acceptable. The helper needs to help them [the client] develop the tactics which will enable the strategy to work" (1982: 92). On occasion research has shown that there may be active resistance on the part of clients to aid offered, since acceptance may well be interpreted as an inability to cope; this appears particularly prevalent around the issue of respite care and informal carers (Twigg et al. 1990).

Research suggests that the coping strategies favoured by practitioners – problem-focused or emotion-focused – will depend on the nature of the stressor under consideration and the resources available to address it. However, researchers have voiced concern over the appropriateness of practitioners' responses. Atkeson et al. (1982) for example, considered that, when working with victims of domestic violence, the individual's psychological state may be overlooked if the concerns of security and safety are viewed as paramount. In contrast, Mitchell and Hodson (1983) warned against concentrating on personal characteristics at the expense of social and economic conditions. The greater understanding of the long-term psychological impact of life events has led to the increased growth of counselling services which focus on cognitive coping processes. However, for Heifetz (1977) this emphasis on feelings is linked to the inability of agencies to offer more practical help in the light of resource constraints.

Thus more recent research within the ESRC/Rowntree Initiative has highlighted how health and social care providers articulate widespread concern about the structural determinants of stress in clients' lives – homelessness, unemployment, poverty, etc. – but in their practice resort to intervention aiming to enhance personal/psychological coping skills at the individual level (Edwards 1995; Edwards and Popay 1994). Several projects in this programme have also explored practitioners' perspectives on the notion of social support. In their study of provider views of the health and social care needs of women caring for young children, for example, Edwards and Popay (1994) found that professionals acknowledged their own needs for social support from colleagues, friends and kin. However, while recognizing that clients may have similar needs, many practitioners felt that clients had to be discouraged from being too dependent on professionals for such support. "A listening ear" was the most prominent model of the kind of social support health and welfare providers in this study felt it was appropriate for them to give – indeed, in some instances it was clear that workers felt this was the only type of support they could give. Other studies suggest that not all service providers accept that social support can mediate the negative effects of life events. Morris for example, quotes the opinion of the director of a Spinal Unit who considers, "people either cope with spinal cord injury or they don't – for those who don't have the capacity to cope no amount of support, psychological or material, will make that much difference" (1989: 190).

Such views may have profound implications for the type of support individuals receive after a life event/crisis. As Dhooper has argued, welfare agencies act as mobilizers, as well as providers of social support. He stated that agencies should aim to supplement informal care, but should also arrange such care, since the "professional may be most effective in focusing efforts on adjusting the fit between needs and network support in addition to delivering services that are beyond the ability of these networks to provide" (1984: 302). The implementation of community care policy in the UK, giving professionals a formal assessment function, means that service providers' assumptions as to the amount of informal support that is available, how formal support might complement this and whether it would be useful and effective will shape the packages of care made available. This has been shown to occur particularly at the time of discharge home from hospital (Anderson 1992; Parker 1992).

Practitioners' perspectives on vulnerability will also be important in influencing the services they themselves provide and the support they are willing and able to mobilize or influence. In the paper discussed in Chapter 1, Titterton (1989) argued that the established model underpinning welfare policy and practice over many decades in the UK assumes vulnerability to be a lasting problem state. However, he cautions against the too ready assumption that people in contact with welfare services are inevitably particularly vulnerable, noting that their behaviour could be part of an information or help-seeking coping strategy. Views about vulnerability will also be linked to ideologies. As Lonsdale (1990) has argued, women may in some circumstances be seen as more or less vulnerable than men depending on dominant assumptions about women's roles. She has shown how disabled women's needs are neglected by agencies partly because of the general invisibility of women in the public sphere and also because of the gendered nature of social roles, which mean that many rehabilitation and domestic services are biased towards men.

A final prominent theme in the discourse around welfare provision and vulnerability is the view that formal welfare services and professional practice are generally delivered in a way which creates individual vulnerability by encouraging dependence. Research has shown, for example, that certain institutions, such as long-stay hospitals and residential homes for the elderly, may encourage and reward behaviour of "learned helplessness" (Seligman 1975; Townsend 1981). Internationally, there have been cuts in public expenditure, accompanied by a view that welfare provision generates welfare dependency although there is little robust evidence to support this view in a situation of large-scale long-term unemployment and low wage economies. As we have already noted, this discourse is played out at the level of individual professionals through a concern that in providing support they do not inadvertently create dependence (Edwards 1995).

Lay Discourses

Everyday understandings of words differ considerably from academic definitions. In common understandings, stress is something that exists and from which people suffer in varying degrees. This has led Wilkinson to comment "thus at a popular level stress is a vigorous concept that has engendered a prosperous industry dedicated to its relief" (1991: 192). As Selye noted

... remarkably few people define the concept in the same way or even bother to attempt a clear-cut definition. The business person thinks of stress as frustration or emotional tension: the air-traffic controller as a problem in concentration; the biochemist and endocrinologist, as a purely chemical event and the athlete as muscular tension. The chartered accountant, the short-order cook and the surgeon consider their own occupation as the most stressful (Selye 1982: 7).

The concept of post traumatic stress disorder has gained some degree of acceptance by the general population due to media coverage of such events as the capsize of *The Herald of Free Enterprise*, the events at the Hillsborough football stadium and the long-term effects of participation in the Falklands and Gulf Wars. Clegg (1988) proposed that receiving news of such events may constitute a trauma in itself; this must be particularly so if relatives are watching live coverage of the event. Media coverage of the Dunblane massacre of 16 school children and their teacher in Scotland in 1996 and the similar tragedy in Tasmania in the same year are testament to the widespread impact such events can have in the age of electronic media.

It should perhaps be pointed out here that some people deliberately introduce stress into their lives, for example by partaking in "dangerous" sports. As Murgatroyd and Woolfe (1982) noted some stress can be "voluntary and predictable" such as that which accompanies being a voluntary worker. Such non-harmful or positive stress, labelled eustress by Selye (1982), appears to be acknowledged by the lay public. Additionally, situations generally perceived to be stressful by practitioners may be viewed differently by those involved. In some studies, for example, parents of disabled children have emphasized the positive aspects of child rearing (Bristol Broadsides 1981; Beresford 1994).

The notion of life events also has a place in everyday discourse; indeed, people use life events as a framework around which to construct the story of their lives. Events such as the birth of a child may be used to provide a focal point from which other occurrences are dated. Alternatively, specific events may be seen as signalling a new phase in the life-course. In the latter case, the event may be seen as biological disruption, as in the event of chronic illness (Bury 1982). The effect of an illness or accident, leading to a long-term medical condition, is that of a break in continuity which may require a reformulation of one's self-concept (Bransfield 1990).

Life events may be perceived as causing subsequent developments either immediately or on reflection. Hence, in Williams' (1984) article on the genesis of chronic illness, two people with arthritis ascribed it respectively to long-term workplace toxicity and a period of extreme personal stress. This ascription was seen by Williams as a process of narrative reconstruction in which the individual repairs ruptures between body, self and world. Research suggests that the extent to which a life event creates a rupture will be related to the age of the person when it occurs and whether or not the event was anticipated (Wheaton 1983).

So far this chapter has presented the concept of coping responses as if this were unproblematic, but the labelling and ordering of the stress-coping process is clearly superimposed by those working in the field. Many people respond to events without considering them to be part of a consciously planned course of actions. Indeed, Straw and Kendrick considered that "people are extremely reluctant, or unable either to see or to articulate the logic of their life stories in terms of planning, control or strategy" (1988: 40). Graham (1982: 103) suggested that a commonsense understanding of coping consists of simply getting on with the task at hand and preferably doing it quietly. This definition seems to be particularly applied to women. Graham proposed that in the context of mothering, coping is something which goes unnoticed until it fails and then the individual becomes visible as someone who is not coping. This idea is echoed in the experience of a spinally-injured woman who felt "there is no space allowed for us to express our grief and other emotions. Instead there is often pressure put on us to 'cope' and if we fail to live up to the standard demanded of us we are categorised as a problem" (Morris 1989: 24). As a result, there may be reluctance to engage in help-seeking behaviour until conditions are extreme, so as to avoid such negative labels. In response, Morris stated that women with disabilities "should consciously resist the pressures to prove we can cope unaided" (1989: 54).

Recent research has also begun to explore the perceived costs of drawing on potential social support and the complex negotiations carried out by individuals in order to realize such resources. Pearson et al., for example, have shown how informal resources are "carefully measured and saved up for emergencies, and on behalf of vulnerable dependants" (1993: 45). They consider that social support is borrowed rather than given, particularly among kin, due to norms of reciprocity. This was confirmed by the study of the negotiation of the onset of disablement in marriage where informants described how they began refusing offers of social support when they recognized the long-term nature of the health condition so as to not become too indebted to friends and neighbours (Seymour 1994). The study also found that utilizing social support can incur real financial costs. Hence one couple were expected to repay relatives' gifts of transport with financial loans from their now regular disability benefits. Other studies suggest that the negotiations which take place around the giving and receiving of social support are predicated on a mutual understanding of the resource being discussed. Cheal (1988) has argued, for instance, that a gift, such as the offer of social support, can only be appreciated if it is recognized as such by the receiver.

Finally, to turn to the sparse literature on the lay perspective relating to vulnerability, it appears that with regard to issues of health and community care, vulnerable people are generally considered to be those living on their own without informal social support or caring resources (Oakley & Rajan 1991). Children are also generally perceived to be vulnerable, while vulnerability in other groups in the population is conditional upon situations – being at risk of violence from others, for example, or even occupational criticism (Button 1991).

Conclusion – Commonalities and Divergence

This review has emphasized the commonalities and differences between disciplinary, practitioner and lay definitions of the key concepts utilized within the new paradigm of welfare research. Interdisciplinary variations in the actual definitions of the terms used seem rare. Where formal models underpin research, most studies appear to have adopted those developed in the Lazarus and Folkman (1984) stress/coping model. Intra-disciplinary differences are most frequently found in psychology where the studies of this subject are most concentrated.

Between the disciplines of psychology, sociology and epidemiology the greatest areas of dissent appear to be in the relative importance placed on social and personal factors and whether the study focused mostly on the causes, the process or the outcome of coping with stressful events. Additionally, within sociology in particular, a growing number of studies are designed to elicit people's own subjective perspectives on the problems they experience, how they do or should cope with these and what support they would find most appropriate. In this research tradition formal definitions are not set beforehand, but rather flow from the accounts given by the subjects of the research.

In what sense then do the issues reviewed here contribute to our quest for a framework which will help us to better understand the links between the personal and historical and the social and material worlds and to connect the study and practice of welfare to personal, psychological and social coping strategies? Three themes are particularly relevant here.

First, there would appear to be growing acceptance of the importance of psychological factors in dealing with any life event. This has had practical implications in attempting to understand the particular way in which people react to circumstances. It has also resulted in agency practices which have paid attention to the importance of providing information to those undergoing medical treatment (Nichols 1984) or counselling, as well as practical aid (Atkeson et al. 1982). Related to this point has been the growing emphasis on individuals as active agents in the development of their own environment. Much of this is related to the importance of cognitive appraisal (psychology) or meanings (sociology) in determining the assessment of action taken and outcome measurement of a life event for any individual. This will be based on personal and social factors and will be context-specific, hence changing over time.

Secondly, there is growing acceptance of the processual nature of the relationship between stress and individual coping strategies. The view that situations and resources are not static, but are constantly being constructed and reappraised mirrors a similar assessment of processes occurring in other substantive dynamics, such as gender. This leads to a more complex understanding of the development of stressful situations as being, not discrete events, but emerging from, and interacting with, the life-course.

The temporal aspects of work on coping with life events requires special emphasis. In academic and non-academic spheres increasing importance is being placed on the long-term nature of this process, both in terms of its operation and the consequences. The point in the life course at which one is exposed to any particular event will affect each stage of the process from appraisal, to available resources, to measurement of the success of the strategy employed. In addition, it is becoming increasingly recognized by academics and practitioners that early life events may have far-reaching consequences, as in the case of child abuse. A final aspect of the growth in attention paid to temporal aspects of the stress/coping process has been the recognition among academics and practitioners of the importance of long-term chronic stressors. It is a moot point whether lay people had to learn this or whether experiential knowledge meant it was already known.

In all the disciplines reviewed, there has been an increasing focus on the role of interpersonal relationships and processes occurring in the domestic sphere. This has shown that people do not experience life events as individuals in isolation, but as members of complex social networks. As a result, people may be positively or negatively influenced in their coping strategies by those with whom they come into contact, both formally and informally. This has led to a reassessment of the nature of social support.

Lastly, the adoption of a more complex processual model of stress and coping has, of necessity, resulted in more sophisticated methodologies. Actual, rather than potential, situations are studied and a greater wealth of detail relating to individual circumstances is collected. A model of personal welfare inevitably requires a focus on inter-individual differences and detailed data collection of personal and social characteristics. This calls for a plurality of methods and more multi-disciplinary work, themes which are addressed in more detail in Chapter 5. But, the work reviewed in this chapter also serves to reinforce the conclusions of the previous chapter. Research into the nature of stress and coping behaviours and to a lesser extent studies which consider the subjective meanings people attached to their experiences of life events and their responses to these, are making an important contribution to our understanding of the creativity of individuals in pursuit of their own welfare and that of others. There is also growing attention to the constraints imposed on creativity by the wider social and material context of peoples lives. However, little of this work makes substantial theoretical and/or empirical links between macro structures and ideologies of inequalities and personal biographies and individual life changes. For this we have to look elsewhere (see Chapter 8).

In terms of the significance of the relationships between service providers and users identified in Chapters 1 and 2 the greatest disjuncture in perspectives identified in this chapter would appear to be between welfare practitioners and service users. Clearly, differences at this interface are important if what are perceived as appropriate coping strategies and what are viewed as successful coping outcomes varies between these two groups. This will have significant and long-term implications for both those facing stressful life events and those attempting to help them cope. Empirical research on the relationship between the differing frames of reference shaping perceptions of welfare needs and appropriate responses among women caring for young children and health and welfare providers is presented in Chapter 7. However, that chapter also highlights that more research at this interface is urgently needed.

Part 3
Methods

Chapter 4

Qualitative Methods and Welfare Research

Chas Critcher, David Waddington and Bella Dicks

Introduction

This and the subsequent chapter move from discussion of concepts to questions of methods in welfare research, some of which were alluded to in earlier chapters. Here we look in detail at the role of qualitative methods in specific areas of welfare research. To some extent welfare research (like much social research) has been dominated by quantitative methods – or at least by the implicit view that research findings based on quantitative data are somehow more trustworthy than those emerging from more qualitative approaches. Yet the research which is most capable of bridging the "old" and "new" paradigms is most likely to have used qualitative methods.

This chapter examines in some detail work utilizing qualitative methodologies in the study of stress, social support and coping. It focuses on the potential of such work, and its pitfalls or unresolved dilemmas. Our discussion is set in the context of wider discussions of methodology, principally in social psychology and sociology (see e.g. Ackroyd & Hughes 1992; Bryman 1988; Smith et al. 1995). The orientation of our discussion is to methodology as the application of perspectives and procedures. We are not directly concerned with the epistemological debates between different versions of positivism and interpretivism; with the theoretical debates between structural or behavioural and action-based approaches in either sociology or psychology; or with the political debates about the purpose of research which are particularly associated with feminist critiques of man-made knowledge. Our aim is much more specific: to identify what qualitative methods have to offer to the study of stress, social support and coping, and to explore the ways in which these have been, and might be, implemented. Although the concepts of stress, support and coping help to form the armoury of the "new" paradigm of welfare research, as Chapter 2 shows, less attention has been devoted to how to collect data in these areas than to how the concepts themselves might be defined. While the theoretical assumptions underlying much research in this area can be criticized, as Fiona Williams demonstrates in her chapter, there are also implications of such a critique for methodological choices and issues. We do not argue in this chapter that qualitative methods should displace quantitative ones; but we do argue that there is a potential complementarity of approaches which will only be achieved when, and if, qualitative methods are granted equal legitimacy in practice as well as in principle.

The Current Status of Qualitative Methods

The perceived role of qualitative methodologies in welfare research can be gauged from two authoritative reviews of the field ten years apart. Depner et al. (1984) identify three possible contributions from qualitative research: as a precursor to quantitative research, especially in the formulation of questions and identification of conceptual categories; as a clarification or exploration of the nuances of interpretations used by sub-groups within a quantitative study; and in a complementary role, where qualitative data humanize the abstractions of statistical data. However, Depner et al.'s acceptance of qualitative data is in practice quite limited: only two out of 15 pages of the review are devoted to qualitative methods, and the rest are concerned with quantitative data. By contrast, Thoits (1995) gives at least equal credibility to qualitative methods, including examples under each of the three headings of stress, social support and coping; noting some specific advances in the analysis of qualitative data; and arguing that qualitative studies offer a route out of the impasse experienced by quantitative methods: "detailed qualitative information about surrounding circumstances, beliefs and personal values is crucial for understanding the meaning and emotional impacts of negative events in identity domains that are important to the individual" (Thoits 1995: 59).

Thoits may overestimate the actual prominence of qualitative methods. One wonders how many of the 3,000 journal papers on stress she cites as having been published in the previous decade, or the 16 methodological reviews identified by Turner and Avison (1992) over a similar period, have actually used or discussed qualitative methods. Thoits' own 1994 study of psychological distress amongst families in Indianapolis is almost wholly quantitative, despite its theoretical commitment to human agency. It does appear that the vast majority of studies of stress, social support and coping, especially in America, remain wedded to a quantitative approach. The roots of this appear to lie in the domination of epidemiology and health psychology in the study of stress. The commitment to hypothesis testing and causal explanation, together with a conception of stress as equivalent to a disease, produce an unremitting positivism, most evident in the volume edited by Kasl and Cooper (1987), where few concessions are made to the legitimacy of a qualitative approach. The net result is that studies in the area as a whole are characterized by all the tenets of a classical positivism: "scientific" sampling, rigorously controlled interview schedules, elaborate measurement scales and statistical analysis of correlation and significance. To consider only those studies which discuss the actual or potential contribution of qualitative methods is to eliminate from consideration many of the major authors in the field. Nor do they fare any better if the criterion is broadened to include some acknowledgement of the limitations of an exclusively quantitative approach. What is even more surprising, especially to those encountering such literature from other disciplines and topic areas, is the almost total confidence in this approach as unproblematic. Orthodox stress research bears a remarkable resemblance to Bryman's portrait of quantitative research in sociology as including a "litany of preconditions for what is warrantable knowledge" (1988: 12). Studies proceed as if there had not been any phenomenological turn in any of the human sciences: "The quantitative imperative still dictates the form of data to be collected and how it is to be analysed" (Smith et al. 1995: 2).

In the rest of this chapter we attempt to dislodge the quantitative imperative in welfare research by looking at how qualitative methods might be defined and used in practice to collect, interpret and analyse data in areas of research concerned with people's responses to stress, their utilization (or provision) of support and their coping strategies.

Defining Qualitative Methods

Qualitative methods cannot easily be defined. Frequently they are defined negatively as "not quantitative" or, more positively, they may be seen to offer resolution of some of the deficiencies in quantitative research. The general objections to an exclusive adherence to quantitative methods, which have been made many times (see e.g. Ackroyd & Hughes 1992; Silverman 1993), are manifold. Not only are concepts defined in advance and rigidly operationalized by the researchers, but no room is left for interpretative options by the subjects whose subjectivity is quite deliberately eliminated by the research strategy. Moreover, the belief that answers given to questions with predetermined categories in an interview situation are necessarily true or valid seems at best optimistic and at worst naïve. In such a context, it could be argued that the genuine effort to eliminate bias may be a specious kind of scientism.

It is from such a critique, often via alternative epistemologies or social scientific theories, that the claim to validity of qualitative methods has been launched. This claim is based on using an approach which allows subjects to express and develop their own interpretations of the situation (sometimes called an *emic* as opposed to an *etic* analysis). Qualitative methods are based on "an approach to the social world which seeks to analyse the culture and behaviour of humans and their groups from the point of view of those being studied" (Bryman 1988: 46). The task of the social scientist is to obtain these points of view with as much fidelity as possible and then to find ways of analysing them. As will become evident, it is at this point that the real problems of qualitative methodologies begin. For while methods of data collection appear relatively unproblematic, methods of data analysis are less well established and therefore prone to idiosyncratic improvisation.

Methods of Collecting Data

Jones has stated the purposes of qualitative methods, in contrast to those of quantitative methods:

> To understand other persons' constructions of reality we would do well to ask them (rather than assume we can know merely by observing their overt behaviour) and to ask them in such a way that they can tell us in their terms (rather than those imposed rigidly and a priori by ourselves) and in a depth which addresses the rich context that is the substance of their meanings (rather than through isolated fragments squeezed onto a few lines of paper) (Jones 1985a: 46).

In his introduction to the same collection on applied qualitative methods, which is very much concerned with social policy issues, Walker (1985) cites as the most relevant methods in-depth interviews, group interviews, participant observation and "projective" techniques, which he sees as sharing "flexibility in execution, deliberate interaction between researcher and researched and a richness of data which stems from their largely textual nature and from their grounding in the language and experiences of the informants" (Walker 1985: 7). However, qualitative research on stress, coping and social support has in practice rarely aspired to the full-blown absorption in people's lives characteristic of ethnography proper, in part perhaps because stress is held to be an individual, or at least private, experience. Hence, in practice for a topic like stress, a qualitative approach means the use of the semi-structured interview. Normally, this implies a lengthy one-to-one interview with a selected group of subjects as the basic method of data collection. For this reason, there is "a 'natural' fit between semi-structured interviewing and qualitative analysis" (Smith 1995a: 9).

We can see how the equation between qualitative methods and semi-structured interviewing operates by taking some examples from stress research. Bograd (1988) conducted such interviews with wife beaters, Parker (1989) with carers of non-elderly disabled adults, Wilson (1989) with those of Alzheimer's sufferers, Zvonkovic et al. (1988) with the underemployed, and Boyce et al. (1988) with adolescent mothers.

Of course, such interviews may be difficult to conduct (and often to arrange), and should not be assumed to be free from the general problems arising from the artificiality of the interview situation. Conventional criticisms or reservations about the interview method centre on possible distortions brought about by interviewees' definitions of the situation. These include reactions to the persona of the interviewer (gender, age, class, etc.), and attempts to justify their own views and conduct or attempts to give the interviewer what they think he or she wants. Even more substantively, there is the underlying assumption that individuals abstracted from their normal nexus of social relations are necessarily the most relevant units of study. These problems may apply most specifically to the survey interview, but in principle they apply also to the semi-structured in-depth interview more characteristic of qualitative methods. As Bryman (1988: 14) has commented: "It is surprising that the widespread acceptance of interviewing in qualitative research has not been given greater critical attention as regards the problem of reactivity."

Glendenning (1983) is one of the few to have noted how interviewees may make complicating assumptions about the researcher's role. She observed that her interviews with applicants to the Family Fund were affected by the interviewees' assumptions that she could or should become their advocate. There tends to be a general assumption that matching the gender of interviewer and interviewee, describing the persona presented by the interviewer and the very length and exhaustiveness of in-depth interviews, are all sufficient to ward off these problems.

Oakley's (1981) critique, shared by Graham (1983b), of the inappropriateness to a feminist research approach of masculine styles of detachment and objectivity in interviewing has more general applicability than to feminist methodology alone, for it reveals and emphasizes that interviews are social transactions, in which there is an implicit exchange. Normally, interviewees offer information, gratis or for a small fee, and in return accept a human interest in their situation, and/or subscribe to a general belief that their participation will help research, which in due course may improve the situation for others. It may be that those suffering from stress are especially grateful for any opportunity to talk about their distress and may be motivated to offer a reasonably honest account, but too much of this may be taken on trust.

Significantly, such problems appear to be most recognized when the interviewees are men. McKee and O'Brien (1983) report that men's responses to female interviewers were both more complex in formulation and overtly sexual than they had anticipated. Interviewing men about their domestic violence, Bograd (1988) and Ptacek (1988), found them to indulge in self-justification, while the interviewers themselves experienced great difficulty in accepting what the men said in view of their admitted and often systematic violence. Some of these issues about the gendering of researchers and responses in domestic violence research are taken up in Chapter 6 by Jalna Hanmer and Jeff Hearn in this volume. The situation of interviewing men about their violence against women, may be an extreme case. Quite different dynamics are likely to be experienced by women interviewing other women about experiences they share, such as childbirth or divorce. This may be altogether a more natural and less threatening situation. The point is that the topic and the shared or discrepant definitions of the situation are likely to have some effect on the validity of the data. Perhaps a start would be to adopt the practice of concluding each interview by inviting comments on the process of being interviewed or even, as ethnomethodologists have done, by re-interviewing subjects about their original experience of being interviewed. The methodological status of their accounts would then be at least a little clearer.

Individuals as the Units of Study

No such strategy would resolve the question of whether the individual is necessarily the most relevant unit of study. Ackroyd and Hughes (1992) have argued that concentration on the "atomized" individual is a reflection of Western individualism in its assumption that social action is located in the individual rather than the group:

> It is a crucial postulate underpinning all the social sciences that individuals are related through associations of various kinds. In short, it is not so much the isolated individual, or even a large number of isolated individuals, that is the focus of interest, but individuals-in-relation-to-other individuals. In this respect then, it can be argued that the survey is too individualistic (Ackroyd & Hughes 1992: 91).

This a priori assumption requires specific justification. In the case of stress, there may be an assumption, in line with the medical model, that the illness is located in the individual patient. But, as radical psychiatry once suggested (Heather 1976), psychological processes are also located in the dynamics of social situation.

Some studies have recognized this, for example by interviewing both parents of a disabled child, wives as well as their unemployed husbands, or both the perpetrators and victims of domestic violence. Occasionally this is done simultaneously but separately, to ensure that each account is unaffected by interjection from the other party. But there are comparatively few attempts to interview a couple as a couple, which would no doubt be seen at one level as failing to obtain each perspective, especially since men are prone to "correct" their wives' views. However, it may often be as a couple, and all the dynamics that flow from it, that the stressor, whatever it may be, has to be dealt with. Of interest here is the experience of Gottlieb and Wagner (1991), whose attempts to interview fathers and mothers of disabled children were in effect modified by the interviewees, most of whom, especially the men, insisted on having their partners present. Gottlieb and Wagner's frankly speculative interpretation of the reasons for this may be questionable, but the point remains that, when given the opportunity to decide the unit of analysis, these parents decided it was a couple.

In a rare discussion of the potential and pitfalls of interviewing couples, Seymour et al. (1996) compare the relative merits of interviewing one partner only, both partners separately but simultaneously, and both partners together in a joint interview. They point out that interviewing both partners requires additional resources and may increase refusal rates. In simultaneous interviews, there are problems in synchronizing interviews and in the ethics of interviewers disclosing to each other what partners have said. Joint interviews may yield data on processes of negotiation between partners and issues of tension in the relationship, though necessarily each member's views are modified by the presence of the other. They also pose particular problems for data analysis, where careful distinctions have to be made about whose contribution is being identified.

There is even less evidence of attempts to interview families as a group. The logistics of this may be simply unviable, but then there should be some recognition that the decision to interview individuals is driven by the pragmatics of the interview situation rather than by any assumption that the individual's account has primacy. Still fewer stress researchers use focus group interviews. We can only conjecture as to why this has not been attempted more often, especially as many interviewees are recruited via helping agencies where a group session would not appear peculiar. The group interview has its own problems, especially in relation to group dynamics and hesitancy about exposure (see e.g. Hedges 1985; Krueger 1994), but it also provides an exchange of experiences and interpretations which the individual interview actually suppresses in its emphasis on the uniqueness of the individual's situation. In short, the qualitative interview of the individual may compound the tendency of quantitative methods' expressed concern to measure individual characteristics by adopting what is in effect a parallel assumption, that the meanings and interpretations to be elicited reside in, and must thus be obtained from, the atomized individual subject.

A generally underused and alternative method is that of observation. Some studies do undertake observation of transactions between the stressed and official agencies such as doctors (Silverman 1993). Others have used observation for clinical purposes, in order to rate such things as the quality of mother–baby interaction. But it is comparatively rare to find any study which actually observes how those coping with stressors actually behave in concrete situations. Oremland's (1988) study of hemophilic boys is unusual in this regard. The potential for widening the focus beyond the interview has been well made by Jahoda in her discussion of methodologies for analysing unemployment. She argues that it is in their daily lives, with the people they meet and in the places they frequent, that the unemployed experience their status. The one-off qualitative interview, much less yet another application of the general health questionnaire, cannot encompass the socially situated meaning of unemployment or, it might be argued, any stressor which affects the public presentation of identity. As Jahoda notes:

> What people feel inclined to put on paper or tell an interviewer does not reveal the full impact of unemployment on their mental state. It is also manifested in the way they conduct their daily life in the family, at the benefit offices, in their consumption patterns, in the streets and in the pubs. In contrast to some studies done in the 1930s, there is in contemporary work little evidence of attempts to gain a fuller perspective by triangulation or the use of unobtrusive methods, two methodological ideas that are more often praised than implemented (Jahoda 1987: 15).

Data Analysis

The complexities of analysing interview data are even more challenging than those of data collection. Interviews are almost invariably taped and transcribed.

The problem then arises as to what precisely to do with what are often massive volumes of raw data. Much here will depend upon the precise role given to qualitative data. Where these are adjuncts to quantitative data, the usual strategy is to extract some quotations or case histories as exemplification of numerical findings, as in Buss and Redburn's (1983) study of unemployment. More problematic is the situation where the qualitative data are all there is; some method has to be found of making sense of the data, allowing for both the identification of common patterns and the specificity of each account.

This problem of processing the data is most often evinced in the product of the completed research report. The invisibility of the process by which data have been analysed requires a lot of trust in the writer on the part of the reader. Some express reservations about granting such trust without sufficient grounds: "The critical reader is forced to ponder whether the researcher has selected only those fragments of data which support his argument" (Silverman 1993: 163). Bryman has specified the nature of the problem for qualitative social science generally:

> There is a tendency towards an anecdotal approach to the use of "data" in relation to conclusions or explanations in qualitative research. Brief conversations, snippets from unstructured interviews, or examples of a particular activity are used to provide evidence for a particular contention. There are grounds for disquiet in that the representativeness or generality of these fragments is rarely addressed (Bryman 1988: 77).

This has been argued to be true for studies of stress, at least as regards domestic violence:

> The manner in which conclusions are drawn from clinical and ethnographic articles is often unclear. Findings are based on data generated in unstructured interviews with small select samples; comparison groups are rarely used and statistical analyses are non-existent (Bograd 1988: 63).

Interpreting the Data

At stake here is the activity of interpretation; how to make sense of others' sense-making procedures. As Jones says: "The analysis of qualitative data is a process of making sense, of finding and making a structure in the data and giving this meaning and significance for ourselves and for any relevant audiences" (Jones 1985b: 56). This can only be achieved by what Smith calls "a sustained engagement with the text and a process of interpretation" (1995a: 18).

The difficulty lies in discovering modes of interpretation which stay faithful to the data and are accessible to the reader. As Bryman and Burgess (1994) point out, this is essentially a process of coding or indexing which, at its simplest, may be no different from the process of coding answers to open-ended questions in a survey. However, the boundaries of the topic may be rather more fluid and the relevant dimensions of the answer less obvious where the texts for analysis are lengthy interview transcripts.

The simplest approach is to read the data for emergent themes and then organize the discussion around generalizations about the themes, interspersed with illustrative extracts. This is the approach adopted, for example, by Lewis and Meredith (1988) in their construction of "caring biographies" for women who had looked after ageing mothers.

The most frequently used method for analysing interview data, at least in the US and until comparatively recently, has been content analysis. This appears to control researcher bias (itself arguably a problematic concept in welfare research) and render the procedure visible. Following the prescriptions of Krippendorf (1980), transcripts are analysed for the presence or absence of salient topics. The discussion is then organized thematically, following the most dominant or salient topics. This is the approach adopted in Bograd's (1988) analysis of men's and women's accounts of domestic violence, in Zvonkovic et al.'s (1988) study of underemployed men, and in Gottlieb and Wagner's (1991) discussion of parenting a disabled child. Little or no attempt is made to enumerate the incidence of topics, which ought properly to be one objective of content analysis. Rarely are the crudities of content analysis acknowledged: the arbitrariness of deciding which units are to be counted (words, sentences, paragraphs, pages) and the tendency to fragment the interconnectedness of themes, so denying the structured nature of accounts.

The work of Brown and Harris (1978) can be seen as a sophisticated extension of the attempt to analyse qualitative data in a quantitative manner, though this does scant justice to the complexity of their method. Their major study appears to occupy an ambiguous position in the field; almost everybody cites it, few seem inclined systematically to criticize it, but almost nobody wants to replicate it, with the exception of Dohrewend and Dohrewend (Shrout et al. 1989), who continue to dispute the precise means, though not the ends, of the methodology. Many commentators appear awe-struck by the sheer scale of Brown and Harris's original study: over 114 interviews with women psychiatric out-patients and a relative, averaging six hours in total; and a survey of 458 randomly selected women as a control group. Every interview was analysed minutely. However, though the women were the only source of data, their reported feelings about stressful life events were not accepted as valid. Instead, the interview material was rated by the interviewer and subsequently by the research team:

Our solution to the problem of meaning . . . has two main components. The first we have already outlined; we excluded any consideration of what a woman said she felt. However, in order to meet the objections concerning arbitrariness and superficiality, we collected background biographical material about each event in considerable detail; and developed twenty-eight scales to deal with aspects of each event (e.g. its expectedness, amount of prior experience, amount of support available to the subject). We used some of these to make a judgement about the likely meaning of the event for the average person in such circumstances without considering her personal reaction to the event . . . by developing what we called contextual scales in contrast to scales of self-report (Brown & Harris 1978: 90).

This method enabled Brown and Harris to chart the frequency with which their sample encountered what they called "provoking agents" and the biographical factors which appeared to make women most vulnerable to depressive reaction. They argued that their method only made more systematic the usual practices of social science: the interpretation by the researcher of other people's behaviour as more or less typical or reasonable, given their situation. However, the general verdict on Brown and Harris's work is that it is highly specialist, requiring a conviction about the methodology and a reservoir of resources beyond most other researchers. It subsequently seems to have been inserted into a specifically clinical and epidemiological context (Brown 1989), which has lost contact with the kind of research discussed in this chapter. Whatever may be the virtues of the "Life events and depression scale", as it has become known, it may disconcertingly remind us that we cannot take accounts on trust, that we do interrogate them and are often reliant on commonsense or professional understandings about perceived overreactions or inability to cope in the face of stressful life events.

More modestly, Boyce et al. (1988) used what they called componential analysis to construct taxonomies of support available to adolescent mothers. This involves a "progressive and increasingly refined elicitation of the categories used by subjects in talking about or referring to some domain of objects, events or persons in their surrounding environment" (Boyce et al. 1988: 1080). What kind of social support from what sources was available or valued was discovered by using the women's own perceptions. Here is a clear alternative to the check-list approach to social support:

> Conventional classification schemes have relied almost exclusively on the perspectives of the investigators and are constructions derived largely from the conceptual architecture of the social sciences. Missing from deliberations on the taxonomic structure of supportive exchange is a serious consideration of a more *subjective* conceptual framework: the taxonomy of social support as seen in the subject's view, unencumbered by social theory (Boyce et al. 1988: 1080, original emphasis).

This represents a sustained emphasis on the potential and largely unexplored contribution of qualitative study to the analysis of social support. The same can be said of Smith's (1995b) demonstration of how the psychological technique of repertory grids can be used to chart perceptions of the self-concept, and perceived relation with significant others, of young adult women in the transition to motherhood.

Grounded Theory

The specificity of the analytical/interpretational methods described above to very particular stressors may partly explain their marginal status. It is the ability to deliver a generalizable methodology which accounts for the popularity of grounded theory. This is closely related to the method of analytic induction – the generation of hypotheses based on a few cases, which are then rigorously applied to each subsequent case. Analytic induction also apparently insists that to be validated, the hypothesis must apply to every single case (Silverman 1993). In the purest form of grounded theory (Strauss 1987), a complex set of procedures is involved in which transcripts are coded at progressively higher levels of abstraction, then conceptual interrelationships are tested by the method of constant comparison and finally theoretical constructs are developed. Charmaz (1995) has detailed how she applied this method to a series of interviews with the chronically ill:

> The distinguishing characteristics of grounded theory methods . . . include (1) simultaneous involvement in data collection and analysis phases of research; (2) creation of analytic codes and categories developed from data, not from preconceived hypotheses; (3) the development of middle-range theories to explain behaviour and processes; (4) memo-making, that is, writing analytic notes to explicate and fill out categories, the crucial intermediate step between coding data and writing first drafts of papers; (5) theoretical sampling, that is, sampling for theory construction, not for representativeness of a given population, to check and refine the analyst's emergent conceptual categories; and (6) delay of the literature review (Charmaz 1995: 28).

Henwood and Pidgeon (1992) have argued in favour of the use of grounded theory in qualitative research in psychology. They argue that good practice should involve: categories emerging from the data, multiple levels of abstraction and theorizing, reflexivity including extensive documentation of the research process, sensitivity to negotiated realities with participants, theoretical sampling and a claim to the transferability rather than generalizability of results. Parker's (1989) study of the carers of non-elderly disabled adults demonstrates the difficulties of both convincing sponsors of the validity of a qualitative approach and the complexities of applying it. Wilson (1989) studied carers of Alzheimer's sufferers, using the computer software package *Ethnograph* to analyse 250 pages of transcripts. These are two rare examples of actually applying grounded theory as a set of analytical practices rather than simply evoking the principles of the approach "as a general indicator of the desirability of making theory from data, rather than a guide to a method for handling data" (Richards and Richards 1994: 149). Like triangulation, grounded theory is more often approved in principle than applied in practice.

Grounded theory is not without its problems. The difficulties include its assumption that theoretical formulation should come from the data alone, presuming an unlikely theoretical agnosticism on the part of researchers, and a tendency to assume that the form of the data, as communicated in interview, is less important than the underlying processes it can be made to reveal.

Concern with the formal properties of language as used in interviews is the very specialist concern of ethnomethodologists and discourse analysts, whose objective is less to establish causal relationships of social phenomena than to discover how interpretations of experience are grounded in everyday rules of interaction and common sense understandings. Silverman (1993: 15) asks whether interview accounts are "true or false representations of such features as attitudes and behaviour" or "simply 'accounts' whose main interest lies in how they are constructed rather than their accuracy?" He concludes that the latter is the only tenable position, with the implication that "qualitative research can no longer concern itself with discovering truths which are unmediated by the situational use of forms of representation" (Silverman 1993: 197).

Applied to the topic of stress, this would involve a radical reorientation of the field away from the causes and remedies of stress towards how it is understood and managed in everyday interactions. It would be an epistemological and theoretical shift of a radical kind, the precise usefulness of which to relieving human misery would remain contentious. However, this has not prevented recognition by some researchers that the status of accounts of stress as communicative forms should be recognized. Thus Riessman (1990) concluded that the accounts she was being offered of the experience of divorce were essentially narratives and should be analysed as such.

Ptacek (1988) argued that men's accounts of their violence towards women were essentially ideological in nature. West (1990) used Cornwell's (1984) conception of public and private accounts to explain differences between his and Voysey's findings about the views of parents of epileptic children. Voysey (1975) discovered a generally positive picture of families coping well and appreciating medical support. In West's own study (1981) the parents were highly critical of the medical profession and felt themselves and their children to be stigmatized. West explains this difference in part by Cornwell's distinction between public accounts, which reproduce official language and assumptions, and private accounts, which are unofficial in language and assumptions. He suggests that Voysey's results are the outcome of a truncated set of interviews, her interpretation by respondents as an "official" figure and the use of mothers as the main interviewee. West conducted a series of interviews of both parents and befriended his subjects over a long period. He suggests that Voysey was presented with public accounts while he eventually elicited private accounts. West argues that all accounts should be treated as artefacts of the situation in which they are produced and that therefore they should be subtly challenged by the interviewer. Their validity will also be enhanced by forms of triangulation, although, as triangulation is intended to check one data source against another, it may succeed in removing some of the most interesting and valuable tensions and contradictions between different data-sets.

What is clear is that a common sense approach to qualitative data, in which the researcher makes wholly intuitive judgements about significant patterns and then exemplifies them (what Silverman (1993: 77) derides as "critical exegesis") is no longer enough. In their own way, qualitative data pose challenges of interpretation every bit as substantial as those of quantitative data, and there are no equivalents of mathematical procedures to resolve them.

Various computer software packages for the analysis of transcripts of qualitative data are now available. At their most basic, these can be used to code, sort and cross-reference sections of transcripts under thematic headings. At their most advanced, they can do more than code and retrieve. Richards and Richards (1994) claim that the NUDIST package they developed can achieve the multiple coding of segments, interrelation of categories, subsequent recoding and enable both the segmentation and contextualization of data. There is consequently opening up a debate among qualitative researchers about the extent to which such packages can be used by the researcher to identify patterns of argument and structures of meaning or whether there is an independent process of creative interpretation by the researcher. Mason is clearly of the latter view:

> Computers cannot perform the intellectual and creative task of devising categories, or deciding which categories or types of data are relevant to the process being investigated, or what is a meaningful comparison, or of generating appropriate research questions and propositions with which to interrogate the data, and so on. Recognizing the limitations of computers in this respect is, I believe, as important as appreciating their benefits (Mason 1994: 108).

The advantages and limitations of interpretative schema, whether provided by computer packages or grounded theory, are still in the process of being identified. At the moment, we can ask only for a methodological self-consciousness amongst researchers about the status of interview data and a clear articulation of the procedures involved. As Bryman and Burgess have remarked:

> Just as qualitative researchers have in the last two decades developed methods of data collection, so the challenge for qualitative researchers in the next decade is to articulate as fully as possible the processes associated with data analysis (Bryman & Burgess 1994: 224).

Otherwise the analysis of qualitative data is likely to reinforce the positivist view that it is in every sense a soft option.

Triangulation

In assessing the relative contributions of qualitative and quantitative methods, it soon becomes apparent that each has the potential to compensate for the weaknesses of the other. Generally speaking, qualitative methods are perceived to have greater validity, while quantitative methods are more replicable. It can also be argued that quantitative methods have more rigorous sampling procedures which produce greater generalizability of results, though much depends on the assumption that defining a sample population is a question of statistical representativeness, where proportionality becomes all important. The counter-argument is that what is important is to identify those with relevant characteristics and sample them until new cases add nothing to the analysis, the basis of theoretical sampling in the qualitative approach.

Despite the suggestion that methodologies with profoundly different assumptions cannot easily be fused together, there is some credibility to the argument that both kinds of methods should be used. This idea that data will be more credible if generated and analysed from more than one perspective is the most basic form of triangulation. Interestingly, some of the strongest advocacy comes from the study of employment or lack of it. Two articles in the Kasl and Cooper (1987) volume (Bailey & Bhagat 1987 and Pearlin & Turner 1987) argue that the qualitative approach has been undervalued in the study of work stress. Jahoda (1987) laments the decline of the multi-method approach in the study of unemployment, and Fryer (1992) specifically argues for triangulation:

> The time has come to reassert the value of descriptive field work, and other qualitative and ethnographic methods, especially in triangulation with quantitative ones. Apart from enhanced methodological adequacy, there would be likely spin offs of a less sterile division of research labour, more contact between researchers and actual unemployed people, more accessibility of research reports to readers and renewed consideration of ethical issues in unemployment research (Fryer 1992: 266).

Specific attempts have been made to combine the two types of data. Oakley and Rajan's (1991) study of social support amongst pregnant women renders statistical data meaningful by extracts from women's accounts, while a different kind of balance is achieved in Riessman's (1990) study of divorce, where the emphasis on qualitative data is qualified by overt measures of gendered differences in depression rates. In a survey of women's mental health in Canada, Walters (1993) selected a sub-set of 32 from her survey sample of 356 for in-depth interview to tease out how they constructed the concepts of stress and depression which had been used unproblematically in the survey itself. She argued that the women's own accounts reinstated what the survey tended to marginalize: the importance of wider influences, from expectations of gender roles to government economic policy, thus creating "a social aetiology of mental health" (Walters 1993: 399).

One of the most substantial discussions of the relative merits of qualitative and quantitative approaches has been provided by Yllö (1988) in relation to domestic violence. She criticizes feminist antipathy to quantitative research: "the creation of a simple quantitative/qualitative dichotomy (especially when posed in patriarchal versus feminist terms) is less than useful. It creates divisions and silences rather than dialogue" (Yllö 1988: 35). Part of Yllö's argument is with the methodological claims of Dobash and Dobash (1988). She does not question their claim to have used a greater range of data than most in the field, but believes that their tendency to dismiss all quantitative research as necessarily sterile and reductive might deprive the field of a valuable research tool. Reflecting on her own experience of researching battered women using both quantitative and qualitative research, she argues that both had their own strengths and weaknesses. For example, the qualitative data suggested that a proportion of battered women may have been abused in childhood, but the precise validity of this hypothesis could only be established through quantitative methods.

Ullah has similarly argued that his ethnographic study of unemployed black youths (1987) was complementary to a longitudinal quantitative survey of a similar group (Warr et al. 1985) in which he was also involved. While the quantitative study demonstrated developing patterns of mental health amongst various unemployed groups, the qualitative data yielded information on variations in what unemployment meant to those affected which could not be captured by the survey method.

There is, then, quite a strong argument that triangulation offers a positive way forward. It is very labour intensive and requires a wide range of skills in the individual researcher or research team. There is always the danger that the attempt to adopt both a quantitative and a qualitative approach will result in neither being adequately executed. A more substantial objection has been advanced by Ackroyd and Hughes, who express some scepticism about the epistemological validity of combining different methods. Part of their objection is that the two kinds of approach utilize opposed "inferential structures" – the processes and assumptions by which the data is taken to stand for, refer to or represent the underlying conceptual reality which is the subject of the investigation. Attempting to cross-check quantitative with qualitative data or vice versa may not be legitimate, because the two sets of data are different in kind, so there is no common basis for assessing their relative validity. Thus if the two sets of data prove contradictory there are no criteria for deciding which, if any, is more accurate. This is the central problem of triangulation, which:

> . . . assumes that there are criteria upon which all agree, and which can be used to decide between alternative theories, methods and inconsistencies in findings. If a survey should provide one set of results, participant observation another and experiments still another, how are we to decide which result to accept? (Ackroyd & Hughes 1992: 173).

Tackling such dilemmas if and when they arise would surely seem preferable to remaining restricted to one kind of data, without any requirement to demonstrate that the findings are more than artefacts of the research method adopted. As Mason has argued, the prime consideration should be "what are all the components necessary for generating a viable and convincing explanation and how do we get to that point?" (1994: 102). A more intractable objection to triangulation may lie in the suggestion that different methods may not be comparable, because they are not seeking answers to the same kinds of questions.

Qualitative Methodology and the Question of Aetiology

One of the key claims of positivism and source of scepticism among its critics is the claim to be able to identify the causes of social phenomena. In the case of stress, as we have seen, this causal emphasis is often taken to be synonymous with the aetiology of illness. Kasl (1987: 307) has put this clearly: "the orientation is invariably etiological – to establish cause-effect relationships – rather than merely descriptive. Often, the goal is to study both the process and the disease outcome." Clearly, qualitative approaches could be regarded as "merely descriptive", unwilling or unable to answer causal questions. Such questions – about which events in which contexts cause more or less stress, which forms of coping are most effective for what kinds of people facing what sorts of problem, and which sources and kinds of social support help to alleviate stress – have particular relevance if the results of research are to be applied to an advocacy of a particular policy intervention. The problem is thus whether qualitative research can help to answer such questions, or whether it can only answer rather different kinds of questions about how people understand their experiences of stress, their capacity to cope and the social support they most value; or how these key terms – stress, coping, social support – are socially constructed.

Perhaps this dichotomy is false, like so much else in the quantitative/qualitative debate. One might suggest that either method is adequate for its own set of questions, and both are vital for the whole problem to be fully understood. Alternatively, it could as well be held that neither method is adequate on its own, even for those questions it appears to be designed to handle. Both interpretations would point to the need for greater co-operation between the two approaches and preferably within the same research project. This position would have all kinds of implications for the composition and constitution of research teams.

It certainly cannot be held that qualitative research necessarily eschews practical policy considerations. Silverman (1993) holds an extreme position in his explicit disavowal of any intention to improve the communication in the counselling of HIV positive patients he observed, arguing instead that the role of the social scientist is to improve general understanding of the processes and contextual constraints of communication. By contrast, Walker (1985) suggests that qualitative methods can act as an important corrective to the often questionable validity of quantitative methods. Ritchie and Spencer (1994) argue strongly that qualitative data can be used in applied research to generate policy recommendations. For example, they found very great variations in the definitions of, and thus responses to, disability amongst those providing YTS schemes for young disabled people. The "adequacy" of the intervention could not be divorced from the understandings of the interventionists of the problem they were trying to alleviate. Charmaz's (1995) work on how chronic illness impinges on self-identity would presumably have relevance to anyone working with the chronically ill. Overall, there is much to be said for Thoits' view, that:

> . . . in order to advance and further elaborate stress theory, we need more qualitative research that focuses on the contexts and unfolding processes of coping and support-giving. In addition to the semi-structured interviews and coding procedures developed by Brown and Harris and Dohrenwend

and colleagues, a variety of new formal qualitative methods are now available for use. These methods combine textual richness with sophisticated analytic techniques, merging important aspects of both qualitative and quantitative practices. This is not to say, however, that the traditional stress model, survey methods, or linear analyses should be abandoned. These are crucial for the replication of major studies, exploring unexamined relationships, and teasing out a variety of causal sequences and time-lagged effects among the multiple factors in our refined stress models (Thoits 1995: 69–70).

Conclusion

In this chapter we have sought to have provided some pointers as to how qualitative research might achieve a higher profile and credibility in the study of stress, coping and social support. There is some consensus amongst those who have considered the matter about how the respective roles of quantitative and qualitative data should be defined and implemented. These might be formulated as a series of propositions:

(1) The methodology should be selected and designed by the nature of the research questions being posed rather than by any principled epistemological or theoretical position.
(2) There should be recognition that quantitative and qualitative methods achieve different research objectives which may be different but equally valid.
(3) Any methodological choice is bound to include and exclude particular perspectives; this needs to be explicitly recognized.
(4) While the criteria for judging the worth of quantitative and qualitative studies may be different, it is incumbent upon any researcher to be explicit, systematic and self-conscious about the procedures adopted, and about their strengths and limitations.
(5) Some form of triangulation is desirable, though not always necessary, even though such an enterprise is resource intensive and requires multi-skilled researchers.

These may not seem strikingly original prescriptions for social science research, but their achievement is a matter of some difficulty in any discipline or field of enquiry. It does not seem to us that the quantitative tradition in the study of stress, social support and coping sufficiently recognizes the restricted nature of the medical model, or the independent value of a qualitative approach. While quantitative research tries to be meticulous about its statistical procedures, the inherent limitations of quantification are rarely addressed, nor are they modified by any routine attempt to collect and analyse qualitative data. On the other hand, the qualitative approach – which has scarcely enough of a presence to be defined as a tradition – may not sufficiently recognize the problem of incorporating causal explanations into an interpretative approach, is ambivalent about its relationship to quantitative approaches, and circles uneasily around the problem of the generalizability of qualitative findings. There is some acknowledgement of the problems of using interview material, though its analysis, in particular, may require less intuitive and more systematic procedures, together with acknowledgement that interview material may require some supplementation with other kinds of data.

Noting the progress of the status of qualitative studies during the 1980s in mainstream sociology, Ackroyd and Hughes suggest that the division between quantitative and qualitative approaches is becoming less and less useful as a way of conceptualizing what are often common issues of research methodology:

> The issues are complex, varied, resistant to easy resolution and, of course, immensely important; far too important to be encapsulated in a simple dichotomy between quantitative versus qualitative research (Ackroyd & Hughes 1992: 31).

This may be a somewhat premature judgement in the study of stress, coping and social support. The case for qualitative research still has to be made in the context of the dominance of quantitative approaches and their positivistic assumptions. It is particularly hard terrain on which to stake out a claim for qualitative approaches. We do not intend to condemn researchers in this area for having failed to resolve the general dilemmas of qualitative research; indeed our own practice as researchers has contributed little to their resolution. The most viable strategy is one which seeks to rescue discussion of methodology from the tendency to either compound inherent difficulties with irresolvable epistemological dilemmas, or to assume that there is one unquestionably established position which can comfortably ignore or marginalize others. The point is less to establish some handbook for research procedures than to refine our understanding and implementation of the processes involved in social research. As Bryman (1988) has argued, the dilemmas of any kind of methodology are unlikely to be resolved by abstract discussion; better quality research is needed.

Better quality research is not merely a matter of methodological rectitude, since it can play a vital part in the development of welfare research as a whole. A major objective of this volume is to help clarify a range of theoretical, conceptual and empirical questions which recur across the whole field of welfare research: into stress and stressors, life-events, and the life course, coping resources and styles, formal and informal support, and varying degrees of vulnerability to stress.

The importance of such longstanding issues in welfare research has been recognized, and the inherited paradigm has been questioned. It has been argued that the old paradigm of welfare, assuming uniformity in the sources of, and reactions to, stress, and universality of welfare provision, needs to be replaced by a new paradigm, anticipating diversity, and a sensitive differentiation in welfare provision. Welfare has been, and needs to be, managed by individuals and groups in more complex ways than was assumed by the old paradigm.

It may be the particular contribution of qualitative research methodologies that they can appreciate and analyse the diversity of experience assumed by the new paradigm. The quantitative tradition tends to insist that concepts must be operationalized, i.e. defined and measured, in an objective manner so that observable statistical patterns may be identified in the causes and effects of stress. By contrast, qualitative approaches inherently emphasize the importance of shared subjective meanings. What constitutes stress, how coping is defined, which kind of social support is valued, are seen by individuals and groups according to the interpretative repertoires at their command. In this sense, the new paradigm's recognition of diversity has methodological as well as conceptual and theoretical implications. New questions require new kinds of answers at both the theoretical and policy level.

For example, the emphasis of the new paradigm on empowerment can embrace the capacity to understand as well as the ability to act. It is a form of empowerment for those experiencing stress to develop as a basis for action meaningful interpretations of their situation, rather than having definitions imposed on them by others, whether welfare professionals or social scientists. It should be a condition of effective welfare policy that it listens to its clients, and of adequate social science that it listens to its subjects. As Riessman notes:

> Investigators have not given sufficient attention to the meanings imputed by the social actor, that is, how individuals themselves interpret the stressors in their lives . . . it is in the interpretation of an event by the social actor that significance may lie, and consequently, the potential for distress and disorder (Riessman 1989: 749).

In what people have to say, we may find clues about how they might better cope themselves, and how others might help them to cope better. In that endeavour, qualitative methodologies may have more to contribute than has hitherto been recognized.

Chapter 5

Social Work and its Evaluation: A Methodological Dilemma?

Geraldine Macdonald

Introduction

This book is concerned with a paradigmatic shift in welfare research, away from frameworks which emphasize sameness and structure on the one hand and individual difference and agency on the other, to a perspective which attempts to synthesize the best of both traditions. It explores how those researching and delivering health and welfare provision can benefit from both approaches, rather than advocating one at the expense of the other.

At first blush this should be an easy adaptation for social work, given its self-acclaimed concern with the uniqueness of individuals and its appreciation of the contribution of structural inequalities to the social problems with which it is primarily concerned. Social work operates where the personal meets the political. Knowledge provided by research within both paradigms is crucial, if social work is not to pathologize individuals whose problems are largely the result of wider social factors, and at the same time is not to be rendered impotent by an appreciation of causal factors outside its immediate sphere of influence. Further, given the oppositional character of methodological debates between exponents of the merits of the two approaches, one might anticipate that social work would have a major contribution to make in arguing the case for a rapprochement between the two camps. However, this chapter begins by suggesting that, on the contrary, social work has done little to bring the two paradigms together in any systematic way, and certainly not in ways which are likely to lead to improved services for social work clients and service users. Taking this into account, it then considers the merits of one particular approach to the evaluation of social work practice – randomized controlled trials (RCTs). The chapter does not consider other, equally relevant, approaches to evaluation. There is, for example, an important role for process evaluation (Patton 1990) and action research. Overall evaluation in social work clearly requires pluralistic methodologies particularly in the context of community development approaches. In confining itself to a discussion of the role of RCT methodologies, the chapter does not seek to devalue these other approaches. But it does suggest that on their own these other approaches are not sufficient.

The Status of Social Work's Knowledge

Social workers typically work with marginalized groups of people who possess little political power and are vulnerable to changes in social policies aimed to keep sweet the less marginalized voter (a politicized disability movement, and better-organized users' and carers' groups in general, may yet give the lie to this generalization). In many areas, such as mental illness, offending, or child protection, neither social workers, nor those who are called their clients – or more bizarrely, service users – have much choice about whether or not they have contact with one another.

In this context, getting it right becomes almost more important than in a free market, where notions of voice and exit have at least some currency. The new paradigm of welfare research, operating as it does at the interface of social policy and personal experience, (linking research on life events, social and personal stress with that on social support, resources and coping) has much to contribute to social work practice. But its acceptance will not be straightforward.

Social work's day-to-day focus on social *problems* makes it especially important for it to operate with a good understanding of the nature and extent of the difficulties with which it is concerned – personal experience alone may prove a distorted window on the world. For example, relatively few parents abuse their children, despite the high percentage of abuse cases on child-care workers' caseloads. Views of child abuse based predominantly on one social worker's work experience, however vivid or however complementary to that of other colleagues (Kahneman et al. 1982) provide no more sound a basis for understanding the factors that precipitate and maintain social problems than data gathered from other clinical or retrospective samples. As Gelles argues:

> [In] early essays on child abuse, and even some of the current essays which purport to document numerous psychological traits associated with child abuse, I find profiles of my students, my neighbours, my wife, myself and my son. It would almost seem that some of these researchers are right when they conclude that child abusers are a random cross-section of the population. However, their research does not tell us anything. Because control groups were not used, there is absolutely no basis upon which to draw any conclusions whatsoever (Gelles 1987: 203).

A sound understanding of child abuse needs to include an appreciation of the extent to which the factors that appear to differentiate the abusive parent from the non-abuser do in fact do so. Gelles's "control group" terminology may be misleading, for a multivariate analysis of data covering the whole population would also serve the purpose (the intention would be to find the predictive factors for those who move to the "abuser" group). It may be that for some very low frequency types of abuse prediction may be an impossible, and inappropriate, goal (Creighton 1985; Macdonald 1995). But inadequate or over-estimated knowledge will result in poor assessments and erroneous decisions. This aspect of the knowledge base relies primarily on quantitative approaches to research, but by no means exclusively so. It is equally important that welfare workers be familiar with those factors that prevent most people, against whom the epidemiological odds are stacked, from adopting socially unacceptable patterns of behaviour, and those which enable others to change. This affords the possibility of building on people's strengths rather than focusing on individual inadequacy, and has implications for the deployment of resources, as well as individual practice decisions, and *modus operandi*. One might, therefore, expect the profession to be an avid, but discerning, consumer of research findings from within both research traditions. To date, however, social work has largely rejected the scientific paradigm, and the argument that this paradigm provides the *best* evidence on the effectiveness of services and methods of intervention. Methodological and epistemological disputes provide a partial explanation for this reluctance and in this, social work is party to a wider debate within welfare research in general. Other reasons are perhaps peculiar to social work as a profession.

What is Social Work?

> The social worker's basic values must relate to individuals, whether he/she works with individuals in a group or in communities, since it is the welfare of the individuals, in a group or in a community, which is the social worker's basic concern even if indirectly (BASW Code of Ethics: 5).

This view of the client as a unique individual is enshrined in social work's value systems (see Biestek 1961). It provides a reason for preferring research which attends to the ways in which individual (or case-specific) factors interact with others (such as social, psychological and biological factors) to increase exposure to risk, or to act in a protective way against risk. Further, given social work's self-acknowledged emphasis on the importance of support – the usual rationale given by those who regularly visit clients for whom they are otherwise doing nothing (Fisher et al. 1984) – one might expect some interest in research which aims to evaluate the effects of such costly interventions and, if they are effective, aims to identify those aspects of social support which comprise the active ingredients for effectiveness (see for example, Oakley et al. 1990, 1994). It is certainly the case that *some* social workers, *some* teams and *some* social work courses can be found which demonstrate just such interests and endeavour to structure their work accordingly. However, they tend to be in a minority. One reason for this lies in the origins of the profession's interest with individual uniqueness (which is ideological and philosophical rather than empirical). (See Clarke with Asquith 1985.)

Despite the positive emphasis put on individuality and uniqueness, a large part of the profession's history has been devoted to operationalizing the dominant political ideologies of the day, and these have tended to centre upon regulating individuals – making them fit in with dominant societal norms, whether in terms of employment, education, child care or culture (Cohen & Bains 1988; Jordan & Parton 1983; Pearson 1989; Roys 1988). Even when the impact of structural inequalities (predominantly seen in terms of class) made itself felt within social work, this had little impact on the shape and content of the day-to-day practice of the majority of staff or educators (Hugman 1991; Rojek et al. 1988). In part, this is not surprising given that many of the early models of social work (social casework, psychoanalytic casework, counselling) had their roots in the clinical experience and theories of individuals (Freud 1930; Hollis 1964; Perlman 1957; Rogers 1951) rather than in psychological or sociological research. One has only to read these texts to understand how the theoretical bases of post-war social work contributed to the framing of social problems in terms of individual pathology. The following extract provides one example:

> The fact that large numbers of people with character disorders live in slum areas is not accidental. Not only do slums spread a kind of contagion and tend to reinforce pathological tendencies, but cheap housing itself operates as a selective factor in determining which families live in a particular neighbourhood or dwelling. Poor housing and blighted neighbourhoods become the receiving ground for persons who are at the bottom of the economic scale, and who, in the main are in this position because of personality difficulties. They are persons who have little success in work and who have had criminal records or a history of family desertion, illegitimacy, alcoholism and so forth. The need for these people to be "dilapidated", like many of their other characteristics, is difficult for the average person to believe or understand. When one works closely with this group of clients, however, one comes to sense that this psychological need plays a large part in determining where they choose to live (Reiner & Kaufmann 1969: 170–1).

The work referred to included a large dose of psychodynamically-informed counselling. Such a view provided an accessible justification to a professional group with little to give by way of houses, income, or other much-needed material resources, but which could always offer a relationship. After all, if the cause of so much lay within the individual, then there too lay the possibilities for change – they had only to be harnessed. It would be difficult to find anything quite so blatant in contemporary literature. Nevertheless, such theories continue to exercise considerable influence (Marsh & Triseliotis 1996) and there is still a tendency to offer therapeutic responses, or more frequently now support, when resources are the key issue.

Recent years have seen an increasing emphasis on the common experiences of people, especially with regard to their membership of oppressed social groups. The attention of policy makers and practitioners has been drawn to the numerous ways in which such divisions systematically disadvantage people. As well as dealing with the consequences of such divisions, social work may itself impose such patterned disadvantage: black families are under-represented in those services which could be described as social care (preventive services and services provided under permissive powers) and over-represented in social control aspects of social work, such as children in care (Batta & Mawby 1981). This is also the case within some areas of the criminal justice system and mental health services, where black people are over-represented both in prisons and psychiatric hospitals (Bolton 1984; NACRO 1991).

Similarly, in relation to women, research into the attitudes and behaviour of social workers towards women suffering domestic violence suggests that their responses are determined by patriarchal views of the factors contributing to this phenomenon and by their statutory responsibilities to children. Women themselves (toward whom no statutory duties are prescribed) have been perceived largely in respect of their roles as mothers or wives (see Chapter 6). Furthermore, it has taken years of persistence from those in the disability movement to make their voices heard by social workers who, despite their long-standing disdain for what they refer to as the medical model of practice, continue to act as if disability was primarily a medical matter, rather than a concept heavily influenced by social and political factors (see Morris 1989, 1991; Oliver 1991, 1996). A small but growing number of those in social work have recognized that as a profession we replicate the same patterns of oppression that exist elsewhere, with very real (sometimes life-threatening) consequences for those we describe as service users or clients (Langan & Day, 1992).

Ethics and Effectiveness

The extent to which traditional scientific methods can do justice to world-views which are not white, male and middle class, is an important issue which is explored elsewhere in this volume (see Chapters 2, 4 and 6). The case made here is that although we need to be cognisant of the dilemmas positivist scientific traditions involve, we also need to examine the potential offered within the scientific paradigm to identify the sort of interventions that would generate most benefit. To reject this potential out of hand may mean we damage the people we seek to help by using ineffective and potentially harmful interventions. In this regard, the recipients of welfare represent a minority group whose voice is rarely heard in relation to discussions and decisions about "what shall count as evidence".

It is not perhaps surprising that the dilemmas presented by the allocation of scarce resources and the exercise of social control functions, have led to an emphasis on ethical issues. However, social work is an irreducibly interventionist occupation, for which a minimum ethical requirement must be that workers be reasonably certain that what they are doing: (1) minimizes harm to the client or others; (2) is legitimated (by statutory or organizational remit and, where possible, by the people concerned); and (3) is the course of action most likely to be effective. Disattention to this third moral constraint of effectiveness leaves social work vulnerable to Wootton's indictment of "the peculiar repulsiveness of those who dabble their fingers self-approvingly in the stuff of other people's souls" (Wootton 1959, quoting Virginia Woolf).

When mistakes or poor decisions are made, people's welfare, and possibly their lives, are at risk (Beckford 1984; Carlisle 1986); families break up (Cleveland Report 1987; Palmer 1993); people are wrongly incarcerated in institutions; and so on. This also makes social work particularly vulnerable to its critics who would wish to delimit state help for those facing severe social and personal problems. Effectiveness in social work hinges on competence, and competence requires both sound knowledge and skills. Like many of the helping professions, social work often finds itself operating in social arenas where little is known, or where the bits of any particular jigsaw have yet to be pieced together. It is often charged with predicting the unpredictable and managing risks that do not readily lend themselves to management by individuals who usually operate at a distance from their clients, and with limited control over the factors which precipitate crises. Social work is not an exact science, but this does not make it an art, to be performed on the basis of flair, intuition and affiliation to a particular school (England 1986).

In the absence of a more certain picture, it is important that social work interventions are based on the best available understanding, and the best available information about what works. To date, social work has tended to be guilty of a general contentment with, or even defence of, a knowledge-base characterized by egalitarianism – namely a rejection of any suggestion that some kinds of evidence are more secure than others. The recognition that social work is a complex human activity has resulted in the idea that its essence is lost if subjected to scientific methodology (Smith 1987). The ideological bias which has underpinned much so-called positivist research, for example its masculinist assumptions and *de facto* denial of the experience and world-view of women and other marginalized groups, has often been used to imply inappropriateness of these methodologies to human experience (Dominelli 1996). Increasingly, however, it is argued that these methods should be used alongside others to address the current agenda around the effectiveness of personal welfare.

Knowledge-base or Knowledge-pile?

Decisions about how to respond to problems are influenced by one's understanding of the causes of particular problems. This is highlighted in any resumé of policies towards young offenders. These policies change depending upon whether delinquents are seen as the product of lax parenting, family breakdown, criminogenic tendencies, or poverty and diminished life chances.[1]

Such views are, of course, not unrelated to dominant ideologies and political preferences, and when social workers act out of step with these they risk the wrath of politicians. An example of this was the media response in the mid 1990s to the news that persistent offenders had been sent abroad on adventure holidays (a response which reflects the "diminished life chances" model of offending). Here is a situation in which research from the structural paradigm (who becomes a persistent offender?) could be combined with that from the individual paradigm (what differentiates those who share these characteristics but who *do not* become persistent offenders?) to provide a better understanding of *how, why,* and *what strategies might prove effective?* We *might* find that adventure holidays, when properly evaluated, offer a cost-effective alternative to even more expensive disposals such as custody, but at present there is little evidence, beyond single cases, as to whether this works or not.

The example of juvenile crime highlights two other key issues in the relationship between research and practice in social work. First, theories and perspectives on causality abound, and these are more often chosen on the grounds of belief or preference, than on the basis of evidence. Some 20 years ago, Sheldon posed the problems raised by leaving such crucial decisions to personal choice like this:

> It too easily leads to the spectacle of any three trained social workers deciding that any one client's problem is the result of either the suppression of his internalized "fun child", an upset in his family dynamics, or his hitherto unsuspected need for three days camping in Wales. Apart from our own feelings about this sort of thing, it must make us politically vulnerable sooner or later (Sheldon 1978: 5).

In other words, not only are theories not created equal in terms of the evidence underpinning them, but some of them are inherently contradictory, and cannot be believed – at least not by anyone who wishes to make a modest claim to clear thinking. Consider the following headings relating to child abuse:

Ethnological and sociobiological perspectives
The psychodynamic perspective
Behaviourism and learning theory
Family dysfunction theory
Sociological perspectives
The feminist perspective
Children's rights

These are to be found in a chapter entitled "Alternative Theory Bases in Child Abuse" (Corby 1992). This overview in a key text reflects the current state of play in an important area of practice. Many social workers appear to think that because human behaviour is complex, we need lots of different explanations to capture the reality of its different parts (distinctions between theories, perspectives and empirical data are often glossed over). We must aspire to something better if we are not to be stuck with what Sheldon referred to in 1978 as a *knowledge-pile* rather than a *knowledge-base*. We need a sophisticated and comprehensive approach to understanding complexity, but not at the expense of rationality.

The second issue which is also illustrated by the juvenile justice example is how we are to evaluate competing theories and research paradigms. As yet there is no consensus as to how this might be done, either in relation to those theories and research which purport to *explain* human behaviour and social problems, or to those which make claims in respect of the effectiveness of intervention in securing desired changes. The *laissez-faire* approach to knowledge that ensues in the wake of this failure to agree ground-rules for deciding these matters leaves workers with rather more professional freedom than our current knowledge base justifies. The situation is made the more serious by the location of social work in a bureaucratic structure in which management – even when concerned with quality audit and assurance – is preoccupied with process, rather than content.

Familiarity with the ways in which gender-bias can compromise the findings of the most scientifically respectable research has led some feminists to the wholesale rejection of quantitative methodology (Hartsock 1983; Rose 1983). Other analyses of scientific research have shown similar processes at work in relation to class, race, sexuality and disability (e.g. Lorde 1984; Kitzinger 1987; Oliver 1990; Morris 1991). As a consequence, there has been a tendency to caricature all experimental methodology as positivist and masculinist, because research conducted within this paradigm has often overlooked important interpretative or subjective aspects of human experience, and has appeared unaware of the particular world-views on which it is based. But to outlaw such methods on the ground of previous convictions invites other errors just as serious. For example, in the course of a book review entitled *Putting the pleasure back into sex*, Jane Ussher writes:

> Research on human sexuality has traditionally taken place within a positivistic framework, focusing on observable aspects of the body and on biology. Arguably, sex researchers adopted narrow experimental methodologies to achieve legitimacy in the scientific community (Ussher 1996: 41).

The motives attributed to these researchers may be accurate, but heterosexually dominated as this field has been (see Wilkinson and Kitzinger, 1993), some areas – such as the physiology of sexual arousal – are arguably robust against ideology. The critical issues are the questions that have not been addressed (*why* questions, rather than *how* questions), the ways in which dominant ideologies have skewed the research process, and the misuse of such findings when used in isolation from personal, cultural and political contexts. Although very closely linked, these are distinguishable from the basic tenets of a scientific approach to knowledge generation which are, potentially empowering to those who participate in research, and whose well-being is subject to the actions of those who apply knowledge – or not.

Few people on the caseloads of social work agencies can afford the niceties of the more esoteric debates encountered in the methodological literature. When considering the effectiveness of social interventions, for example, those who argue solely for either quantitative or qualitative research are equally misguided, because both approaches are crucial to the understanding of social and personal problems. The key point here is that the positive outcome associated with quantitative or objective changes (for example in behaviour) depend on more qualitative dimensions related to the meaning attached to such change. In child protection, for example, changing parental behaviour may be essential, but not sufficient, to secure the well-being of a child. In order to work appropriately and effectively with parents who experience difficulties in managing their children or meeting their needs, it is necessary to know what it is like to be a parent in a particular set of circumstances with a particular life history; to know the range of things likely to help; and to be able to tailor these so that they are acceptable and meaningful. In conflicts of interest between parents' welfare and that of their children it is important to know where priorities lie, to be able to minimize feelings of guilt and inadequacy, and to ensure that what can be cherished is preserved. Even here, in areas where values and principles of good practice appear pre-eminent, there is a role for securing the best available evidence about the ways in which principles can be operationalized — as well as checking that these values and principles of good practice are shared by social work clients themselves. In short, to disregard the experiential standpoints of key players is unreasonable, and sometimes dangerous, even when, to all intents and purposes, we have achieved what we set out to do, for example securing a cessation of violence from a mother towards her young son. But knowing the best way of effecting such changes in mother–child interaction is equally important, and as the following section argues, scientific methodology has an especial contribution to make in the latter regard.

Grounds for Rapprochement

The central concern for this book is to build links between two relatively distinct perspectives in welfare research. Clearly, there is more to paradigmatic divides than the kind of data collected. Some feminist critiques of science have raised concerns about the distorted world-views produced by historically masculinist research (Hartsock 1989). Feminist critiques of social welfare and psychological research have highlighted the dangers of an uncritical acceptance of research findings, and indeed the weaknesses inherent in positivist approaches that do not attend to these issues of hidden bias (see Harding 1990 for a succinct overview). But in welfare practice, either/or choices between scientific approaches and other methods of theory generation may have serious implications for action. Rejecting the former in favour of personal preference may have significant consequences for clients and service users. How else are the relative merits of particular standpoints to be assessed when these conflict, if scientific principles are not accepted?

Empiricism does not provide an escape route from theory to truth: observation is never theory-free, and theories are not free from subjectivity or other forms of bias. However, empiricism does provide one way of making explicit the theoretical underpinnings of our conceptualizations, hypotheses or assumptions about problems (and solutions). It also provides the possibility of controlling for some of these influences when seeking to test the relative usefulness of different interventions. We need to be able to ask and answer the question "What works best with these sorts of difficulties and within these constraints?"

If a rapprochement between qualitative and quantative approaches to evaluation were to be attempted, four principles to conserve might be: (1) that, as far as possible, researchers make explicit the assumptions and values underpinning the questions they ask and the methods they deploy, and take care to carry this through to the analysis and interpretation of their data; (2) that the methods used should be robust against charges of invalidity, both internal and external; (3) that researchers should not employ methods oppressive either to researchers or to the researched; and (4) that research should be oriented towards the production of knowledge in such a form and in such a way as can be used by users themselves. The last two points are drawn from Oakley's (1989) suggested ground-rules for feminist researchers, but offer a guide to good research generally, particularly in a field like social work and social welfare, where the nature of the task is, in part, to address oppression and its consequences.

Evaluating Outcomes

Discussions about research methodology appear to be at their most heated when related to the evaluation of services. This is perhaps because other factors come into play. After reviewing some of these particular characteristics of social work practice, this chapter will conclude with an overview of outcome-research in social work, and its implications.

Firstly, it is extremely difficult for those in social work and similar professions to disinter the personal from the professional: what we do is through the medium of our personalities and the relationships we establish. The well-evidenced importance of process variables, such as relationships and worker characteristics, in social work interventions (see Beutler et al. 1995; Orlinsky et al. 1995) has helped shape a view that these are the most important contributors to effective helping. This has reinforced the idea that it is appropriate to select theories and methods of working on the basis of personal preference, or acceptability; hence the catch-phrase, "it works for me". Social workers generally consider *what* is done to be less important, despite growing evidence that this does in fact matter considerably (Macdonald & Sheldon with Gillespie 1992).

Secondly, the evaluation of social interventions presents problems not encountered in other, more clinical settings. In real-world settings, social problems come packaged with unique histories and in unique constellations – hence, in part, social work's emphasis on individual uniqueness. The many influences on the trajectories of personal and interpersonal problems, many of which do not lend themselves to monitoring (let alone control in a research sense), have led some to argue that scientific methodology is too blunt an instrument with which to attempt such a delicate and complicated undertaking as the evaluation of social work. One extreme form of this argument is the position that social work is an art, rather than a science – a stance which has elicited from two antagonists the retort:"if social work is an art, then let it be funded by the Arts Council" (Brewer & Lait 1980). The position taken in this chapter is that it is the very complexity of social work which makes rigorous, scientific evaluation essential to accountable practice, and which requires researchers to develop questions and methods which enable us to interpret the meaning and implications of quantitative data.

An important reason for taking outcome research seriously is the cautionary tales of deterioration effects evident in the literature over many years – people who got worse as a result of the good intentions of would-be helpers. This sometimes happens despite reports of immense satisfaction from clients about the way in which they were helped (see McCord 1982; Miller 1962). Further, financial resources have been allocated to projects and services (and wholesale changes made to policy and practice) on the basis of no evidence whatsoever – a situation not confined to social welfare.[2] Sometimes this is ideological and political – as with Youth Treatment Centres. Sometimes it is simply a response to the evidential vacuum resulting from a failure to take seriously the importance of basing interventions on sound evidence, or to ensure that, where this is not available, evaluation runs in parallel with service developments.

The following hypothetical situation highlights some of the key issues in the evaluation of social interventions. Suppose a particular family centre wishes to evaluate a discussion group aimed at improving the parenting of a group of parents whose children have been placed on the Child Protection Register because of neglect. Suppose the programme runs for eight weekly sessions and is considered by the workers and parents to have been a success for those who did not drop out. These judgements are based on the self-reports of the parents, the workers' observations of parents' increasing self-esteem, and improvements in the apparent well-being of the children (who have been cared for in a crèche during the parents' group). But before asserting that discussion groups work we need to be as certain as possible that these improvements have in fact taken place, and that they are attributable to the discussion group. It is very difficult to do this unless we have mechanisms for ruling out competing explanations.

The parenting of the people involved might have improved simply with the passage of time and increased confidence in their parenting ability. (There is evidence that psychological problems will improve spontaneously over time in many cases (see Rachman & Wilson 1980).) The children might have become more manageable and interesting as a result of weekly exposure to skilled crèche supervisors. Alternatively, other external factors might be responsible for changes, such as improved income support, or more help from social services due to their children's registration, such as extra day care. Conversely the apparent improvements may not be real. They might, for instance, be due to the fact that in the course of the intervention parents had learned the right things to say, having been asked the same kind of questions at the beginning and end of the programme, and become familiar with the expectations of the workers – their behaviour may not have changed. Workers' familiarity with the parents may have led them selectively to perceive or emphasize those aspects of parents' behaviour with which workers were most concerned, and about which they had limited information at the start of the programme. Finally, the parents who completed the eight sessions might have been highly motivated – parents who would have improved anyway. Alternatively, the parents of those who dropped out might have improved as much as that of those in the programme.

These alternatives constitute reasonable "Ah, but . . ." reactions when claims are made that a particular programme is responsible for change in the absence of robust evaluation. The difficulties of demonstrating effectiveness arise whenever social work does something that produces apparently clear outcomes, whether good or bad. It is their ability to allow researchers and research consumers to postulate causal connections between intervention and outcomes that give Randomized Controlled Trials (RCTs) the edge over any other form of evaluation. The random allocation of research participants to one of two or more groups, with the intervention under investigation then provided for one and not the others, allows us to control for selection bias and bias arising from the influence of extraneous variables. That is, RCTs ensure that we do not pick those who we think are likely to respond well, and if other factors are exerting an influence they will be doing so in *both* groups – therefore any differences identified between the groups can be more confidently attributed to the intervention. When not controlled for, these sources of bias undermine the attributive confidence of research, that is, the degree of confidence that reported changes are attributable to the intervention in question (see Campbell & Stanley 1973).

RCTs do not remove all the problems. For example, we may well worry about what our intervention actually is; if a discussion group is effective, is its effectiveness due to the discussions, the worker's directions, or the companionship of others? We need to ensure that the measures we use are meaningful and that changes they record are not due to bias on the part of those gathering the information. But, like other aspects of enquiry, these are problems we have to address irrespective of research design. RCTs simply ensure that, once we solve them, a causal link between an intervention and an outcome can be confidently argued to exist.

The research synthesis with which this book is concerned involves a shift from a preoccupation which locates explanatory narratives in the attributes of category membership to one which does more justice to individual difference, encapsulated in historical and experiential narratives without losing social context. Within this framework, it might appear that RCTs in particular, and quantitative approaches in general, are at odds with research which focuses attention on individual difference and identity. This is not so. In part the antithesis is artificial because of the differing nature of the task: RCTs are concerned with the effectiveness of *interventions*, whereas explanatory narratives based on individual difference are concerned with *current states* and the acceptability of interventions. More centrally, accurate assessment of the impact of interventions on individuals is congruent with the underlying concerns of those who are sceptical of the ability of scientific methods to treat individuals seriously.

If we take seriously the contention that broad categorical attributions provide inadequate accounts of individuals, it follows that simply matching groups using conventional socio-economic attributes of individuals will be insufficient to control for between-group variation. These categories fail to capture socially significant information which may help to determine behaviour. This means that evaluation strategies which rely on control groups based on matching are by definition less secure than those which rest on randomization. The logic of the research paradigm, which emphasizes individual difference and which attends to the links between life events, social and personal stress and behaviour, entails acceptance of the RCT as the optimal and most defensible way of determining how we, as professional helpers, can effect beneficent (not merely benevolent) change.

Concerns about Randomization

The process of randomization has been deemed to be a practical and ethical obstacle to the use of RCTs in evaluating social interventions, though more often by those who provide rather than those who use such interventions (Paley 1990). By comparison, those representing users seem to grasp the significance of RCTs with ease (see for example, Oakley 1989). The starting point for RCTs is that often we simply do not *know* what works, or works best. Those who reject RCTs appear not to notice that their rejection usually occurs against a real-world context which operates like a large partially random (as opposed to randomized) uncontrolled trial. For some people, it seems that ethics are only a problem when we are asked to do intentionally what we do *de facto*, or to endeavour to learn from naturally occurring experiments.

The realities of social work mean that it is not always possible randomly to allocate clients to different services or wait-list control groups, for ethical and practical reasons, although the intransigence of both sets of difficulties may be exaggerated (Macdonald & Macdonald 1995). The likely cost of RCTs, the desirability of large samples, and the fairly loose relationship that often exists between our understanding of social problems and the responses we make to them (for example, child abuse) mean it is neither possible nor sensible to place all our evaluative eggs in this basket. What is essential is that *all* research designs deployed in outcome research pay heed to the sources of internal validity that RCTs are best able to control, and that results from studies which do not involve RCTs are treated with appropriate caution. An understanding of the strengths of the RCT, and its ability to control the sources of bias that otherwise render research findings inconclusive or misleading, provides a template against which to develop other research designs when RCTs are not possible (e.g.

quasi-experimental and non-experimental methods), and more appropriately to interpret their findings.

In principle, non-experimental studies could provide secure bases for judgements if we were certain in our understanding of particular problems. For example, if we knew with certainty what factors combine to produce child physical abuse, and we could measure these and their interaction, then we could rely on statistical measures to control for their influence on outcomes. Unfortunately, few areas of social welfare enjoy such an empirically sound and comprehensive knowledge-base.

Judgements on Social Work

How do we fare when the empirical basis of what we do is scrutinized? Child protection is a high profile activity, and one which brings into sharp focus the need for both quantitative and biographical or qualitative data if practice is to be effective and empowering to children and adults involved. Social workers have a major role to play in this area, both procedurally and in terms of interventions.

However, good evidence to direct and inform this work is lacking. In a search of upwards of 50 journals, Macdonald et al. (1992) identified 96 studies which evaluated social work practice, either alone or in conjunction with other professionals. The majority were American, and together the studies covered some 18 client groups or problems, and used upwards of 16 methods of intervention. Remarkably few – 13 – comprised attempts to evaluate child protection work. This dearth of empirical data about a major area of social work activity was mirrored in other key areas of practice, such as work with the mentally ill, with juvenile offenders, and with older people.

This picture in respect of child protection is also true of studies in which other professionals are the practitioners, and whether one restricts oneself to RCTs or not. For example Fink and McCloskey (1990) identified only 13 studies which met what they regarded as minimum criteria of methodological rigour. These included: clearly defined outcomes and valid measures; explicit criteria for including and excluding participants; and randomized assignment to experimental and control groups (p. 189). Only four of these studies were published after 1985.

In their review of evaluation of child protection work, Oates and Bross (1995) used a number of inclusion criteria to select studies: more than five subjects in the sample; one of three methods of comparison (randomization, matched control group or the use of a pre- and post-measure of effectiveness); and at least 15 per cent of the participants in the sample known to have been physically abused. These authors uncovered only 25 papers in 10 years which met these minimum requirements, none of which were concerned with routine service provision. Given the huge investment in this area, and the stakes involved if we make wrong choices (including decisions to do nothing) we should perhaps be less worried about the tyranny of the quantitative method and more worried about the lack of solid evidence on which to base our practice.

Conclusion

This chapter has argued for a rigorous, empirically based approach to the evaluation of social work as one of the helping professions. It has further been argued that this approach fits better with a new paradigm for welfare research which is concerned better to understand the relationship between creative human agency and structural constraints and opportunities. Although profiting from such a new welfare research paradigm, it is also important to see that its roots lie far back in the tradition of empirical sociology. "We are safe in saying that personal life-records, as complete as possible, constitute the perfect type of sociological material, and that if social science has to use other materials at all it is only because of the practical difficulty" (Thomas & Znaniecki 1958: 6).

It has been argued (Carr-Hill & Macdonald 1973) that the temporary eclipse of this focus arose not from an opposition between quantitative and non-quantitative approaches, but from the retarded development of appropriate analytic quantitative tools for handling event sequences. When both are properly understood, the concern with individual difference is easily compatible with the need for interventions to be tightly defined and controlled in order to demonstrate effectiveness.

Notes

1   Scott's (1970) book *The Making of a Blind Man* described a similar process whereby differing dominant ideologies about the nature of blindness (a personal handicap or a socially constructed disability) shaped national policies and individual professional practice in the USA and Scandinavia.
2   Recent research evaluating the introduction of Total Fundholding in the NHS represents the only official evaluation of the extensive reforms introduced into the NHS from 1990 by the Conservative government (see for example Robinson and Le Grand 1994; Mays et al. 1998; Glennerster et al. 1994).

Part 4
Social Relations of Welfare

Chapter 6

Gender and Welfare Research

Jalna Hanmer and Jeff Hearn

Introduction

So far in this book we have been focusing on general theoretical, conceptual and methodological issues within welfare research. In this chapter we turn to consider the same issues, but in the context of a specific concern with the relationship between gender and welfare research. This chapter is, in one sense, a case-study of how a framework for welfare research might be developed which more adequately links the new focus on individual human agency to the older focus on social structures of power and control. But it is more than this. It is also centrally concerned to describe the complex and pervasive relationship between welfare and gender and so points to the centrality of gender inequalities to all welfare research. The chapter has three main aims. First, it briefly considers the ways in which gender, gender relations and welfare have been conceptualized in research to date (referring back to the more extensive discussion of these issues in Chapter 2). Secondly, it examines the work of the ESRC/Rowntree Management of Personal Welfare Research Initiative from the same perspective. Finally, we move on from this to outline a more adequately gendered approach to welfare research – focusing in particular on two central concerns: women's experience of poverty and the study of violence.

The central argument of the chapter is that one of the main weaknesses of mainstream social science, including welfare research, is that non-gendered constructions and accounts have been explicitly valued over gendered versions. One of the main impacts of the development of feminist knowledge has been to show how gender-absent accounts are valued over gender-neutral accounts, which in turn are valued over gendered accounts. This bias is particularly reflected in a preference for non-gendered methodology in all forms of theory. The tendency to favour gender-absent accounts is also one of the major ways in which gender domination, specifically men's domination of women and children, has been, and is, maintained in social science research.

106

Approaches to Welfare Research

Welfare research necessarily studies welfare, and thus studies its gendering, whether explicitly or implicitly. Welfare and welfare research are fundamentally about processes of social power and inequality. In this chapter terms such as gender, gendering, gender power, gender organization, gender relations, non-gendered approach, non-gendered construction and accounts, gender interest, and even genderedness are used. These terms are not restricted to a limited definition in which gender is only understood as a social variable unbounded by theory, but encompass difference and inequality between women and men, including oppression and exploitation. Attention is drawn to three forms of relation between gender and welfare research: gender-absence, gender-neutrality and gender-presence. Gender-absence and gender-neutrality are dominant theoretical (and political) positions within the social sciences. We see these terms as descriptive, not as analytical, even though those who utilize these positions generally would not agree. Because gender-absence or gender-neutrality in social theory is impossible to obtain, presentations in these traditions do not eliminate power relations between women and men, but rather only serve to obscure them. Gender-absence differs from gender-neutrality in that to be gender-absent is to presume to make no distinction between women and men: it is the "people position". Gender-neutrality recognizes that there are women and men, but fundamental interests are conceived as equal or complementary or different but in a fixed or given way, and therefore not in need of further recognition. Gender-presence prioritizes the importance in social theory of being women and men. The feminist project in social theory is to transform the production of knowledge from an epistemology rooted in gender-absence or gender-neutrality, with the implicit or explicit acceptance of the male view as representing the total of humanity, to an epistemology rooted in gender presence, and the acknowledgement of women's and men's differential interests, life experience and life chances socially structured through inequality, oppression and exploitation.

Gender power and inequality are some of the most important and pervasive forms of social power and inequality. As Scott has noted:

> Gender is a constitutive element of social relationships based on perceived differences between the sexes, and gender is a primary way of signifying relationships of power . . . As a constitutive element of social relationships based on perceived differences between the sexes, gender involves four interrelated elements: first, culturally available symbols that evoke multiple (and often contradictory) representations . . . Second, normative concepts that set forth interpretations of the meanings of the symbols, that attempt to limit and contain their metaphoric possibilities . . . a notion of politics as well as reference to social institutions and organizations [is] the third aspect of gender relationships. The fourth aspect of gender is subjective identity (1986: 1067–9).

Welfare is an umbrella term covering a very wide range of experiences, policies and situations; accordingly, gender relations may be significant in different ways within different welfare arenas, for example, in families, labour markets and the informal care sector. The idea of welfare also may be gendered in another sense. Welfare refers to the well-being of people; yet *well-being* may be interpreted in particular and restricted ways. The concept usually refers to public, particularly state, definitions of experiences that are assumed to be located primarily in the private, domestic or community spheres.

Doing research on welfare introduces many further questions of gender power. These include the gender organization of universities and other research bases; the appropriateness of different methods and methodologies in researching different gendered situations; the gender and gender relations of researchers; and the significance of gender in epistemology – in what counts as knowledge in the first place. Thus, attention to gender also demands inquiring into theory, politics, methodology and practice, and the connections between these.

Differential Constructions of Gender in Research

Gender may be constructed in research in a variety of ways. Non-gendered approaches, including the *gender-absent* and supposedly *gender-neutral*, are *implicitly* gendered. Gendered approaches, including those that are more or less explicitly gendered, may adopt any of the various theoretical approaches to gender (for example, positivist, psychoanalytic, discursive). They may use different disciplinary or inter-disciplinary traditions or frameworks. Different disciplines and disciplinary traditions vary in the extent of their implicit/explicit genderedness. Most of these traditions have been adept at *excluding* women's accounts, particularly women's experiential accounts. Thus, much social science remains gender-absent. *Gender-absence* in this context means one of the following:

- not noticing the way gender operates in a situation; gender-absence may be understood as a problem of the observer's perspective, in particular prioritizing the male position;
- not seeing gender as a fundamental feature which interacts with, and modifies, other social divisions and social experiences;
- making specifically gendered and taken-for-granted assumptions in observation or analysis, for example, seeing all paid workers as *he*, or all carers as mothers;
- trivializing gender.

Approaches presented as *gender-neutral* are more explicit in arguing one or more of the following:

- that their methodology does not need to deal with gender;
- that their methodology can be applied to any situation, regardless of its gendering;
- that gender is noticed, but is a minor factor or variable relative to the major themes or explanatory frameworks of the study.

The preference for gender-neutral accounts is illustrated in the way in which methodology, particularly non-gendered methodology, is valued over theory, either gendered or non-gendered (see Davies & Roche 1980 discussed in Chapter 2). A major characteristic of non-gendered approaches is the false separation of experience, methodology and theory.

In the face of the long-established gender-absence within social science, considerable work, particularly within feminist scholarship, has been devoted to making women more visible, to redressing that invisibility and/or reconceptualizing gender in more thorough-going ways. There are clearly very many ways of thinking about gender. Different approaches include: seeing gender as biologically-determined; as the social construction of biological differences; as psychological differences (developmental/cognitive/psychoanalytic); as social roles (i.e. sex/gender roles); as fundamentally rooted in power and power analysis; as a form of categorical thinking (often as sex/gender classes); as discourse; and as practice (see for example, Connell 1985, 1987; Oakley 1982, 1985). Of particular interest is the conceptualization of different forms of sexuality and sexual experience, which parallel Marxist formulations of economic class as the consolidation of differential forms of labour (MacKinnon 1982, 1983, 1987, 1989; see also Dworkin 1974; Stoltenberg 1990). In this view, gender is itself truly a social construction, not just a social construction of sex and sexual differences.

Some writers have focused on more particular issues, such as the way *sex* and *gender* are often used to mean the other (Stanley 1984), or the relationship of theories of gender to gender politics (Walby 1988). One of the crucial issues that distinguish different approaches to gender is whether gender is seen as one of several fundamental social divisions underpinning social life, individual experience *and* the operation of other social divisions, on the one hand, or as just one of a string of social factors defining an individual's response to a situation, on the other. Studies that simply refer to women or to women's experiences do not necessarily constitute a fully gendered approach. They may, for example, treat women (or gender) simply as a variable, rather than as constitutive of, or located in, some social-structural formation; alternatively, studies may be conducted on women for pragmatic reasons. This tendency was discussed more fully in Chapter 2 using the work of Brown and Harris (1978) as an example. As Roberts (1979) has noted, however, studies which seek to demonstrate women's experiences can illustrate the inadequacy of non-gendered approaches, even when adopting one.

Gender in the Stress, Coping and Social Support Literature

Titterton's review (1989) of the literature dealing with stress, life events, coping, social support and vulnerability has already been described. As the discussion in Chapter 2 highlighted, gender, along with other dimensions of social inequality, is either inadequately treated or totally absent from much of this work. As Hilary Graham (1991b), has commented of Titterton's review: "It powerfully [because inadvertently] demonstrates the fact that the area does not use gender as a category for analysis." Stress, coping and social support have the potential to be fully gendered concepts, but it is necessary to develop an understanding of the ways in which gender is relevant to each of them. Some examples of the work which might contribute to this endeavour were discussed in Chatper 2. Other studies include those by Aneshensel et al. (1991); Baum & Grunberg (1990); Beloff (1986); Broverman et al. (1970); Ernst & Goodison (1981); Hamilton & Fagot (1988); Phoenix (1991); Roberts (1981); Slavin et al. (1991); Showalter (1987); and Ussher (1991). Many of the salient points from this literature have already been made in earlier chapters (see especially Chapters 2 and 3) but it is worth summarizing here the most important issues to arise out of the new paradigm research from the perspective of gender inequalities.

In relation to the work on stress and coping there would appear to be four key points to be highlighted. First, in much research, gender – in terms of being a woman or man – appears to be completely absent from the analysis. Secondly, where gender or sex is a variable, there may be no exploration of the extent to which it shapes the operation of other variables, for example, the experience of stress and/or the mediation of people's response to it. Thirdly, and more positively, some studies of stress have focused more directly on gender and gendered relationships (see for example, Mitchell & Hodson 1983; Snyder & Scheer 1981). Fourthly, the focus on stress as a process in which stressors, stress mediators and stress outcomes are all interrelated (Pearlin et al. 1981) also appears to offer some useful applications, in the sense that the idea of the stress process does at least raise the possibility of considering the pervasiveness of stress in a way that interrelates with the pervasiveness of gendering. A useful survey of this perspective is found in Pearlin and Turner's (1987) review of the family as a context for the stress process. However, the interconnections of gendering and stress are left unexplored. Indeed, there is a sense in which the very idea of stress is assumed to be characteristic of men, such that it can be thought of as a masculinized concept (Hanmer 1978).

Like the literature on stress and coping, the social support literature is gendered to some extent but in ways no-one appears to have analysed systematically. As noted in Chapter 2, being a woman or man is invisible or is treated as not directly relevant. Key social support texts not discussed earlier include Cohen & Syme (1985), Duck (1984), and Gottlieb (1981). Relevant texts on marriage and friendship include Allan (1979, 1989) and Duck (1990), while Raymond (1986) focuses on friendship among women, and Miller (1983) and Nardi (1992b) focus on men's friendship.

Much of the information in the social support literature can be reconceptualized as being implicitly about either men or women, even when it is not explicitly described as such. Thus discussions of, say, participation in voluntary organizations, or caring, are necessarily gendered, not only in terms of the differential involvement of women and men, and different types of women and men, but also in the construction of what is meant by caring or a voluntary organization.

What is to count or not count as social support is not so obvious when gender and other social divisions are introduced. There may be several reasons for this. For example, women and men may see social support differently, particularly in terms of their relationships to husbands, wives and partners, colleagues in paid work or other public domain organizations, and friends. Working outside the home may give access to more social contacts and potential support, especially in large organizations. Yet such work may be alienating, impersonal and isolating. Moreover, men's participation in the public domain is often on very different conditions from women's, both in terms of women's double (childcare), triple (care for elderly) or quadruple (emotion labour) burden, and in terms of women's lesser structural power in organizations. Similarly, domestic carework, whether full-time or not, is likely be experienced very differently by women and men with their differential potential for support and isolation. Men may have access to more social contacts, yet often seem to have less close friendships; in contrast women's restricted participation in the public domain may be accompanied by more close friendships.

Although the very notion of social support itself rests on gendered assumptions and arrangements, the concept does at least engage with the *social* aspects of gendering. At its simplest, the technical notion of social support is an attempt to abstract *support* from *social relations*. To put this another way, a relationship which is described as supportive may also be stressful and oppressive. Similarly, that which is described as supportive may also be violent and abusive.

It was argued in Chapter 2 that the literature on stress, coping, and social support emphasizes methodology at the expense of social structure, power, lived experience and subjectivities. Accordingly we have been critical of these concepts of stress, coping and social support, particularly in the way they have been used within an implicit functionalism. As noted in Chapter 2, some work does attempt to attend to such issues, recognizing gender and other social divisions as social relations which shape the experience of stress and mediate responses to stress and stressful experiences. Notable here would be Ann Phoenix's (1991) study, *Young Mothers*, which considers how black African-Caribbean and white women experience and cope with their lives and Berry Mayall's research *Keeping Children Healthy* (1986), which looks at how mothers care for young children and focuses on how class inequalities affect mothers' caring practices. A third example is Mama's book *The Hidden Struggle* (1989b) which documents the responses of statutory and voluntary agencies to violence against black women. These studies are sharp reminders of the limits of an individualistic approach to stress and coping, and the need to place such concepts in the social context of power, domination, exploitation and oppression.

Differential Constructions of Welfare

The idea of welfare has complex historical roots. It refers in some ways to the well-being (or lack of it) of people in civil society. Paradoxically, the idea of welfare comes from observation of, and intervention in, the lives of those who are presumed not to have it (welfare). In many European countries the state has often been seen as the main actual or potential *provider* of welfare, as in the notion of "the welfare state". Accounts and explanations of welfare can also be thought of as gender-absent, gender-neutral or gender-present. This applies to both their construction by authors and interpretation by readers. The conscious construction of accounts by authors as gender-neutral may be read as gender-neutral by certain readers or as gender-absent by others. Moreover, the actual idea of welfare can itself be understood as implicitly gendered. The concept of welfare has been constructed largely through the state's organization of domestic life (Wilson 1978) – processes which are themselves gendered.

In the development of welfare policy and the tradition of research that has studied this policy, there has been both a dominant non-gendered/gender-absent approach and a subordinated gendered/gender-present approach. The latter has been increasingly important in feminist critiques of welfare; in these women are recognized as numerically dominant in both the production and provision of most welfare services, and their consumption and use of those services. The history of welfare policy development and its study can be understood as a continuing dialectic between those non-gendered and gendered practices, accounts and readings.

The dominant traditions for theorizing welfare and the welfare state have already been briefly discussed in Chapter 1. From the perspective of this chapter the crucial point is that they have been largely non-gendered. In response, feminist approaches to welfare and the welfare state have emphasized the gendering of welfare and the welfare state, but again in diverse ways. This literature raises a large number of issues and critiques (see for example Dale & Foster 1986; Hallett 1996; Pascall 1986; Ungerson 1987; Williams 1989; Wilson 1978). Notable amongst these are:

- the liberal tradition of service-giving, around the issue of increasing equality of provision and opportunity;
- the gendered function of the welfare state, as in Marxist feminism;
- the gendered public political struggle that in some countries at least produces the welfare state, in others more limited public provision;
- the welfare state and welfare services as gendered labour processes.
- the differential as well as common experiences women have of the welfare state according to class, race, ethnicity, sexuality, disability, age and marital status.

All of the above partly represent gendered reworkings of non-gendered traditions. Other strands within feminist work on the welfare state reformulate the analysis in more fundamental ways (Holter 1984; Glendinning & Millar 1992; Millar & Glendinning 1989; Walby 1990). Key themes in this literature include:

- the emphasis on welfare and the welfare state as unequal gendered structures of caring, public and private, paid and unpaid;

- the welfare state as the site of the social construction of women's economic dependency and poverty;
- the emphasis on the body and women's control of the body, as in the women's health movement;
- the importance of having a voice in the way welfare is provided and organized;
- the emphasis on the processes of reproduction in both biological and non-biological senses;
- the importance of women-only services;
- the emphasis on sexuality and violence;
- the contradictory experiences of welfare for women – both enabling and constraining their lives.

These reformulations problematize the division between the public and private domains and explore the various ways in which women are highly represented as both providers and users of welfare services.

One of the most important insights of feminist scholarship in the welfare domain broadly defined has been the re-conceptualization of work, in particular the reformulation of the relationship of *work* and *non-work*, and the recognition of non-work *as* work. This is most clearly seen in early work on the recognition of domestic labour, unpaid labour and care work (Oakley 1974; Delphy & Leonard 1977, 1992; Delphy 1984; Dalla Costa & James 1973). Following Goffman's analysis of "people work" as work in the text *Asylums* (1961), Stacey (1982) developed this concept in terms of gender, and has highlighted men's domination of both women and people work. Related concepts include childwork (Hearn 1983), emotional work (Hochschild 1983), solidary work (Lynch 1989), and carework (Finch & Groves 1983).

The literature on care and caring is now considerable. It has emphasized the material distribution, sources and consequences of carework as well as the attitudinal status of caring about someone (Dalley 1988; Graham 1984, 1991a, 1993; Morris 1993; Parker 1990; Ungerson 1987). The materiality of care has been argued to include not just physical effort but also emotional costs (Parker 1990). Thus care is work; it is gendered and often stressful. The performance, the burden and the associations of care all fall disproportionately on women; this is both a cause and a consequence of the undervaluing by men of both women and care. Differential, gendered valuations of care, whether paid and unpaid, are reflected in the gendered structuring of the state, welfare professionals and welfare services. The professionalization of caring has led to the creation of hierarchies and bureaucracies, which men can manage and control and within which they can easily fit (Hearn 1982). Current moves towards community care in the UK and the deinstitutionalization of caring internationally by no means change this unequal gendered structuring. In some ways they may even reinforce the power of men as managers and resource controllers, while women are engaged in relative isolation in the caring tasks. In addition, those who are cared for are often women too, and often represented as dependent, passive and without agency.

Theorizing welfare must also involve the theorizing of the state. All theories of the state have been gendered, both in their practice and in their dominant constructions. Gender-neutral models predominate (see Hartmann 1979; MacKinnon 1989). Feminist work has analysed the patriarchal state (see Connell's review (1990) of some of this work and Barrett 1980; Burstyn 1983; Burton 1985; Eisenstein 1981; Knuttila 1987; MacKinnon 1982; McIntosh 1978; Walby 1986). Connell (1987) examines the following major propositions. (Connell's work glosses over major differences among these feminist theoreticians. Some of the major differences are in square brackets.)

- The state is constituted within gender relations as the central institutionaliza-tion of [men's] power; gender dynamics are a major force constructing the state, both in the historical creation of state structures and in contemporary politics.
- As a result of this history, the state is a bearer of gender; each empirical state has a definable "gender [men's privilege] regime" that is the precipitate of social struggles and is linked to the wider gender order of the society.
- The way the state embodies gender [men's privilege] gives it cause and capacity to "do" gender; as the central institutionalization of power, the state has a considerable, though not unlimited, capacity to regulate gender rela-tions in the society as a whole.
- The state's power to regulate reacts on the categories that make up the structure being regulated; thus the state becomes involved in the historical process generating and transforming the basic components of the gender order.

Finally, there are important connections between gender, welfare and patri-archy. The concept of patriarchy has attracted great attention and debate (see, for example, Walby 1986, 1990). It has been used in a variety of ways to refer to the rule or domination of men, whether as fathers or more usually as a general social group or gender class. The concept of patriarchy does, however, bring some difficulties. These include the difficulty of separating such gender arrangements from other social arrangements, especially the economic relations of capitalism. Patriarchy can be seen to reinforce a kind of theoretical dualism. Other difficult-ies may include the tendency to use patriarchy in an analytically imprecise way, or, more occasionally, in an analytically over-precise way (Alexander & Taylor 1980; Hearn 1987; Millett 1971; Rowbotham 1979). Although these problems remain unresolved, the concept of patriarchy does at least recognise the *structural* relation of women to men.

Recent work on patriarchy has developed in two related ways. First, there is an attempt to specify the complexities of patriarchy in terms of different sites of patriarchal relations (Walby 1986; 1990), types of specifically patriarchal rela-tions (Hearn 1987, 1992), and the contradictions of patriarchal and other relations (Ramazanoglu 1988). Thus, for example, patriarchy may be seen to operate in terms of the family/household; capitalist enterprises; the state; sexuality; violence; and culture. Secondly, a differentiation is made on historical grounds, particularly in the shift from family or private patriarchy to social or public patriarchy. This distinction is made by Jane Ursel (1986) in relation to wage labour; by Brown (1981) in relation to monopoly capitalism; by Hernes (1987, 1988) in relation to the post-war state; and by Borchorst and Siim (1987) in relation to the welfare state. The Scandinavian work on public patriarchy by Hernes (1987, 1988) is particularly important, as it relates the movement of men's power towards the public domain directly to the growth of the state and the welfare state. In this scheme, the state is analysed as an institution to which women (and men) relate in three major ways: as citizens, clients and employees. This particular analytic perspective is alive to both the emancipatory potential of the welfare state for women, and the dangers of women's dependence on the state and their lack of involvement in state decision making.

These qualifications of the concepts of patriarchy also mark a further shift in the development of feminist work on the welfare state. This is in the identification of the different ways in which women are constituted through social policies of the state, as citizens, clients and employees, according to their class, race, ethnicity, sexuality, age and disability (Gordon 1990; Hallett 1996; Langan & Day 1992; Williams 1989). For example, the campaigns to establish refuges for black women and children escaping domestic violence exposed not only sexist practices in relation to domestic violence, but racist assumptions about the nature of African-Caribbean and Asian family life and the needs of African-Caribbean and Asian women within them (Mama 1989a and b). In other words, women do not experience the welfare state in the same ways and the state may respond differently to different groups of women. This acknowledgement of the multiple identities and divisions which structure women's lives has made the search for a *single cause* of women's oppression (capitalism, patriarchy) less pressing than it once was (Nasir 1996; Williams 1992a).

There are some interesting affinities and reinforcements between these various positions on gender, the individual and society, and welfare. For example, non-gendered approaches to welfare and the welfare state have tended to individualize women and men, while gendered approaches to welfare may collectivize women and men, or construct women and men in relation to both social structures and individual experiences. Welfare can be understood as a shorthand representing the public organization of the reproduction of that which is assumed to pre-exist in the private realm. It is thus concerned with public definitions of the private. Through welfare, reproduction is placed in, and under the control of, the private realm. Welfare is the public organization of reproductive labour in its fullest sense and a representation of organized gender divisions. Indeed, in many ways the concept of welfare is underpinned by gender divisions. Public domain definitions of that which is assumed to be primarily private, for example, health, are riven by gender. Gendered differences apply in the very ideological structuring of the public and the private; the different meanings of locations – for example, as managers and fathers.

The Management of Personal Welfare Research Initiative: Diverse Approaches to Gender

As noted in Chapter 1, the concerns that gave rise to this book arose during discussions among the researchers working on projects funded within the ESRC Rowntree Foundation Management of Personal Welfare Research Initiative. In some senses this Initiative was located within dominant institutional constructions of personal welfare; its management was discussed in Chapters 2 and 3. But in another sense the Initiative was unusual, in the gender composition of the researchers – more women than men, its more collective ways of working, and (at least in relation to some projects) making gender a more explicit theme and focus of analysis. The different projects which made up the Initiative included examples of approaches located in different theoretical traditions and were underpinned by different constructions of gender and its salience, and of welfare and the state. The traditions ranged from the gender-absent to the gender-present. Using the concepts of stress, social support and coping as a unifying model is problematic because, as we argued earlier, these concepts originate in largely gender-neutral intellectual traditions. It is easier to problematize the gender-absent and gender-neutral approaches of the stress, support and coping model when the topic is inherently gender-sensitive, as, for example, in the study of violence to women from men. It is much less easy to do this when the traditional approach taken to the study of the topic is gender-absent, as for example, in the study of caring for disabled children. However, there is a literature which is relevant to all the projects that problematizes the concepts and social behaviour of husbands and fathers within family and those of wives and mothers as family carers.

Four of the projects focused particularly on processes of care; a fifth concerned changes in communities; and two centred on violence and abuse. Three projects in the Initiative – The negotiation of coping, disablement, caring and marriage; and the two on Social support and the health and welfare of vulnerable children – shared an interest in the gendered nature of caring within the family (Glendinning 1985; Graham 1983a, 1984; Land 1990; Parker 1990; Ungerson 1990). Health was also a shared concern across all the projects, although in somewhat different ways: caring for those who are vulnerable or ill; the experience of being vulnerable or ill; and the origin of work on health and disablement in the field of medicine.

The project on Coping and the care of a severely disabled child involved qualitative in-depth interviews with the main carer of the severely disabled child. Two interviews were carried out with each carer. In 19 of the 20 cases, the main carer was the mother, in one the main carer was the father. The majority of research on parents of children with disabilities has focused on mothers as the primary care-givers. The reason commonly given for this is that mothers are regarded as the main carers of the child, and are therefore more likely to be directly affected by the daily strains of caring tasks. This field has generally reflected the importance given to the mother–child dyad in child care and development theory. For these reasons, some research has been constructed *as if* gender issues are not particularly salient. There is also a growing literature on the situation in which fathers are the main care-givers, and where mothers and fathers operate a caring partnership (Bristol & Gallagher 1986; Lamb 1983; Parker 1986).

Women's role as carers in the family has been studied within the analysis of the family (Finch 1989; Social Care and Research Seminar 1986), and from the viewpoint of the skills and tasks involved in their provision of family care (Ungerson 1987). The social policy implications of women as primary carers within the family have also received attention (Dalley 1988; Land 1976; Pascall 1986; Ungerson 1987). Gender differences in coping and stress have also been explored (Hamilton & Fagot 1988; Vingerhoets & Van Heck 1990). Additionally, the experience of disability, particularly of women, is a growing area of study (Lonsdale 1990; Morris 1989; Oliver 1990) as is the gendering of age (Arber & Ginn 1991).

The project on The negotiation of coping, disablement, caring and marriage involved separate in-depth interviews with each of the spouses where one of them is experiencing a major chronic disability. The two projects on Social support and the health and welfare of vulnerable children explored gender relations in rather different ways. The project looking at service-providers, mainly women at the level of service delivery, used ethnography and observation to focus on the gender construction of professionals and decision making. The study of service users deployed secondary analysis of an existing dataset which included self-completion questionnaire and interview data provided by mothers, to consider the measurement of, and relationship between, stress, life events, social support and service use. These studies also sought to compare the perspective of service providers and users on the problems experienced by poor women with young children, the role of social support in their lives and views about appropriate service responses. As discussed in Chapter 3, there is relatively little work of this type in the welfare research field; some of these data are explored in Chapter 7.

The study on Mining communities under threat considered a number of issues around gender relations: men's and women's different responses to the threat of mine closure; closure and the survival of informal support networks; the potential for the development of enduring changes in gender roles; and youth unemployment and gendered coping strategies. The dominant model of gender used here is gender difference. A partial recognition of gender recurs within community studies, although the ways in which this is expressed varies considerably (Bell & Newby 1971; Frankenberg 1966). Frankenberg's (1976) work remains of central importance, as it critiques the development of gender analyses within specific community studies, from rural Ireland to metropolitan London and points in between, including a study of a mining area (Dennis et al. 1956). Frankenberg criticizes community studies for either ignoring the relations of production in home and community, or treating the home as solely a unit of consumption (see Young & Willmott 1957; Willmott & Young 1960).

The two projects on Violence, abuse and the stress coping process, which we directed, place gender in an absolutely central place in their conceptualization, organization and operationalization. Gender is not just a variable in relation to the explanations of violence and abuse; rather violence and abuse problematize the notions of stress, social support and coping. The first project involved women interviewing women about their experiences of violence from known men; the second involved men interviewing men about their experiences of being violent to known women. In-depth interviews and questionnaires including measures of social support and coping were followed up by interviews with the staff of various welfare agencies, for example, the probation service. These projects are discussed in more detail in a later section of this chapter.

The projects in the Management of Personal Welfare Research Initiative raised a number of general issues in their treatment of gender. (These are explored more fully in the sister volume – Popay et al. 1998.) First, how did projects understand both the state and gender? In the studies on violence, the conceptualization of the state was particularly important, because of the focus on welfare provision which included the voluntary as well as the statutory sector. As previously noted, the state is constituted within gender relations, and as a bearer of gender it embodies, regulates and contributes to the formation of the gender order. The gender order is also structured by the wider society which relates to the state in complex ways. The topics in the Initiative related in different ways to the gender regime of the state. Secondly, disciplinary location, methodologies and concepts were both shared and different across the Initiative. Theoretical approaches included socialization, sex differences and sex roles, as well as approaches emphasizing power, conflict, oppression, exploitation, dominance, structural relations, discourses and subjectivities. Thirdly, some of the factors, issues or concepts identified for detailed examination in one study were also found in the others: for example, sexuality, violence, women, men, girls, boys, age, community (of interest, if not geography), and physical and mental conditions.

In an important sense, the projects funded within the Management of Personal Welfare Initiative reflected the diversity in concepts, method and theory evident within the wider welfare research field. Within all the individual projects a plurality of methods were utilized but there was a considerable emphasis on interpretive methods and the social construction of meaning. More generally the theoretical and analytical approach to gender was more or less adequate, in the sense of linking together a concern with individual agency, material conditions and gendered structures of power and equality.

In the final section of this chapter we want to briefly review two substantive areas of welfare research. The first, feminist research on women and poverty, provides a background literature which is key to the development of a more gendered approach to welfare research. The second, our own research on violence, offers insights into the key features of such an approach. The second example also differs slightly in its emphasis. Whereas a gendered approach to poverty has concentrated on the material consequences for women of gender inequalities, our research on violence explores unequal gender relations through the subjective accounts of both the women who experience violence and the men who enact it.

A Gendered Approach to Welfare Research: Women and Poverty: An Essential Context for Welfare Research

The literature on women and poverty provides an essential context for research on gender and personal welfare. Women are at a greater risk of experiencing poverty than men (Glendinning & Millar 1992; Oppenheim 1990). The possibility of poverty shapes the experiences of women who never become poor, just as the possibility of rape controls women's lives in the direction of living safely. The actual experience of poverty has a powerful effect on people's well-being, but there is ample evidence that poverty affects men and women differently (see Payne 1991).

Glendinning and Millar (1992) have argued that the bulk of poverty research lacks the gendered approach which is essential to an adequate analysis. The sources of research funding influence the nature of the research that is carried out. Charitable trusts fund a certain amount of research on poverty, including work with an explicit gender interest. However, a major area of the work on poverty is contract research for government departments. This is designed to meet departmental needs, and usually does not include looking at men's and women's experiences separately. An exception is work on the take-up of benefits for the DSS which finds gender differences in reluctance to claim benefits; within households the research also found that women have responsibility for claiming (Corden & Craig 1991).

Work on poverty traditionally uses households or families as the unit of measurement; it is far more difficult to collect data which take members of households as separate units. By and large, women are the managers of poverty. Bradshaw and Holmes (1989) looked at women's and men's experiences separately in two parent families where the man was unemployed; they found that it was the women who identified lack of money as the major problem. Women's stress related to being in debt, but men's did not. Research into social security changes (Barnardo's 1990) has reported that women bear the brunt and absorb the tension of poverty (Colmen & Sadiq 1991).

Classical texts on the conditions of poor people reveal a long history of unequal distribution of resources within families (Orens 1979). In the past women felt it necessary to look after the breadwinner, giving him a greater share of the essentials as well as the small luxuries of a little tobacco or the occasional beer, which often left other members of the family short of basic necessities. There are two issues here: men's control of resources; and women's management of these. In a context where men's wages were barely adequate to feed families and women's wages were still lower, keeping the breadwinner happy and fit for work was a priority.

Research on contemporary families shows that the unequal allocation of resources within families is still with us, and that it is not just a feature of poor families (Morris 1990; Orens 1979; Pahl 1980). Women in apparently well-off households may experience hidden poverty (Vogler 1989). Unequal access to other resources such as space in the house, the use of a car and occupational benefits of various kinds brings into focus the separate experiences of men and women within the family (Brannen & Wilson 1987). Further evidence of the hidden poverty of women in families comes from a small study of lone parents by Hilary Graham (1984). Graham found that women often felt better off as single parents, despite the fact that, as a family unit, they were poorer. Some women are literally better off when they have exchanged dependency on a man for dependency on the state (Everson 1982; Homer et al. 1984).

Economic dependency is a key concept in looking at women's access to an adequate income (see, for example, Dex 1985; Glendinning 1983; Lister 1992; Parker 1990). Behind dependency lies the relationship between time and money. Heather Joshi (1989) has shown the effect on a lifetime's earnings of children as a major demand on women's time. Women are expected to spend time converting money into usable resources; their time is often taken for granted; and poverty involves women putting in time where others would use money. Using public transport, going to jumble sales, cooking from basic ingredients – all these are time-consuming but money-saving activities (Balbo 1987; Land 1990; Lister 1990). In considering women's relationship to poverty, it is important to take account of several aspects of the relationship between men and poverty. First, there is the impact of male-dominated state institutions and employing organizations on women. Second, there is the impact of men's experiences of poverty on women's experiences of poverty. Third, there is the specific structuring of income and resource distribution within households and families (Brannen & Wilson 1987; Burghes 1980; Glendinning & Millar 1992). This last issue relates directly to the importance of the social construction of men as fathers, husbands, and breadwinners, who are involved in the control of money and resources.

The realm of paid work is extremely important for the social construction of men and masculinities. While increases in unemployment may mean that men spend more time at home, this does not necessarily mean a change in men's behaviour. Loss of jobs may mean loss of status, increased frustration, domestic difficulties, and even the reassertion of *specific* or new forms of masculinities through violence (Cobb & Kasl 1977). There is also evidence that men's unemployment has disproportionately negative effects on wives, girlfriends and other women (Beuret & Makings 1986; Hunt 1980; McKee & Bell 1985, 1986; Morris 1985). Changes in the internal workings of households and families, the absence of fathers, and some men's loss of interest in the role of breadwinner (Ehrenreich 1983) do not necessarily undermine the associations between masculinity and the control of money (Hearn 1987).

The poverty literature is largely, but not entirely, about working-class experience. More recently there has been an emphasis upon the differential risks of poverty faced by particular groups of women – especially lone mothers, minority ethnic women, disabled women and above all, older working-class lone women (Glendinning & Millar, 1992). However, the focus of the work on women and poverty (indeed, poverty in general) can be criticized for focusing too much on the poor and not enough on the people and processes which keep them poor. Additionally, from the perspective of this book, much of the research, including feminist scholarship, has failed to adequately recognize and address the possibility of creative human agency among women and men experiencing poverty. That is to say, how people who are poor negotiate the different resources and opportunities available to them, how they understand their poverty in material, cultural and emotional terms, how far their lives and experiences are constructed in terms of the discourses of poverty – "the poor" or "the underclass" (issues which are elaborated in Chapter 8). There are, however, notable exceptions here, with publications from the Child Poverty Action Group (see, for example, Oppenheim, 1990) and Graham (1993) giving voice to women themselves and despite the limitations, the work on women and poverty is a rich source of detail about the different ways in which women encounter poverty. Facing life problems against a backdrop of poverty puts particular limits on options in coping with these. Balancing time devoted to managing poverty, the demands of other problems, economic dependency, unequal access to household resources, insignificant earning power and absorbing the stress of poverty, are all potential determinants of women's responses to life events – and their ability to manage their own and their children's welfare.

The Study of Violence

Feminist practice, research and theory demonstrate the extent and importance of men's violence to known women (for example, Binney et al. 1981; Dobash & Dobash 1979, 1992; Mama 1989a and b). The fact that women are most at risk of violence from men with whom they have a heterosexual relationship is a matter of great personal, political, policy and theoretical urgency. It is also a social phenomenon that challenges much conventional "malestream" sociological wisdom, in particular around the separation and interrelation of agency and structure, of primary and secondary social relationships, and the pervasive idea of the ungendered individual in the family. It was from this perspective that we designed and undertook our two linked projects on violence as part of the Management of Personal Welfare Research Initiative. Project 1 addressed women's experiences of violence from known men; Project 2 addressed men's experience of violence to known women. Both projects also examined the policy and practice of agencies, their management and workers, that deal with the area of men's violence to women. This involved interviews with service providers and managers exploring in particular the follow-up of individual contact with agencies, where the individual gave permission. Sixty women and sixty men have been interviewed in the first instance, and follow-up interviews and/or examination of records have been conducted. The findings from these projects have been extensively written up elsewhere (Hanmer 1993, 1995, 1996; Hearn 1993, 1994, 1995a, 1995b, 1996). In conceptualizing and undertaking this research, issues of power and politics permeated the research process. These apply to the subject matter of the research, i.e. men's violence to known women; the disciplinary location of the research work; and the relation of the research to existing paradigms around social policy.

The conceptualization of this research involves the recognition that gendered power relations are basic to the study of violence. First, violence and abuse were central concerns; they were not incidental or secondary or developed in passing within other work. Second, gender relations were explicit. The recognition of gender relations rather than just gender is important. It expresses the notion of gender as relational or interconnected with other social divisions and phenomena, and as matters of social relations not just actions. Third, violence and abuse are directly connected with gender relations. Violence and abuse cannot be understood outside of gender relations, and, moreover, gender relations, including the very idea of gender, involve references to violence. The research design was developed in order to obtain data on women, men and the agencies with which they have contact, that could be compared on a number of dimensions relating to personal experience and social context. These include the very different experiences of women and men and the responses of others to them, issues such as the impact on women and men of violence in relation to definitions of violence; the impact on women and men of violence in relation to income, housing, etc., the relationship between the gendered intervention of agencies, structuring help seeking and giving, and the social location of women and men.

The research design involved a replication of a United States study of 60 women in a battered women shelter, and their patterns of stress-coping in relation to social support (Mitchell & Hodson 1983). Our study was in part (Project 1) a replication of this US research in a British context and in part an extension by applying the same pre-coded questionnaire with a minimum of necessary adjustment to men (Project 2). Project 1 had two subsamples consisting of 30 Asian women and a general sample of 30 mainly white women. The Asian subsample included women with and without English language skills. The sample of women was also structured longitudinally. As violence against women in their homes produces different needs and responses in women over time, the sample in Project 1 included two subgroups, women living in refuges and women in the community. The sample in Project 2 was not stratified into subgroups although there were variations to be explored between men obtained from different agency sources. Men, too, were at different points in time and places in relation to their violence, for example, in men's programmes and in prison.

The combination of methods used (unstructured and semi-structured interviews, precoded interview and interview/case records from agency staff) meant that a more diverse and in some ways more complete picture of men and men's violence could be obtained. This is particularly important as some men may not tell or may not be able to tell others about their violence. This could be due to minimization, lack of awareness of the effects of their violence, lack of re-call, and so on. In many cases, the information from the pre-coded interviews would give a very limited indication of what had happened. This appears more

122

obviously in the description of the violence, social networks of men concerned, contact with agencies, and so on, and in the interrelationships between various aspects of men's accounts. For example, one man said in the open-ended part of the interview,

> I wasn't violent, but she used to do my head in that much. I picked her up twice and threw her against the wall, and said, "just leave it". That's the only violence I've put towards her. I've never struck a woman, never, and I never will.

> . . . When I held her I did bruise her somewhere on the shoulder, and she tried making out that I'd punched her. But I never did. I never to this day touched a woman.

This kind of detailed construction of violence is not apparent in the pre-coded part of the questionnaire, and indeed it would be very difficult to produce a questionnaire that fully addressed the meaning of such statements. While "picking up", "throwing against the wall", "holding" and "bruising" do not appear to be constructed as violence, "striking", "punching", and "touching" do. Accordingly, the use of qualitative and quantitative methods together, and triangulation of accounts between men and agency staff provide a sounder methodological basis than reliance upon one method alone (Brannen 1992).

The study of women was concerned with a variety of dimensions: how the experience of violence is structured for women and affected by differences in women's personal and social situations and the response of others, particularly around language (English and non-English speakers), culture/class, and race/racism and how the responses of others differ, creating positive and negative outcomes for women. The initial plan for access to women was via one women's aid refuge and one black women's refuge. Both women currently resident and rehoused in the community were to be approached through each agency. In practice acquiring the sample of Asian women required approaching a number of other agencies offering accommodation and contact with women in the community, while the other agency was able to provide all the women needed for the general sample. Women in the community were largely interviewed in their own homes, although some of the Asian women were interviewed in other contexts, such as place of employment.

Acquiring women for interview and the experience of interviewers varied between the two subsamples for a number of reasons. The refuge providing the general sample was larger with more resident and rehoused women, and these women were more trusting about research, the implications of taking part, and in general felt safer than women in the Asian sample. Thus women in the general sample largely felt at ease when talking about their experiences and trusted the researcher to keep their tape-recorded interviews confidential as promised. They viewed talking to another woman as a positive experience, as time for themselves. This view of the interview process could be shared by the Asian women interviewed, but it could also be seen as intrusive and dangerous as women did not know who the interviewer was, why she wanted this information, and what she might do with it. While sharing many aspects there are important differences between the two subsamples of women in the type of violence experienced and from whom, its personal and social meaning for women, and the response of agencies (see Hanmer 1993, 1995, 1996).

However, while the behaviours women understood to be violent, harassing and threatening varied, there were common elements that made sense of women's differing responses. An earlier study (Hanmer & Saunders 1984) explored how women define violence. A common strand running through the events was an inability of the woman to control the initiation of the behaviour and the subsequent interaction. This became the definition of violence, threat and harassment. Women put differing importance on behaviours than do the law, police and courts. It seems that the greater the uncertainty about the outcome, the more terrifying the encounter. Associated criteria used by women to assess whether or not a situation is violent are: whether or not others were present, the time, the place, prior knowledge of individuals or groups of men as violent and whether or not the woman knew her assailant. Specific violent events experienced by women are not sealed off into private versus public domains. Types of violence, threat and sexual harassment include visual only encounters, for example, being chased; or verbal, e.g. threats, insults; or physical, for example, assaults, including sexual. This definition of violence incorporates diverse accounts.

Men's accounts of violence are also diverse, but fundamentally different. Men overwhelmingly refer to physical violence. Although some men do refer to emotional, verbal or psychological violence, even these references are often related to the threat of physical violence or are constructed as if they are physical violence in their reduction to incidents. For men, violence to known women is generally constructed as:

- physical violence that is more than a push – holding; restraint, use of weight/bulk, blocking, throwing (both things and women) are often excluded;
- actual conviction for physical violence;
- physical violence that causes or is likely to cause damage that is visible or considered by the man to be physically lasting;
- physical violence that is not seen as specifically sexual; sexual violence is seen as separate (cf. Kelly 1988).

Thus men's violence to women is for men a combination of physical force, legal effects and personal effects. Men separate violence from sex/sexuality. Visual violence, including pornography, is excluded from how men talk about violence to known women. Men's definitions of violence in relation to control, "loss of self control" and "lack of control of anger" are particularly interesting, when considered alongside violence as social control of women, and the use of controlled force towards women.

As already noted, the Management of Personal Welfare Research Initiative emphasized the importance of considering the extent to which individuals, groups, families and communities differentially cope with lack of welfare. This meant a specific focus on issues such as coping mechanisms, stress and social support. Our specific focus on violence and abuse problematized all of these concepts. Stress has a history in relation to studies on violence, particularly in relation to men. It has been used as an explanation for men's violence and as a basis for therapeutic intervention. The concept of stress is less likely to be used in relation to women as explanation: in this view, women are not stressed, but cause stress. It is also a class-based concept insofar as it often refers to the stress faced by middle-class people (for example, businessmen) whose behaviour and responses to external demands are described as stress-related. This works because stress is said to come from outside, i.e. life events over which individuals have no control, including social constructions such as "she caused him stress". Violence certainly causes feelings of stress as negative, but to say this is to recognize that some men enjoy violence; it can be exhilarating, exciting, thrilling, passionate. Stress has different meanings based on whether one is receiving violence or being violent, but this has not been the focus of research on stress.

Our study also problematized the concept of coping which may mean carrying on as before by tolerating, accommodating, accepting the situation or changing the situation by leaving, separating or modifying personal behaviour in a long term way. Coping with violence means avoiding or dealing with violence, potential violence and the threat of violence. In relation to the concept of coping, the problems facing women who are abused and men who abuse are different. Coping well for some men can mean not giving up violent behaviour while for others giving or trying to give violence up can mean not coping as well, in the short term at least. Coping for women means gaining more control over their lives and involves survival strategies.

Social support also needs to be looked at critically. Support for women can mean help in stopping a man's violence, for example by moving away. For men, removing the woman or themselves can be experienced as a lack of support for their activities. If intervention to assist the woman is not forthcoming, then this is non-supportive for women but can be supportive for men. The way agencies may approach this issue is to redefine the meaning of support (which individual men may not want or may be ambivalent about and therefore do not experience as supportive) and/or to support the man during changes in his life, which may be multiple, such as separation, divorce and/or custody issues. For women a major issue is agencies that interpret their remit as not intervening in violence against women if it is defined by the agency as not being their responsibility. In relation to women and men, agencies may provide social support, affect what happens to individuals, refuse to provide services, provide negative services or punishment. For these reasons social support is not a unified concept, but has particular meanings in particular situations. Most obviously, a woman whose partner or husband has been or is violent is unlikely to receive social support from him. Notions of family support also become problematic when understood in relation to violence and abuse. What is called social support in some conceptual frameworks can be very dangerous in condoning or not acting against violence, or even in being violent or potentially so. This can of course also occur when women leave or attempt to leave families, extended families or communities.

Our research also raised a number of important issues for the study of policy. Policy development in relation to men's violence to women is usefully informed by two interrelated principles: the recognition of the universality of men's violence and potential violence; the recognition of differences between men in terms of violence and potential violence.

One of the most important findings to come from our study of men who have been violent to known women is the diversity of men, men's violence and relation to violence. While all the men were in some way involved with violence to women, and all were involved in relations of power and dominance over women, these unities and commonalities have to be understood alongside differences. There are a number of ways of describing these differences among men in relation to violence to known women. First, there is the question of men's location in relation to agencies, in particular the criminal justice system. Secondly, there are differences in terms of the violence. Thirdly, there are differences in the men's relationship to violence. These three differentiations overlap to some extent. Paradoxically unities of men's power are maintained through difference, and differences are obscured in the maintenance of unities (Collinson & Hearn 1994).

This diversity of men's violence to women has major implications for policy. Responding to this diversity of men's violence and potential violence involves some very difficult policy decisions and choices. In particular there is the continuing need to address what is to be done about men who are a continuing threat to women. On the one hand, all men or all men who have been violent to known women remain a continuing threat to women. This applies even after the end of a relationship, as evidenced when men attack ex-partners. On the other hand, men do appear to vary in the kind of violence they have done or are likely to do. Responding to both the diversity of men's violence and to the continuing threat of men means strengthening, rather than diluting, the legal framework and legal enforcement. Unless men's violence to known women is prosecuted at least as stringently as other violence, patterns in repeated assaults will not be fully apparent. While different kinds of policies are currently being developed for different men, in practice knowing which men will respond to which initiatives is unclear. Arrest and sentencing is conducted largely on the basis of type of offence and now, ability to pay, rather than likely future threat to women. Psychiatric services for certain men may attend to the psychological state of the man rather than to violence. There is a need for making violence to women a much stronger focus of the work of probation officers, social workers, doctors, psychologists and other professionals.

Women come into contact with a range of statutory and voluntary agencies in their search for assistance. The single most intractable problem for women is to find agencies that will help. Agencies may have policies that focus the work elsewhere; ignore or do not think violence against women is relevant, or not very relevant to their work. Agencies may not see it as their function to unreservedly support the woman in what may be defined as a family matter. Even if agencies have a neutral or mildly positive attitude to women living in, or who have left, violent situations, there may be a lack of understanding of how women's needs are structured by their experiences, in particular the needs for safety and security for themselves and their children. Not only are agencies important in the development of actual and potential polices on men's violence to women, but they also have the effect of structuring the social lives of women and men. They structure the meaning of violence by both omission and commission in policies and practices. The historical and cultural construction of violence may specifically shape the personal circumstances and future courses of action for women and men in relation to violence. Agencies are gendered, and present gendered understandings of violence are directly related to policies, and practices. Formal agencies generally operate from men's definitions, which in this context means men's definitions of violence. In the case of state organizations, men's control and definitions, both in general and of violence, are particularly dominant. This applies in both state bureaucracies and the legal system. Alternative definitions, policies and practices have been developed through women's organizations in relation to violence against women. Such contested definitions and meanings of violence, implicit and explicit, apply not only to agencies and their policy development, but also to academia and social theory.

Finally, our research raises many questions for social theory, and specifically how the social is theorized. These include the reformulation of historical and cultural definitions and the meaning of individual action, organizations and social structure; the place of experience in the creation of knowledge; the rethinking of power; and the deconstruction of "the self". One example of such questions concerns the way in which violence is generally not understood in social theorizing as a characteristic form of interpersonal or structural relations. The most usual model of interpersonal or structured relations is of the "rational individual", with a "unified self", who conducts his or her affairs in a liberal and reasonably tolerant way. This model informs much study of families, groups, organizations, and so on. In this situation, violence is portrayed as relatively isolated exceptions to normal life. Violence often does not even figure prominently in debates in social theory on power. In such formulations violence is not understood as integral or embedded or imminent in social relations, and social relations are not understood as characterized by violence, actual or potential. Thus when a man is violent to a woman "he loves" or "is married to" or "has an equal relationship with", the violence is portrayed as aberrant.

These features are parallelled almost exactly in men's account of their own violence and *men's social theory*. Violence occurs as "incidents": it is literally "incidental". It is understood as occurring as exceptions within non-violent ordinary, normal life. This is comparable to national, international, inter-ethnic violence on a mass scale that may occur after many years of living "peacefully" as "good neighbours", as in the former Yugoslavia and previously in Lithuania and elsewhere. Such challenges to social theory, indeed the bringing of violence into the centre of social theory, in turn represent a challenge to sociology.

Something similar can be said about gendered relations and power. It is now legitimate to bring gender into the sub-disciplines and topic areas of sociology, and other social science disciplines. However, this is often predicated on the assumption that social cohesion between women and men is basic and therefore existing theoretical frameworks continue to be used. Work that challenges this cohesion is marginalized, or simply not taken up in a larger way (for example, Delphy & Leonard 1992; MacKinnon 1982; O'Brien 1981). When violence is understood as fundamental to gender and power and is recognized as adhering to all social relationships then a different kind of social theory is required; one that simultaneously deals with differences, conflict and forms of violent contact. Clearly, this perspective has profound implications for the body of welfare research reviewed in Chapters 2, 3 and 4.

Towards a More Adequately Gendered Approach: Concluding Comments

Welfare research is a contested area, and nowhere more so than in terms of the development (or lack of development) of gendered approaches. In shaping the ESRC/Rowntree Foundation Management of Personal Welfare Research Initiative, the Titterton review (1989) pointed the funded projects towards the concepts of stress, social support and coping. However, these concepts are located in particular social theories which themselves only partially, if at all, explain the range of gendered social phenomena explored in the Initiative. Although there is some discussion of *mediation* in the literature on stress and social support (such as in social support mediating the experience of illness), the concepts of stress and social support are largely presented as unmediated experiences. In particular, stress and social support are represented as possible external occurrences that happen to people. But certain experiences can be conceptualized as not just causes or sources or predictors or exacerbators of stress, *but as stress itself.* Violence and abuse are not just stressful, but are stress in itself. This poses a major, and clearly gendered, conceptual problem for any notion of stress as something that exists separate from material experience. Seeing violence and abuse, and, indeed, other social experiences *as stress* questions the idea that it is possible to have unmediated experience at all (Game 1991).

Differences in theory and in the recognition of gender in different areas of study within welfare research manifest themselves in terminology, concepts, theoretical approaches and methodologies. The topics under study may affect the adoption of gendered (or gender-neutral, or gender-absent) theory in a number of ways. First, the nature of the trauma itself may be of relevance. It is necessary to overcome victim-blaming in order to see the trauma; this may not be easy, as interests based on power and privilege may unconsciously take precedence. Secondly, the distribution of effects by the event on women and men may be seen as requiring explanation; this will not be easy if the gendered behaviour or event is naturalized or normalized. Thirdly, historical movements, for example, feminism, and critiques of imperialism and racism, make some events apparently political; alternatively, the event under study may appear to be apolitical. Fourthly, a possible approach may be to ask what is adequate about the theory in which the event is embedded; this may be easier in relation to some methodologies than to others.

One of the crucial underlying issues is whether gender is seen as one of several fundamental social divisions underpinning and influencing social life, or as just one of a string of social factors defining individuals' responses to their situation. Thus, studies that simply refer to women's experiences do not necessarily constitute a fully gendered approach. They may, for example, treat women (or gender) simply as a variable, rather than constitutive of, or located in, some more social-structural formation.

This raises the question of what might constitute a more adequate treatment of gender. In our view, necessary features of an adequately gendered approach to welfare research would include at least eight key features described below.

- Attention to the variety of relevant feminist approaches and literatures; these provide the methodology and theory necessary to develop a gendered account of welfare.
- Recognition of gender differences as both an analytic category and experiential reality.
- Attention to sexualities and sexual dynamics in the research and the research process; the deconstruction of taken-for-granted heterosexuality, particularly in the study of families, communities, agencies and organizations.
- Attention to the social construction of men and masculinities, as well as women and femininities, and including understanding masculinities in terms of relations *between* men, as well as relations *with* women and children.
- Attention to an understanding of gender through its interrelations with other oppressions and other identities, including those of race, class, age and disability (see Hearn 1992; Hearn & Parkin 1993; Williams 1989, 1992b).
- Acceptance of gender conflict as permanent, and as equally as normal as its opposite; examining resistance to this view should lead to the centrality of theorizing on the family and the place of the family in social welfare.
- Understanding that gender and sexuality and their relationship are historically and culturally acquired and defined.
- Understanding that the close monitoring of gender and sexuality by the state (the official biography of individuals) is not accidental, but fulfils the purposes of particular social groupings.

Without the development of a more adequately gendered approach in welfare research, issues of gender, power and inequality will not only fail to be studied, but will also be reproduced. The long established traditions of gender-absence and gender-neutrality in welfare research need to be counteracted by gender-sensitive studies in order to achieve a thoroughly analytical approach. As presented in the literature reviewed by Titterton (1992) and discussed in other chapters the new paradigm fails to provide an adequate framework from this perspective.

Acknowledgements

We are grateful for the information and advice given by the following researchers: Sara Arber, Janet Finch, Hilary Graham, Teresa Hampson, Mike Levi, Ruth Lister, Mavis MacLean, Eileen McLeod, Sarah Matthews, Russell Murray, Helen Roberts, Hilary Rose, Susan Smith, Jane Ussher and Alison Watt. We are also indebted to Errollyn Bruce for contributing to the initial literature review which informed this chapter, to Graeme Baylis and Pam Todd for library work, to Linda Arbuckle and Marina Sarjeant for the preparation of this manuscript, to Jennie Popay for editorial work and to the other researchers in the Management of Personal Welfare Research Initiative for information on their projects and discussion of the issues.

Chapter 7

Service Users' and Providers' Perspectives on Welfare Needs

Jeanette Edwards, Ann Oakley and Jennie Popay

Introduction

Earlier chapters have stressed the importance for research, policy and practice of understanding people's own definitions and experiences of welfare needs and risks and their preferred ways of dealing with these. But they have also highlighted the dearth of research directly addressing these issues. In Chapter 3, for example, Julie Seymour describes how stress and life events are conceptualized across disciplines as context dependent processes – processes which are best defined by the person experiencing them. Yet relatively little of the research reviewed so far allows people to express their own views on the stress and life events they are experiencing in their own words. Similarly, several authors have identified the relationship between providers and users of welfare services as key to our understanding of issues of appropriateness and effectiveness. However, relatively few studies have explored the relationships between the perspectives of these two groups. The research that does exist highlights the importance of this area as a focus for future work.

Recent work, for example, has highlighted the ways in which people's own understandings of their health, and what constitutes risk, may challenge professional definitions of the same issues. This work has considered, for instance, the interface between lay and professional perspectives on environmental hazards and the outcomes of, and priorities for, health care (Bowling et al. 1993; Brown & Mikkelsen 1990; Hill et al. 1996; Popay & Williams 1994; Williams & Popay 1994). These include examples of both qualitative and quantitative research. Within the NHS there have also been some noteworthy attempts to develop a "user's" voice. For example, there is a substantial social science literature on women's experiences of medical maternity care (Cartwright 1979; Garcia 1982; Garcia et al. 1988; Oakley 1980). At a policy level, recent years have seen an increasing emphasis within health and social services on the need to listen and respond to the views of service users (Audit Commission 1992; DoH 1989a and b; DoH 1997). Interestingly, the limited research that has focused on the way in which service providers in health and social services construct their clients' problems suggests that users may have very different perspectives on health and welfare needs across a wide range of services (Barnes & Wistow 1992; Becker & MacPherson 1988; Dhooge & Popay 1988; Edwards 1995, 1998; Edwards & Popay 1994). There is also some research on the diverging views of service providers and users on what constitutes effective coping behaviour (Murgatroyd & Woolfe 1982). But there is an urgent need for more systematic research focusing on the meanings lay people attach to the wider canvas of welfare needs and the experience of care, and how this perspective relates to that of the people providing services.

This chapter is a modest attempt to contribute to this endeavour. In it we explore the discourses around welfare needs, risks and the experience of services in a sample of mothers and another of midwives and health visitors. These service providers and users were involved in two separate but linked research projects – combining data from the two studies allows for an exploration of areas of divergence and convergence between lay and professional discourses.

Both projects were part of the ESRC/Rowntree Management of Personal Welfare Research Initiative which began in 1991. They were concerned in various ways to explore the notion of social support. In particular, they focused on providers' and service users' views on the support needs of pregnant women and mothers of young children and the role of statutory and voluntary health and social services as providers of social support. Social support is clearly something that formal health and welfare services are theoretically able to provide, but there is little information on how this role is articulated and experienced by either users or providers. Both studies sought to privilege the experience and voices of people living and working mainly in areas experiencing considerable socioeconomic disadvantage (Thompson 1963). The studies utilized a number of different research methods. The analysis presented here therefore drives forward the increasing move within social science to combine insights and knowledge from both quantitative and qualitative research – also a prominent theme of earlier chapters in this book.

The Studies

The *provider study* collected data from a sample of health and welfare workers concerned with the provision of services to pregnant women and mothers of children under five in two localities within Greater Manchester. The *user study* was based on samples of mothers in Derby, Stoke-on-Trent, Reading and Tunbridge Wells. Although the service providers worked in different geographical areas from the service users, from the analysis presented here there is much that binds the different localities together. (For most of the analysis the user data were restricted to the two Midlands samples – Derby and Stoke-on-Trent – which could be argued to be geographically and socially closer to the population drawn on for the provider study.) Professional discourses, and the social and economic point in history at which the studies took place, are shared across geographical space. Likewise, although specific places have particular geographies and socio-economic histories, it can be argued that women's needs for certain types of services will be shared, to some extent at least, by pregnant women and mothers of young children wherever they live in Britain.

The provider study was based in two areas of Greater Manchester – named for present purposes as Banton and Tarrow. Although adjacent geographically, these are served by different health and local authorities. Each area has a population of approximately 12,000 people who are primarily white, working-class. A subsequent extension of the study explored similar issues among service providers working in an ethnically more diverse neighbourbood of one of the districts. Both Banton and Tarrow are described by service providers as having high levels of material and social deprivation, characterized by poor quality housing, low or fixed incomes, high levels of unemployment and poor quality and quantity of local services.

Fieldwork for the provider study was conducted between October 1991 and December 1992. It included semi-structured interviews with 84 providers, including all the social workers and social work assistants, health visitors and community midwives working in the two areas, plus community support and family centre workers in Banton and paid and unpaid workers in two voluntary sector organizations in Tarrow. Hospital health professionals and general practitioners were not included in the provider study. The survey was followed by a period of ethnographic fieldwork with each of the occupational groups. Four to six weeks were spent with each of the organizations with the fieldworker accompanying workers during their working day and making fieldnotes based on observations of, and conversations with, workers. For the purposes of this chapter we concentrate on the views of community midwives and health visitors in both Banton and Tarrow.

The user study involved secondary analysis of data from the Social Support and Pregnancy Outcome Study – (SSPO) – a randomized controlled trial of a social support intervention in pregnancy carried out in four centres in 1986–8. The intervention was given by research midwives, who provided a 24 hour a day contact telephone number, and carried out home visits.[1] During these visits they discussed anything of concern to the mothers and used a semi-structured interview schedule to collect social and experiential data. The SSPO study has been reported on at length elsewhere (see Appendix II in Oakley 1992a; Oakley et al. 1990; Oakley et al. 1996 for a full list of sources). The women who took part in the original study were all pregnant and had previously given birth to a low birthweight (<2,500 gm) baby; 77 per cent of them were working class on the basis of their own or partner's occupation and 19 per cent had unemployed partners. Five hundred and nine women were enrolled in the study. Women randomized to the social support intervention were offered three home interviews during pregnancy: 238, 235 and 224 women were interviewed at the three different times. The women were sent two postal questionnaires, one six weeks and one a year after delivery (response rates to these were 96 per cent and

78 per cent). The data drawn on in this paper are taken from the postal question-naires and from the home interviews. Several particular case studies are drawn on heavily as being illustrative of themes general to the sample as a whole.

Service Providers' and Users' Perspectives on Need

Women's Accounts of their Needs

Women's perceptions of their needs in relation to health and welfare services and other sources of support were central to many of the conversations that took place between them and the research midwives providing the social support intervention in the user study. The women were also asked direct questions in the home interviews conducted by the research midwives as part of the intervention, and the postal questionnaires. Four prominent and related themes emerge from these data: the importance of support in women's lives; the interlinking of different kinds of need; the relationship between information and the social relations of care; and women's concerns regarding the status of their knowledge about their own health and that of their children. Some of the main types of help women felt they needed during pregnancy and the first year of a child's life are listed in Table 7.1. The two lists strikingly illustrate the importance of support in women's conceptualization of their needs and the intermeshing of different kinds of needs. A third of the women in the user study said that they needed more continuity of care during the current pregnancy, 28 per cent wanted more sympathetic medical care and 20 per cent felt that mothers of small babies would be helped if they received more support and help from health professionals.

The intermeshing of different types of need evident in the lists shown in Table 7.1 is also apparent in the accounts of women's experiences given during interviews with the research midwives. These accounts point strongly to the relationship between women's needs for acceptable and appropriate information and the social relations of care.

Table 7.1: *Women's expressed needs*

During pregnancy	During children's early years
More continuity of care	More support/help from health professionals
More sympathetic medical care	Family support
Financial help	Cheap easier-to-obtain small clothes
More medical care	Support group
Help with housing	Help with feeding
More help from friends	More help/advice from Special Care Baby Unit
More family help	Better information
Domestic help	

Because of a previous history of pregnancy loss, Jackie Hinson went into hospital in her next pregnancy to have a stitch put in her cervix. In the following interview extract, it is clear that she needed more information. But she links this with the need to be treated with sensitivity and with respect for her own knowledge about her body:

> When I came from theatre I was bleeding, and they never told me I would be bleeding . . . I never had anything like that explained . . . and that worried me . . . and then all of a sudden they say "Well you've got to stay in bed now, Mrs Hinson," and I said, "Why?" And they said, "Well you've got to unless you want to pick your baby up off the floor!" . . . I mean it was really cruel . . . They didn't explain a thing to me, I mean I didn't even know what a stitch was . . . They said what it was but they never even told me if I could have intercourse when I came out of hospital or anything, they just said whatever you do, don't wear tight clothes and don't do any strenuous work . . . which I knew, you know yourself if you've got problems, you don't go round being crazy!

What women reported was that often their experiential knowledge of their own health and that of their children was devalued or ignored by health professionals. Jackie Hinson illuminates this process when she talks about her experiences of returning home with her previous premature baby, who was later diagnosed as having epilepsy:

> . . . and then my health visitor came to see me, she was new, the health visitor, and I always blamed her for Tom having gastroenteritis. I didn't like her, she was snotty, I didn't like her at all, and she never weighed him every time she came to see him, she had got the proper prem scales, but sometimes he would be asleep and she would just have a look at him . . . [but] she was supposed to weigh him every time she came. I tried ringing her the day Tom took poorly, she hadn't turned up twice, two times in four days she didn't turn up, and I kept ringing the clinic and I couldn't get hold of her, I was getting worried about Tom, he was starting to vomit, and I was ringing all day and then when the doctor rushed him into Children's and found out how much weight he'd lost, I thought well, she could have stopped that . . . you would think she would make more of an effort, being new at the job, and with such a small baby . . . And then, like his fits, I tried talking to her about his fits and she says, "oh it's just a paddy, just ignore him, it'll go away". Then when the doctors told me how serious it was, I thought how could she say that?

In many of their accounts women were asking for explanations. Without this they were worried, angry and/or unclear as to what they could and could not do. They indicated that such explanations needed to be provided with sensitivity – technical competence and accurate information alone were not enough. Another woman, Maya Lester, was similarly distressed at the lack of sensitivity she perceived to have been exhibited by some of the professionals providing her antenatal care, and her comments parallelled the findings of many other studies of the antenatal services:

> I felt like a number, I just felt I was a statistic, you know, that I wasn't a human being at all. The only person who ever treated me as though they really cared and was concerned was a Sister on the ward and some of the – mainly the student nurses, I found they had much more compassion than the older ones . . .

Maya also points to the absence of eye contact and appropriate body language in the meeting with the consultant:

> Mr Mortimor was efficient and I thought that was the sign of a good doctor, but when I went to see him last week I suddenly realized that he was only concerned about filling the records in, well that's how I felt anyway, he didn't even – he was writing his notes, he didn't even look up at me, it was as though he was talking to nothing, you know . . .

It was common for the women in this study to experience practices in professional–client encounters which they saw as breaking the normal etiquette of social relations. But these accounts do more than highlight the importance of etiquette. They also emphasize the importance to women of the need to develop social relationships over time with service providers if the people who provide their care are to be truly supportive – as Maya Lester commented.

> You never saw your midwife, I didn't see the midwife until I came out of hospital with the low-birthweight baby . . . you know, she didn't come to introduce herself or anything . . . I think you have got to have somebody you can really talk to when you're pregnant, like now, it's the same mid-wife I had with Rosie and we get on really well, I mean we can talk, like, like next door neighbours' talk, do you know what I mean?

Accounts such as Jackie Hinson's also illustrate how the experience of formal health care can have unintended negative consequences for women's health and wellbeing if it is not provided in a positive and holistic way. At one point in her interview, for example, Jackie Hinson made a connection between what she experienced as unsupportive treatment from health workers and her subsequent confidence and capacity as a mother:

> . . . when I had Tom I had to leave him in the SCBU . . . and the midwife – I had three different midwives when I came home because it was a bank holiday – stopped me going to see him. She said I was doing too much, because I had one at home . . . and my husband wasn't helping me at all with . . . anything – he never helped me. Apparently with your discharge after you've had the baby you can tell if you're overdoing it . . . the colour of the discharge . . . and they said I was overdoing it, so they banned me from going to see him. And then I did get depression, it lasted for about a year, I can honestly say I don't think I really loved him till he was about a

year old, and it just clicked one day. I never used to sit and cuddle him, and I think that because I had nobody to talk to and I don't think I was going to see him regularly enough . . . I used to ring the hospital three and four times a day but it just wasn't the same as actually being there and seeing him. I couldn't go in the bus, it was two hours with Lucy as well . . .

Several issues are raised by this narrative. One is the tendency for health professionals to work with narrow definitions of health, focusing on specific physical indicators rather than a more broadly based notion of wellbeing. Jackie Hinson was told not to visit her baby in hospital for the sake of her own physical health, but for her, the resulting separation had a long term impact on her emotional wellbeing and feelings about motherhood. She also points to the significance of material constraints in her reference to the 2 hour bus journey – an issue returned to below.

Another crucial issue she raises is the relationship between the health services and family/community support. The absence of support from her husband exacerbated an already difficult situation. Deficiencies in the type and level of support provided by family and friends were a common theme in women's accounts. As Bonny Howarth observed:

I don't think my friends understand me. I think they think I can carry on now I'm pregnant in the same way as before, I don't think they understand that I've got a fulltime job now even, because most of them don't work . . . they haven't gone back to work, but I'm the only one probably, in our group of friends that did. And they are involved in school activities and all the rest of it, which I am, but now I feel I have got to put the block on that a bit because I don't feel like going to PTAs, and I don't feel like doing things in the evenings, like I used to . . . I could do with less hassle. That if I don't feel like doing things there is no pressure to do it. I mean I feel that there is pressure sometimes to carry on . . . making demands and thinking that I can carry on . . .

Similarly, Maya Lester, when asked who had been the most helpful person in her low birthweight pregnancy, answered:

There was nobody. The next door neighbour used to look after me, she was ever so nice, she was an elderly woman, she had got three children, grown up, and she used to nip to the shops for me and look after Rosie for an hour while I went to sleep in the afternoon . . . I wasn't in contact with any of my family, I was just a loner, my husband was at work all the time or at football, we never saw him, and my mother-in-law I never got on with . . .

As this quote makes clear, women's needs for support and help are felt and articulated within the broader context of both constraints and resources: the stress and difficulty of their lives, on the one hand, and the social relations and resources available to cope with these, on the other. When informal support is lacking, women's need for socially supportive care from service providers may increase. However, the issues of dependency engendered by an enhanced need for professional care may have important effects on women's emotional well-being, which in turn can impact on their own and their children's health. In discussing her own experiences with health professionals Bonny Howarth elaborates on the significance of power relations:

> I think it's partly because you don't understand . . . you ask questions and then wish you hadn't. Because you're not really understood properly . . . what can you do? You tell them you are not happy about certain things and they don't really respond . . . there isn't any time . . . I mean what should happen is that they should give you time to talk about what you're not happy with . . . There's no sort of, well, how do you feel about what I've said? . . . I mean you have the examination, they give you the information, and then it's cut off. So you do feel powerless and helpless and you become passive . . . They almost force you to behave in a passive way. You keep on being assertive when you don't really understand and the energy is just wasted.

Providers' Accounts of Mothers' Needs: Support, Self-Esteem and Social-relations

The service providers articulated the needs of women living in poor material circumstances in somewhat different ways from the women themselves. In response to questions about problems facing families with whom they worked, for example, providers often commented on the social isolation of many of the women they served. This was particularly the case in Banton, where providers pointed out that many young families had been rehoused there out of the inner city and away from family and friends. One health visitor who had worked in Banton for over ten years described how, throughout the 1970s, there had been an influx of households from demolished or renovated inner city estates and a more recent migration in young families:

> So, if you were a young girl who lived on the . . . [estate] or somewhere like that and you were pregnant and you wanted a place of your own and you put your name on the waiting list, you would be offered [Banton] . . . so you come here and you've just got loads of young families, the schools are bulging at the seams, playgroups have got waiting lists as long as your arm, and we haven't facilities . . . It's inner city in a green field site. We've got fields all around us but it's still got inner city problems.

Social isolation was linked to poverty and material circumstances. Community midwives and health visitors painted a picture of complex and interrelated problems:

I think it's a combination of unemployment, no money, living in poverty-stricken houses, poor repairs to them, overcrowding, lack of support within their own relationships and, a lot of [the] time, just single parents with no community support, no friends, no one to baby sit – things like that. Not many nursery places. Not many groups around. Not a lot of community spirit.

The providers in this study acknowledged a need for the women they work with to be treated with respect and recognized that they do not always get it. However, the health visitors and midwives tended to see GPs, hospital doctors and, to a lesser extent, social workers, as providers who did not respect the views of local women. Significantly, health visitors considered the practical advice they themselves offered about, for example, getting children to sleep or weaning, potty training, or dealing with temper tantrums, to be supportive. Such support, they thought, helped women feel less isolated and helpless, to deal with their children more confidently, and enabled them realize that certain problems are common and not unique to them. They also emphasized the importance of praise, of reassuring mothers that they are doing the right thing.

In the words of a community midwife:

I think some of the parents I'm in contact with do a better job than me. They're wonderful. They're marvellous. I don't know how they do it, and I tell them. You know, they're never told when they're doing a good job . . . I tell them when they're doing a good job, even when they're not – to be honest. You know. I always say, when . . . "what beautiful children you've got, they're so lovely", and they'll go, "ooh, they're bleedin' swines!"

These ideas about confidence and self-esteem were, however, linked to notions about the proper management of children which were themselves part of professional/expert discourse. The effects of poverty may be acknowledged (for example, "poverty is stressful"), but a particular outcome – the mother's parenting – is placed to the fore ("stress causes poor parenting skills"). This is well illustrated by a health visitor, talking about setting up a clinic for sleep problems in toddlers, who noted, "It's surprising how many women are manipulated by their children. They need to be reassured and told they can effect change; they can do something about it.". A different health visitor on a separate occasion pointed out that it was: "surprising the number of parents who cannot say no to their children and who feel they have not the right to say no" – a situation which again, in her view, was related to low self-esteem amongst mothers.

Aspects of the social relations of care were also evident in providers' accounts, and there was an awareness of the power differentials involved. Some community health service professionals, for example, were particularly aware of the dangers of being expected to perform a monitoring role. Describing a "first-parenting" scheme to one of the health visiting teams under study, a health visitor interested in implementing such a scheme emphasized that, "Visits are not for checking up on the care of the baby or for the health visitor to tell them what to do. But they are intended to help towards a greater understanding of their child's development and for parents to enjoy their children.".

Monitoring was thought by health visitors and community midwives to be the role of social services, and some ambivalence was expressed about their role in child protection. While they argued that families "in need" require support from community health professionals, monitoring was thought to add pressure to families already under stress. A midwife extended this view from families to the community, agreeing with the views articulated by women in the user study that judging a mother's actions and practices is often far from supportive:

> You see I find, it's awful, it's a general thing but constantly Banton within its little network – they are all being judged. We're judging everything, social services are judging it, their peer groups are judging them, their mothers are judging them. I mean, this happens in all our lives but they're constantly being judged and I think they know they are.

The Significance of Material Resources

Women's Perspectives: Felt Needs and the Material Reality of Everyday Life

The impoverished circumstances in which many of the women in the user study were living meant that they frequently mentioned inadequate material resources as producing concrete, immediate needs. As Maya Lester commented:

> . . . I have got to get out of this house . . . I hate it . . . Rosie is continuously having colds, there's damp everywhere . . . there's a lot of repairs that want doing to it and I just can't get any of them done . . . the only heating we've got is in here, well I'm a kitchen person and I can't think of anything better than sitting in the kitchen, that's what I like to do but it's just too cold, you can't do it . . . I do not want to spend another winter here, especially not with a new baby. I mean I thought my mum's house was bad enough but compared to this you know it was like comparing the Antarctic to Barbados . . .

Maya also pointed to the stress of poverty itself: the ways in which inadequate material resourcing of women's reponsibilities as mothers can lead to a great burden of debt management:

> I mean, they expect you to live on the money you get off Social, it's impossible . . . they expect you to live on £10 a fortnight, you just can't, they pay your rent, fair enough, but you've got gas, electric . . . Rosie was premature, therefore when they allowed me money I had to buy prema-ture clothes; they won't allow me any money to replace her clothes, I mean now she's fifteen and half months old she's just going into second size clothes and they're not cheap items . . . it's like if she needs another pair of shoes, we've got to find the £6 to get them . . . I mean Rosie was

desperate for clothes . . . my mum, she's on widows' benefit, she gets less money than us and how the hell she lives on it I don't know, she ordered Rosie two pairs of dungarees and two t-shirts out of a catalogue, £7 each, and that was just for the dungarees, But that's the way we have to do it because I can't afford to go out and pay that money all at once. The only way I can do it is a bit of money a week, that way means you're always in debt one way or another . . .

Maya's narrative also illustrates how worries about money can trigger tensions and arguments in domestic relationships.

. . . to have a decent style of living you need some money. I mean we're alright at the moment because we've got a little bit, but in a day or two there'll be nothing left, and then of course you start worrying because you don't know where to turn and that causes us to argue . . . because neither of us knows where to turn and then we both start blaming each other.

In this example domestic disputes focused on attributing blame for a situation over which neither partner felt they had much control. In many instances, women's accounts also illustrated how having responsibility for young children meant they often found themselves in a position of trying to negotiate with male partners a fair share of household resources for themselves and their children. Marilyn Palmer tells the research midwife about her own domestic division of labour:

We had a big argument, me and Derek, a few weeks back because last time you were here I didn't get the shopping money . . . I used to pay for the shopping when I was at work so since I stopped working Derek has to pay it. He used to come with me and pay the shopping bill and keep whatever change there was. Well, we had a big argument because I find I can't manage to buy – I mean he doesn't buy Amy's clothes, all Amy's clothes I buy, he doesn't buy anything for her, all the toys I buy, he doesn't think to buy things for her, it's as if she is just my child. And we had a big argument about it a few weeks ago. I said I can't manage on just the child benefit once a month, and I want £5 a week extra plus the shopping money in my hand so that what's left I can keep, and he said that was impossible . . . I mean I don't like losing me temper with him, but it's the only way. You know, he threw at me that he pays the mortgage, the bills, this and this, what more do you want from me? But as I said to him it's his child as well and there's another child on the way . . .

The impact of material conditions and stress on maternal wellbeing and confidence, so prominent in the narrative accounts of these women, is borne out by quantitative analysis of the user study data. The chances of women in the study experiencing low emotional wellbeing are increased when income is low, and low emotional wellbeing is almost four times higher among women reporting recent life events. Low emotional wellbeing is also associated with poor physical health both for women (Oakley & Rajan 1990) and children (Oakley et al. 1993).

Providers' Perspective: Poverty, Individual Behaviour and Personal Biographies

The material circumstances in which many service users lived in the provider study meant that health visitors and community midwives could not help but be cognizant of the effects such circumstances would have on the lives of mothers and young children. When asked what they thought were "the two or three main problems that affect the welfare of children under five" in their geographical area, most of them made some reference to difficulties associated with material disadvantage, in particular to lack of money, poor housing and unemployment. However, references to poor material circumstances were often linked to individual behaviour and the quality of social relationships, which in turn were associated with individual biographies (see Edwards & Popay 1994).

Providers made it clear that they were aware of the increasing financial difficulties facing many of the families with whom they worked. Some, however, pointed to the management of money as being more significant than poverty *per se*. "Ignorance, I think. Ignorance. And I think lack of education, because I wouldn't say money. Lots of them seem to have babies coming and could very much use it wisely but, money [is] spent on cigarettes and things that have no value whatsoever to, you know, the babies."

The term *deprivation* was used by service providers to cover both material and relational aspects of social life. One worker explained it thus:

Deprivation, in all its senses, poor housing, poor finance, it's poor socialization . . . Poor role models . . . And a breaking down of family. I don't know, maybe I'm a bit sort of romantic in thinking that maybe family relationships were better in the past, maybe they weren't, but I tend to think perhaps they were. Now people don't have the same support.

The notion of a *cycle of deprivation* features in some service providers' comments. In the case of families whose children are deemed to be at risk of neglect or abuse, parental difficulty is attributed to parents' difficulties in childhood with their own role models. In the words of another health visitor:

. . . it is a very deprived area. I think there's children that their actual basic physical needs aren't being met, and I think some of that's to do with poverty and some of it's also to do with this cycle of deprivation, whereby the mothers haven't had a role model that . . . that it just goes on perpetuating.

This quotation shows how in some professionals' accounts poverty can be separated from, and contrasted with, problems located in personal biographies and abilities. This separation appears to shape professional practice. Perhaps the most vivid example of this is afforded by the prominence community health service providers give to the discourse of parenting skills in their construction of the needs of the women with whom they work (Edwards 1995).

Both community midwives and health visitors identified a lack of parenting skills as a problem for some of their clients. Although the language was that of parenting, most of the specific comments and examples related to mothers; fathers were notably absent both from the conceptualization of parenting and from the routine work of most of the providers in the study.[2] The concept of parenting skills was clearly tied in with ideas about a cycle of deprivation, though there were a number of different variants on the theme. In some instances, for example, the idea of parenting skills was related to the age of mothers, in others to the lack of good role models in the older generation. Providers also related skills of parenting to stress: ". . . parenting skills, for a variety of reasons, really, maybe their own upbringing, I mean, a bit of a generalized statement, but . . . or a deprived upbringing. Also the stress of maybe being a single parent.".

Despite these perspectives, in their day-to-day practice service providers responded to people in complex multifaceted ways. This reflects to some extent a movement between a largely professional discourse shared between the respondents and the researcher and an everyday life discourse service providers shared with parents. For example, after visiting the home of a baby who had been placed on the at risk register because of a previous injury, the researcher asked a health visitor directly about the poor parenting she had mentioned as a feature of the family. Her reply was that, "It's because they [the mother and father] don't know any better; they've both been in care themselves and are in a circle trying to fight to get out of it.". However, during the visit, the health visitor reassured the parents that, given the present care of the child, social services would not initiate care proceedings. She explained the reason for, and described the content of, a series of meetings planned between social service staff and the parents, looked at recent photographs of the baby, admired her new clothes, and listened to the couple's plans for their future.

Though all the community service providers in this study gave prominence to the need for better parenting skills among some of the poor women with whom they worked, there were professionals who criticized the dominant tendency among service providers to individualize problems. One health visitor, for example, criticized what she perceived as an emphasis on cleanliness and health, and pointed out that people "do not necessarily have the money to buy cleaning equipment and some do not have refrigerators . . . still, in this day, there are families who do not have facilities".

Another described her concerns that lack of money had an adverse effect on women's health preconceptionally and during pregnancy, which in turn affects the health of children. Similarly, whereas health visitors and community midwives were more likely than other workers to raise the issue of diet alongside material poverty, poor diet was itself often contextualized by poverty. This is illustrated by the replies of a health visitor and a community midwife to a question from the researcher on what they thought were the main problems facing families with whom they worked. "I think poor housing, low income and poor diet." "Obviously I think unemployment. Diet – I think for all we are doing, a lot do not get a very good diet." Some of these service providers understood that living in poor material circumstances can mean that local service users have very different priorities from those held by middle class health professionals. As one health visitor noted, "Is health a priority? It may be that housing or the dole will take priority. They put up with a lot of illnesses. [We] need services they will use – play bus for immunizations, transport, health clinics in community centres."

Similarly, providers could also be sensitive to the constraints poverty imposes on people's ability to access services even when they share the professionals' priorities, in terms of prevention and child health screening, for example. This is evident in the experiences of a health visitor in Tarrow visiting the home of a woman whose baby had failed a routine eight-month hearing test. The woman had two other children, was herself deaf, and had missed two appointments for a follow-up specialized hearing test for the baby. The health visitor commented that, as far as the clinicians were concerned, further appointments were simply not made after two DNAs.[3] She noted that she herself may therefore be the only person concerned about missed health appointments. The purpose of the home visit was to finalize plans to take the woman and her children to the Centre the next morning. On the way to the woman's home, the health visitor noted that the Centre which carried out this specific hearing test, a 15-minute car journey from the woman's house in Tarrow, required two buses and one hour's travel on public transport. She argued that help with transport should be the role of the health visitor if that is what women need. Clearly, such help would also have been of considerable benefit to Jackie Hinson when she faced a two-hour bus journey to visit her baby in the Special Care Baby Unit. However, this health visitor expressed a fear, shared with other providers in this study, that increasingly such tasks were seen by managers to be wasteful – not the role of qualified health professionals and difficult to justify in terms of time and outcomes.

The Role of Services

Women's Perceptions: Accessibility on Providers' Terms

When women in both studies talked about their needs for information, support and care sensitive to their material circumstances, they were often simultaneously commenting on both health and welfare services. Because the focus of the original user study was on pregnancy care, the majority of comments about met and unmet needs in relation to service provision concerned hospital doctors, GPs and midwives. Table 7.2 shows how women rated health professionals in helpfulness compared to other social support resources. Almost a quarter (22 per cent) of mothers mentioned either midwives or other health professionals as the most helpful people; however, 40 per cent also said that health professionals were the least helpful people. During the child's first year the importance of formal service providers declines considerably – during this time the most important people are partners and mothers, followed by other relatives and friends/neighbours. Importantly, only 2 per cent of women mentioned the GP and only 2 per cent health visitors as most helpful during the child's first year. Although a

Table 7.2: Women's views on the most and least helpful person

Source of support	Most helpful during pregnancy (per cent)	Least helpful during pregnancy (per cent)	Most helpful in child's first year (per cent)
Partner	43	4	56
Mother	13	0	18
Midwife	10	14	–
Other relative	9	4	11
Friend/neighbour	–	–	9
Other health professional	7	7	–
Health visitor	–	–	2
Social worker	–	–	<1
Mixed	4	2	–
GP	3	7	2
Hospital doctor	2	12	–
No one	9	50	–
Other	–	<1	<1
Total answering	100	100	100
	n=244	n=240	n=355

similarly low proportion of women found social workers the most helpful, this has to be seen in the context of the fact that social workers are likely to be in contact only with a very small proportion of women, even in this disadvantaged sample. Asked whether they would have welcomed more help from GPs or health visitors, 5 per cent of women said yes to more help from GPs and 10 per cent to more help from health visitors (not shown in table). Qualitative data from the interviews provide important insights into the processes that may deter women from using formal services as a source of support during stressful periods of their lives. For example, Bonny Howarth described the support available from the services as "accessibility but on their terms":

> I don't think you can talk to anybody about little worries. I mean they say to you, the midwife says to you, "here's my home phone number, ring any time", but I didn't feel able to do that. Perhaps that was my problem, perhaps it was hers in the way that she said, "ring me any time". I don't know . . . And there were occasions when I came back from the hospital when I used to think, Oh they've said this to me, I would like to ask her about that, but I wouldn't, I would wait until she came . . . there was accessibility, but on their terms really . . .

When asked if she thought medical care could be improved, Bonny highlights again the importance these women attach to etiquette in social relations and to time in which to develop relationships with people providing services:

> I think they should be more available to you, to talk to about everything, and more approachable than they actually are . . . It's the sensitivity. I mean, I think perhaps the midwife who is going to be looking after me could have perhaps come here and introduced herself . . . and told me a bit about her role, something just to make it a bit more friendly . . . I mean all you ever see of them is at a surgery behind a desk with all the technical bits on the desk that you don't understand, so it's very off putting . . .

The "little worries" which Bonny refers to above and which many women may have, can be essential data for both mothers and service providers in providing appropriate care for young children. They can, for example, act as early warnings of more serious problems, as Jackie Hinson's account of her son's gastric problems and fits, described earlier, so powerfully illustrates. Jackie Hinson's understanding of the health visitor's responsibilities towards her and her son seemed to differ from the health visitor's own interpretation; Jackie wanted her baby weighed regularly, even if this meant waking him up. She expected the health visitor to come when the health visitor said she would. She would have liked to have been able to contact her when needed. Most fundamentally, though, she wanted the health visitor to listen to *her* definition of the kind of care needed by her son.

In the women's accounts provided so far in this chapter the value they attach to health service providers listening to them has been a recurrent theme. Other data from the user study demonstrate how widespread this concern is. The women were asked about what they particularly valued about the social support intervention provided during the research. The relative ranking of different elements varied between the four centres. In relation to the role of the research midwife, around three-quarters of the women at the two centres in the Midlands – from which the data presented here were taken – reported that the most important thing was that "she listened" (overall the figure was 80 per cent). The fact that they felt they could talk to the research midwife was second in importance at one of these centres and the advice she gave at the other. The other things they valued included the information provided by the research midwife, continuity of care and her "helpfulness". The majority of women – over 90 per cent at both centres – said that being able to phone the research midwife at any time was a good idea. Responding to an open-ended question about their experiences with the research, feeling increased confidence and/or reassurance about one's role as a mother were identified as important by 22 per cent and 14 per cent of the women, and 55 per cent and 39 per cent of the women expressed a preference for having someone like the research midwife visiting them after the birth.

The research midwife's professional training was last in the order of priorities in the two centres: only 36 per cent and 27 per cent of women considered this important. Indeed, some of the study women expressed the view that the help of the research midwives was particularly appreciated because in the context of the study they were *not* professionals – that is, they were unconnected with the professionalized health and welfare services. The research midwives also perceived themselves to be closer to the women than other service providers. As one midwife noted, "They're anti everybody, but not me . . . She said she told me about this Visa card [debt] because I'm not *from* anywhere. That's not the first time I've been told that. It's like husbands having jobs that social security don't know about, and all this sort of thing.".

Providers' Perspectives: Listening, Befriending and Resource Constraint

The recognition by providers that some of the women with whom they worked had few people to turn to for help and advice was reflected in the way they themselves defined their role. Listening featured prominently in the response of midwives and health visitors to questions about the meaning of support. A community midwife in Banton linked this theme to the open access phone line her service provided:

> After we've transferred women over, we give them the GP unit phone number . . . they can ring most 24 hours a day, seven days a week, bank holidays, everything, if they feel they ever need to talk to a midwife about the welfare of the baby or themselves . . . two o'clock in the morning whatever, crying baby service, a stress service, colic, what you like, we're there.

Support was seen as a means of offering opportunities for people, usually women, to talk. This perspective was vividly illustrated in the following comment from a health visitor:

> I think one of the ways, one of the main ways, of offering support is listening. Particularly if – if women, who are at home, because if they are on their own then that's probably an unknown element in their life, that people actually sit down and listen to what they've got to say. You know, somebody listening is quite important.

However, while health visitors and community midwives understood that one of the needs of women they work with is to have somebody who will listen to them, they also understood that this was not always enough. As one health visitor said in response to a question about what offering support meant to her:

> Listening to their problems. It may not actually be help-orientated but would have a bearing on the family's general well-being . . . Like a mum with two children who is living in an upstairs flat, you know, there isn't really anything practical I can do to help the situation. I can at least listen to her and understand the situation.

It is evident from some of the definitions of supportive work presented by service providers that such work serves purposes above and beyond that of providing support at a particular point in time. In some instances, the work was seen as enabling providers to establish a relationship with the mother. During a clinic organized by health visitors and attended by a community medical officer, one health visitor described the routine weighing of babies and recording of weights on centile charts as "bread and butter stuff" which had the advantage of "building up a relationship" and allowing providers to get to know mothers and babies. Similarly, the following quote from a midwife talking about the benefit of a maternity drop-in centre illustrates how this involved making contact with "hard to reach" groups:

> Hope perhaps they're going to be reaching some of these girls [sic] that won't go to the GP's surgery . . . and I think they find that doing antenatal clinics up there – not clinics as such – but they're doing antenatal exam-inations, women that they wouldn't normally get their hands on . . . girls that wouldn't normally attend.

In some instances, providing support for women was undertaken in part at least as a way of ensuring the welfare of children. In other cases, supportive work was ideally directed at the baby, which would indirectly help the mother. As one health visitor described it, "Support . . . it's with the baby really. To see that the baby's settled. Because in my mind, if you've a baby that's eating and sleeping and content, you've then got a good basis for the mum to relax and get on with life and enjoy that child and get on with it."

Health visitors pointed to the importance of visiting antenatally; as one health visitor put it "to build up a rapport", while another pointed out that such a visit would provide the opportunity to get to know and understand "the situation" of the mother.

While they stressed the relevance and importance of providing support for the women they worked with, service providers recognized a variety of constraints on the support it was possible for them to offer. Lack of time due to excess case-loads and/or under-staffing was one of the most important perceived constraints. One community midwife described what her work had been like before two colleagues were away, one sick and the other on maternity leave:

> You could kind of think about your caseload and go back to your practices and go through little things, or there'd be a little bit more communication that you might just have time to do within the primary health care team. Or there were a little more ante-natal and off-spec visiting – well that's what I used to do. Those have gone. They have gone. That's what I have personally found very frustrating, because personally speaking, I used to do a lot of socializing with my women – well they're not my women – the women I'm in contact with. And I feel very frustrated that I personally am not able to do that. And I know personally much less women in this last, sort of, nine months than I've ever known before and I'm frankly a bit worried. Because if a problem's mentioned I don't know if I may help . . . I've prided myself on befriending and I'm not befriending [now].

Health visitors spoke of the frustration of only reaching what they called "minimum standards". They recognized that building up a relationship with those to whom they provide a service was a crucial element in their work, not only to help socially isolated mothers, but also to be effective in their role as "promoters of health". Yet time to do this, they felt, was at a premium.

Time to listen and befriend was also felt to be threatened by the increasing emphasis on the measurement of work and concrete outcomes. This has to be placed in the context of ongoing changes in community health services, and in particular the transition to fundholding general practices. Health visitors argued that the supportive listening aspects of their interaction with their clients could not be measured in ways that would impress their importance on management. As the majority of providers in the study were women, and the interactions they talked about were for the most part with other women as mothers, this point refers in part to the undervalued and largely unrecognized work that women do in maintaining and smoothing social relationships in all spheres of social life (see e.g. Miller 1976).

Another constraint recognized by providers was the expense of a health visiting and community midwifery service. One management response to this, to provide less qualified assistants, was seen by some as "de-skilling" health care professionals. It has created concern among community health and social service providers about the effects on continuity of care and a holistic approach to health and welfare.

This issue was aired in a Banton health visitors' team meeting. The topic of "skill-mix" or "grade-mix" was raised in the context of moves to use less qualified assistants to perform tasks that do not require the qualifications of a health visitor. The debate focused on the potential of such arrangements to free health visitors from routine undemanding tasks, and on the contrasting possibility that health visiting would "lose its holistic approach" if skill-mix were introduced along these lines.

A final and important limit which health visitors and community midwives placed on their work had to do with what they felt they were able to achieve. They were aware that in some cases they were simply unable to provide the kinds of resources which would make the quality of life for some women and their children better. As this health visitor put it:

I think when you are supporting someone you need time and you need provision of services and the resources. I think one problem we have is, it's just that we come across so many different sorts of problems, there's not always an answer really to what people are asking you to give them help with . . . I also think support is also being able to do something about the situation as well and I don't think we always can do . . . Sometimes I'd like to be able to, with a new mum, spend a day with her. I'd like to do some ironing for her . . . physical support . . . maybe helping to keep their hospital appointments. It's those sort of things that really are not within the time that we've got and some people would like a friend and I'm not sure, you need time to build up a relationship with friendships and, I don't know we're necessarily here for that – or somebody to say, "you sit down I'll make you a cup of tea", that's all you need sometimes.

Discussion

Both similarities and differences are evident in the perspectives of the health service users and providers drawn on in this chapter. The user study highlights a number of dimensions to women's accounts of their main needs in relation to the services: sympathetic, supportive care and practical help which recognizes the close links between emotional wellbeing and physical health, and the importance for children's wellbeing of services which facilitate the ability of their mothers to cope, often in seriously constrained material circumstances. To some extent, providers' perceptions of the problems facing families with whom they work – financial difficulties, lack of social and supportive relationships and lack of information sensitive to women's circumstances and respectful of their experience and knowledge – clearly mirror users' concerns, and can be mapped onto the elements of support which providers understand to be part of their role. However, there are also points at which perceptions differ markedly, reflecting perhaps the way in which service providers draw on and feed into different discourses – both lay and professional. Whereas what providers feel they can do for their clients reflects in part their understanding of client needs – and resonates to some extent with clients' views – their views on their roles are also crucially delimited by features of their own occupational identities and tasks.

This opens up the potential for direct conflict between service providers' identification with the views of health and welfare needs expressed by mothers on the one hand, and their views and perceptions resulting from their professional training, background and working conditions, on the other. In this context, the concept of a frame of reference is useful as a way of understanding the convergence and divergence in the two sets of attitudes and experiences. The notion of frames of reference as applied to the analysis of users' and providers' standpoints was originally developed in work on maternity services (Graham & Oakley 1981). It embraces both the notion of a system of values and attitudes, and that of a reference group – those individuals and/or groups who are a significant influence on these attitudes and values. The general frames of reference within which the health service users and providers perceive health and welfare needs are overlapping, but also differentiated. Conflict between service users and providers can be understood as resulting in part from this differentiation. One consequence is that any perception of commonality has to struggle with a framework of difference.

A major difference in the two frames of reference is the personalization of the problems of poverty evident in some of the providers' accounts – the tendency to locate the source of the problem within individual biography rather than, or more often in addition to, material circumstances. Women in the user study did not relate their problems primarily to their own personalities and backgrounds. Instead, they located the difficulties they faced in their immediate and pressing circumstances and wanted services which addressed these sensitively and specifically. The community midwives and health visitors in the provider study oscillated between emphasizing the constraints of poverty and stressing the relevance of their clients' personal histories and abilities. This is not to suggest that personal biographies are irrelevant to women's current circumstances, but rather to high-light the disjuncture between professional constructs of personal biographies and women's accounts of the nature and genesis of the problems they experience.

Another point of divergence between users and providers concerns support needs. For users of services, support was not an extra desirable element to the services they wanted, but an integral part of these. But among providers there was an ambivalence as to whether listening and befriending should be con-sidered as the legitimate role of health and welfare professionals. Many service-providers did argue that they would like to provide more of the practical type of help valued by women in the user study (for example, transport) or more of the emotional kind of support highlighted by users (such as befriending). They also recognized the need to give information clearly, sensitively and with respect. But supportive care tended to be seen as an optional extra. Some service providers also argued that the constraints of time and caseloads prevented them from pro-viding the kind of support they would envisage as ideal.

Providers' perspectives on women's needs are partly shaped by their need to feel that they have a role. Bull and Shaw (1992) have argued that some causal accounts in social work refer to factors which cannot be changed, and which in a sense justify the inability of providers to change things and hence act to play down their responsibility. Faced with cumulative and apparently overwhelming obstacles to achieving positive health and welfare outcomes, providers need to feel that there are some things they can do. This may be increasingly the case as professional discourses are superseded by, or amalgamated with, managerial dis-courses which privilege notions of efficiency and effectiveness, as opposed to caring and listening. Thus, an emphasis in situations of extreme material depriva-tion on the importance of parenting skills allows service providers an area – that of parent education – in which they feel able to exercise their own profes-sional skills with some hope of positive effect. Where providers use the concept of "a cycle of deprivation", their concern is also with how such a cycle can be broken, and with some of the ways in which the services they provide may help to break a chain of cause and effect; educating parents (mothers) is seen as one major way of breaking the chain.

However, there are differences linked to gender between the findings reported here and Graham & Oakley's (1981) earlier study exploring the differing percep-tions of maternity service users and medical professionals. The earlier study com-pared a female client group with a predominantly male provider group – in the present study most of the service providers were female. Evident in many of the current providers' comments is an identification as women with the needs of the mothers they serve. However, this common identity competes with the social distance flowing from the constraints of their professional training, struc-tural position and working conditions. This results in a greater shared area within the two frames of reference than was found for the earlier study. But there are also significant areas of disagreement, which are illustrated by data from the women and the midwives providing the social support intervention in the user study. For example, in 49 per cent of cases where the midwives considered at their first home visit that the women were experiencing high levels of stress, the women rated their own levels of stress as low. Conversely, in 70 per cent of cases where the midwives rated stress levels as low, the women said they were high. The midwives and the study women also disagreed about the extent of the midwives' helpfulness. In 36 per cent of instances when the women felt the midwives had been helpful, the midwives disagreed, and in 49 per cent of cases where the women thought the midwives had been unhelpful, the midwives reported that they felt they had been helpful. The tendency for the research midwives to consider themselves helpful when the women thought they were not is stronger than their tendency to perceive themselves as unhelpful in situations where the women thought them helpful. Such dissonances are likely to reflect differences in underlying perceptions of user needs and the relevance of professional help to these.

The data drawn on in this chapter suggest that the need to address differences in user and provider perspectives on health and welfare needs and ways of responding to these is particularly acute in relation to family social support resources. Users and providers both stressed the limits of family and kin support as a resource available to stressed and disadvantaged mothers. They also acknowledged the tendency for this form of help, where it does exist, to introduce burdens of its own.[4] The support of formal service providers is most needed where there are few other social support resources, combined with high levels of stress (Madge 1993; Tudor-Hart 1971). Yet it is also in these circumstances that professional care may be most counter-productive, because it is based on definitions of need that are not derived directly from the standpoints of service-users (Scott-Samuel 1980).

There are many implications from this research for the planning and provision of health and welfare services. Some can be read from the providers' accounts of what they perceive to be current threats to their ability to provide client-sensitive care. In a situation in which services are being reorganized and subject to tightened accounting, appraisal and managerial structures, health service providers will not find it easy to become more sensitive to users' perceptions of their needs. Given constraints of time, workload and pressure to measure their outcomes in quantitative terms, supportive work, such as listening, may increasingly be thought of as an unaffordable luxury – despite the fact that research points strongly to its health-enhancing role (Berkman 1984; Broadhead et al. 1983; Rogers & Elliot 1997; Dean 1986; Gottlieb 1981; Popay et al. 1998).

To the extent that strategic planning in the health and welfare field succeeds in incorporating a users' perspective, as current policy emphasizes (DoH 1997; NHS Executive 1992) the divergence between the frames of reference of users and providers explored in this chapter will become more visible and salient. The resolution of these tensions will inevitably involve a challenge to the power and status of health and welfare professionals and to their assumed right to define the nature of legitimate knowledge. This knowledge challenge points to some of the critical implications of the analysis presented here for the future of welfare research – the primary focus of this book.

These implications for welfare research are evident at the level of both theory and method. Any future framework for welfare research must address the need for a more sophisticated theorizing of people's own perceptions of their welfare needs and their experience of provision. This requires greater attention to the unique contribution of qualitative research and to more effective methods of combining the insights to be gained from combining different research methods. In this context, however, it will be important to move beyond the over simplistic dichotomy, evident in much previous research, and continued in this chapter, between the notions of service user and provider. Just as people are multiply positioned in relation to structural axes of class, gender and race, for example, so they may occupy, at one and the same time, particular positions such as service user and provider. It is important that welfare research in the future should give more attention to the relationship between lay and professional understandings of welfare needs and the experience of care – linking the experience of welfare subjects to both professional discourses and institutional arrangements. However, it must do this in a way which encompasses and explores the complexity of people's relationships with welfare risks and provision. In the next and final chapter we consider in more detail the concepts which offer some potential to move us forward in the search for a more adequate framework for welfare research in the future and begin to fill in the contours for such a framework.

Acknowledgements

We would like to thank the people who participated in the study as both users and providers of health and social services; Cathy Pratt, for her initial work on the provider study, Tony Crowle for technical help with the database for the user study, Patty Peach for transcribing interview material, and Jackie Lee, Sandra Stone and Christine Saunders for help with preparation of the manuscript.

Notes

1 The research used midwives to provide the social support intervention and to collect data, but they did not provide clinical midwifery care – these are termed research midwives in the text.
2 This is also a general trend in policy discourse around child-care and divorce (Edwards 1998; Piper 1995; Smart 1991; Williams 1998).
3 DNA = Did not attend (clinic appointments).
4 The changing social relations of informal care are discussed in detail in Janet Finch's book (1989).

Part 5
The Future

Chapter 8

Balancing Polarities: Developing a New Framework for Welfare Research

Fiona Williams and Jennie Popay

Introduction

Reviewing Harold Wilson's account of the 1964–70 labour government, E. P. Thomson commented that "the book starts badly but it gets a great deal worse as it goes on" (Thomson 1971: 50). Damning criticism indeed. Hopefully external judgements on this book will not be quite so withering! Our own view, as editors, is that the book started by highlighting some of the tensions and dichotomies that currently characterize theory and practice in welfare research and this complexity has deepened as the book has unfolded. In this final chapter we therefore highlight those elements of the complex terrain traversed in earlier chapters that we consider to be most salient to our pursuit of a new, less dichotomized framework for welfare research. In the second section we consider some existing concepts which might help to mediate between these tensions and dichotomies. In the course of doing this, we also point to dimensions of theoretical adequacy which could inform a new paradigm for welfare research. In the third and last section Fiona Williams begins to sketch out a framework for this new paradigm.

Polarities, Dichotomies and Balance

This book has unashamedly focused on theory and method within welfare research rather than the sphere of policy and practice. It has also been concerned with only part of the wider canvas of research activity that is rightly labelled "welfare". However, the tensions and dichotomies within research, which we have been exploring, lie at the heart of current debates about the future direction

156

of welfare policy and professional practice. They also have a powerful shaping influence on much, if not all, welfare research – whatever its specific focus.

The outer perimeter of our concerns is set by what, for our purposes, might be termed a primary dichotomy, discussed in the first chapter, between research paradigms in which structural and policy analyses are foregrounded and paradigms which seek to prioritize the individual welfare subjects. The problematic interface between these paradigms has provided much of the material for this book. Earlier chapters have highlighted how research in the latter mode has tended to neglect the influence of the social and economic context within which individuals act and failed to explore the significance of the meanings that welfare subjects attach to their experiences and action. In so doing such research has individualized and privatized issues which are essentially both public and private – social and individual. Equally problematic, and again with important exceptions discussed in earlier chapters, research in the structuralist mode has tended to neglect individual experience and agency, leaving the recipients of public welfare as, at best, shadowy, largely forgotten inhabitants of the research terrain. In the past this dichotomy has been represented in analyses of poverty in terms of an individualist (blame the victim) approach versus a structuralist (blame the system) approach, supported by the political right and left respectively. We are not arguing for a middle way, since both of these approaches have limitations. Rather, we are arguing that the dichotomy requires transcendence.

The salience of this dichotomy for the future of welfare policy, and the importance of finding analytical and practical ways of bridging and going beyond the divide, was vividly illustrated in the UK in the winter of 1997. In mid-November, the new Labour Government, engaged in a wide ranging review of the benefit system, confirmed its intention to abolish two special benefits for lone parents, which were worth between £5 and £10 per week for women caring alone for dependent children. At the same time press reports pointed to an emerging power struggle between Harriet Harman, the Secretary of State for Social Security in the new government and Frank Field, the specially appointed Minister for Welfare Reform. But, as a Guardian article at that time noted:

> . . . the battle is about more than just personalities. Brown [the Chancellor and reportedly an ally of Harman] and Harman see welfare as essentially a problem caused by a malfunctioning economic and social system . . . Mr Field has a different starting point . . . he believes that people's behaviour must change too. Drawing deep on Labour's Christian socialist and mutual-society roots . . . he favours self-help and would like the government to foster mutual organisations which would assist people to make their own welfare provision (White 1997: 12).

This representation of Harman's and Field's positions may be overstated in this media construction, for Field himself has written of the "two opposed assumptions about human nature and behaviour which have crippled thinking on British social policy for so long – on the right that the poor deserve to be so because they are lazy, on the left that they are immune from the faults of laziness"

(Field 1997: 61). We are not, in this book, particularly concerned with the moral description of poor people's behaviour (as lazy). Rather, we are concerned with the fact that they and other welfare subjects are acknowledged as having the capacity to act and also with understanding the dynamic processes that link their behaviour to the system of which they are a part. If research is to have any impact on the direction of welfare policy in the future, then there is an imperative on the research community to move beyond such paradigmatic dichotomies.

To do this, a number of fine grained and closely inter-related tensions in the focus of, and methods employed within, different welfare research paradigms must be addressed. These have been threaded through the preceding chapters, but they merit brief restatement, here. At the epistemological and methodological levels, earlier chapters have rehearsed the many ways in which different research paradigms have embedded within them assumptions about the nature of legimate knowledge and, flowing from this, about the appropriate ways in which such knowledge or understanding is to be captured. As the chapters by Fiona Williams, Julie Seymour, Jalna Hanmer and Jeff Hearn, and Chas Critchner and colleagues illustrate, for example, a great deal of the research identified by Michael Titterton as the basis for a new paradigm for welfare research – that concerned with coping, life events and social support – is located within social psychology, quantitative sociology and epidemiology. Much of this work is premised on the notion that the purpose of research is to reveal factual, scientific realities. It gives primacy to individual character traits and behaviours and makes use of quantitative methods which require and dictate the use of standardized social categories, such as social class and ethnicity, and measurable outcomes. The same epistemology underpins much research located within the structural paradigm, which also has a strong tradition of quantitative methods, with inevitable consequences for the ways in which aspects of social and individual life are conceptualized and represented empirically.

A smaller research enterprise, which would sit uncomfortably within either of the two broad research paradigms discussed above, has also been identified in previous chapters. Here, a model of research as the "surfacing of facts" and scientific realities is replaced by a model which is concerned to glean meanings from multiple discursive realities. Qualitative research methods predominate, although sometimes alongside or within quantitative research designs. Recounted experiences and interpreted processes are the focus of attention rather than relationships between predetermined analytical categories and measured outcomes.

As Geraldine Macdonald's chapter illustrates, these epistemological and methodological dichotomies are not just the stuff of academic debate. They are also apparent in the world of professional practice – in this case in debates about how social work is to be evaluated. Most straightforwardly, the debate about the relative merits of experimental versus experiential evaluation of social interventions is about the salience of different research questions – the former concerned with the efficacy and effectiveness of interventions and the latter with appropriateness and acceptability and the relationship between them. However, more fundamentally and more problematically, the debate about different approaches to the evaluation of social interventions, also reflects the contested nature of legitimate knowledge about the social world and points to the difficulties of resolving what are often competing and perhaps irresolvable knowledge claims. As Chapter 7 highlighted, for example, lay and professional experts can have different perceptions on welfare issues, particularly on the nature of needs and how they are to be met and including questions about the appropriateness and effectiveness of interventions. These can, and often do conflict.

Conceptual and theoretical tensions within welfare research to some extent mirror epistemological and methodological dichotomies and to some extent move beyond them. Whereas, for example, the importance of the notion of individual difference is now widely recognized within the welfare field, it is variously conceptualized in the research literature as reflecting and/or shaped by pathology, personal experiential diversity, more or less random social variation or as a manifestation of structural inequality. Similarly, the relationships between notions of identity, subjectivity, agency and socio-economic circumstance re- main largely untheorized. Additionally, though time, in its many manifestations – social, biographical and historical – is now accepted as pivotal to our under- standing of welfare processes, discourses and outcomes, (and operationalized in notions such as life course and cohort effects) the significance of different dimensions of time, and more importantly the relationship between them and individual experience, remains relatively unexplored.

Despite the prominence in much of the discussion so far of dichotomies and tensions in welfare research, earlier chapters have also identified research which has attempted to move beyond these divisions. Some research, for example, has endeavoured to grant the recipients of welfare both voice and agency and to locate and understand people's accounts of their experiences and behaviours within the context of wider structures of power and control. In the next section of this chapter we consider some of this research in more detail as we seek to answer the question, in analytical terms, of how it is possible to recognize individual variability and creative human agency without losing sight of the dynamics of social structure. The final part of the chapter attempts to incorpor- ate some of these mediating concepts and dimensions of theoretical adequacy into a more encompassing framework for welfare research. This framework seeks to acknowledge the dynamic between the creative human agent and the social structure as well as an understanding of individuals as complexly and multiply positioned, engaging with, and acting upon, the diverse policy landscapes that they inhabit. We are, in essence, seeking a balance between existing, and to some extent divergent research paradigms, accepting that there will be differing views as to where the equilibrium might be struck.

Developing Mediating Concepts

This section starts by looking at research studies which have attempted to link agency to structure through the use of normative guidelines and resources. It then moves on to focus on other concepts which link the welfare subject to their capacity to act – these are autonomy, control, identity and experience, exploring examples of forms of identity creating the basis for both individual and collective agency. The final two concepts discussed – welfare discourses and risks – represent aspects of the structural context which mediate the relationship between the individual welfare subject and that social structure.

Normative Guidelines and Resources

The first two exemplar studies highlight the importance of subjective experience, meanings and interpretations in understanding the link between individual action and structure. Both attempt to apply aspects of Anthony Giddens' structuration theory (Giddens 1979) to an explanation of people's management of their or others' personal welfare. In so doing, we suggest that these studies develop key concepts which mediate the relationship between agency and structure.

In Chapter 2 it was suggested that the debate as to whether socialization patterns or role-constraint explained better the differences in stress and coping between women and men, reflected the paucity of conceptual tools to understand the relationship between individual experience/action and social structure. In other words, the positioning of these as either/or explanations cannot help us bridge the relationship between the individual and the structural. There is little sense from much of the research on women and stress of women consciously acting out their lives or finding some way through the maze of constraints and contradictions. In much of this research, women, and working-class women in particular, appear as either conditioned or constrained, and probably depressed, their happiness and stability contingent upon a particular constellation of apparently unrelated variables. It is possible to find alternative representations of women's lives in the feminist work on informal care (Finch 1989; Graham 1983a; Ungerson 1987), although this deals with the role of *supporting* rather than *social support* itself. It is thus not generally seen to be part of the literature on stress/support/coping. Here we focus in particular on Janet Finch's work on normative guidelines and timetables.

Janet Finch's *Family Obligations and Social Change* (Finch 1989), develops an understanding of why and how support operates within family and kin. From the point of view of women, this is crucial because women are so central to processes of care and support. However, caring and supporting work carries both costs and benefits in women's lives, and is also interwoven with patterns of social and economic inequalities. Finch takes as her starting point the formulation by Giddens (1979) of the significance of the relationship between social structure on the one hand and the possibilities for independent human action on the other:

> Giddens' view of social structure is that it provides *resources* which people can use when they are interacting with others in daily life. In that process social structure is also reinforced and reconstituted. We need to see human

beings *acting purposefully* in their use of such resources, although the outcome of their actions may have consequences which they did not intend.
In the context of theory, Giddens rejects the view that patterns of action
are straightforwardly imposed on people, including those theories which
tell us that people internalise the norms of society and then produce
appropriate action . . . *People need to, and are able to, explain what they have
done and why they have done it* and this in itself forms part of the action. We
all do this by drawing upon our understanding of how the social world
works, by using the *same shared knowledge* of our society which we use to
formulate our conduct (Finch 1989: 87–8, our emphases).

In terms of social structure, Finch looks at factors including changes in law,
social policy, economy and demography. When she turns to the human agent she
focuses more on the "sense of obligation" than simply on patterns of support
and exchange (Finch 1989: Ch. 5). In order to hook individual action (or an
explanation for it) into social life she explores questions of norms and obligations, again following Giddens' ideas. He argues that norms and obligations are
central to human interaction. When people act purposefully and strategically in
relation to others this represents an attempt to "mobilise obligations". In this way
people help to reproduce and mould sets of norms and obligations, but in their
own specific ways, specific to who and where they are.

Finch develops the concept of *normative guidelines* to help explain the factors
shaping how people act. In her study, they are the principles through which
people give and receive care and support within the family. These guidelines do
not contain answers for people, in fact they may create conflicts: how far, for
example, do the emotional needs of children conflict with the emotional demands from parents or partners? Finch also introduces the concept of both
biological change, or life course, and social change into her analysis through the
concept of *normative timetables*: "the proper thing to do" changes over both an
individual's lifetime as well as being shaped by social and cultural changes. At
each point of her analysis, Finch explains how these guidelines and timetables
are cut across with gender differences: for example, women have a clearer sense
of obligation towards family or there may be differences in the way men and
women deal with the moral obligations they face. Importantly, Finch's concept
of normative guidelines is drawn from people's own explanations, understandings
and behaviours, rather than, as in some of the studies we looked at earlier in this
book, being a reduction of aspects of behaviour into discrete variables subject to
social divisions.

Although Finch's analysis develops the dynamics of the relationship between
agency and structure and is informed by a notion of social divisions – in this case
gender divisions – her work points to two areas in need of further development.
First, her use of gender remains largely undifferentiated in terms of intercutting
divisions of say, class, race and ethnicity. This is a point she acknowledges, and
her work provides a good basis from which this could be developed. Secondly, it
could be further argued that she overgeneralizes a particular heterosexual norm

of family life and it thereby becomes difficult to acknowledge those who may, at times, stand outside the normative guidelines. Not everyone lives in families; households based on same-sex relationships may find it easier to negotiate support outside the boundaries of kinship (i.e. from friends) rather than within. Nevertheless, the emphasis, in Finch's work, and especially in later work with Mason (Finch and Mason 1993), upon the way in which people negotiate their commitments, responsibilities, sources and beneficiaries of support, provides a basis for investigating these processes in same-sex relationships and households where responsibilities and roles are less fixed by institutional and legal structures. This point is made by Weeks, Donovan and Heaphy in a literature review for an empirical study into the structure and meanings of non-heterosexual relationships in Britain, which they have termed "families of choice" (Weeks et al. 1996).

The second exemplar study we draw on to explore the potential of mediating concepts is the research undertaken by Jonathan Gabe and Nicki Thorogood (1986) on the use of tranquillizers as a resource. The aim of this study was to illuminate the meaning of tranquillizer use for working-class white and Caribbean women. This aim is set within a critique of existing work on stress, support, coping and well-being and their relation to tranquillizer use. The authors make four main points in this critique. First, that existing work categorizes individuals in terms of particular attributes (e.g. class, gender, depressed, not depressed, coping, not coping) which are then aggregated in order to find co-relationships. This means that individuals are not treated as members of a particular social group whose relations are structured unequally (class, gender, race, etc). Secondly, that analytic variables are treated as related but discrete, rather than as internally-related and mutually constitutive. Thirdly, they argue that existing work assumes that relationships exist between variables rather than questioning *how* this relationship has arisen. Fourthly, they note that subjective meanings about social phenomena tend to be treated as psychological attributes to be drawn from uniform and formal questionnaires. This, they suggest, underestimates the differential and problematic nature of experiences and meaning, as well as their relationship to a specific historical context.

The authors also identify the need for a "middle range" concept to bridge agency and structure. Here they use the concept of *resource* but distinguish their use from its use in the stress/support/coping literature (e.g. Pearlin & Schooler 1978) where it is seen as a psychological attribute. Instead they, like Finch, refer to Giddens' structuration theory and his use of resources (and rules) as the structural properties which individuals draw on in everyday life. Here, resources are both the medium and outcome of social life, and represent the interdependence of structure and agency. They are both enabling and constraining. At the same time, resources are not inert objects but part of social relations. Resources are the vehicles of power – through which power is exercised and structures of domination and subordination reproduced. In addition, Gabe and Thorogood use the concept of "management" rather than coping.

Their data are drawn from two separate but related studies in Hackney: one on the use of benzodiazepines by middle-aged white women; the other on the relationships between health beliefs, health behaviour and the structural position of Caribbean women. They focus on data from 45 white working-class women and 15 working-class Caribbean-born women all aged between 40 and 60. Of these, 32 of the white women were users of benzodiazepines and 13 non-users; nine of the Caribbean women users and six non-users. The studies involved indepth interviews up to four hours long using a life-history approach. The interviewers picked up on issues of health, illness and tranquillizer use and the women were asked to relate these to social circumstances. They were also asked about work, housing and family circumstances and, in the case of the Caribbean women, about their experiences of racism. Content analysis then drew out thematic categories.

The resources which the women themselves said they used in the management of their daily lives, besides benzodiazepines, were housing, social support, leisure activities, cigarettes, alcohol and religion. The authors present their particular findings about these resources, first, in terms of their general structural dimensions, for example general race/class/gender differences in employment and unemployment, and secondly, in terms of the extent to which these resources were experienced as enabling and/or constraining. So, for example, long-term users of benzodiazepines were ambivalent about the drugs, viewing them as both enabling but also addictive; short-term or non-users were more likely to mention the dangers.

Overall they found that the white women used benzodiazepines more often and for longer than the Caribbean women and were more likely to see them as enabling. Their explanation for these differences was multi-faceted. One aspect of the explanation was the nature of the other resources available. For historical, cultural and economic reasons Caribbean women were more likely to have a full-time job and view this very positively; they were also more likely to have children living at home and find their daughters particularly supportive. In addition, Caribbean women were much more likely to go to Church and to regard that as a very supportive resource. The authors suggest that the lower rate of health service use among Caribbean women may be because the health service is experienced as racist or subordinating; this may also reduce the women's use of drugs as a resource. The white women had far less access to the resources which Caribbean women used and/or those resources were not seen as sufficiently enabling to do without tranquillizers. For example, the white women were less likely to have a full-time job, and more likely to have ambivalent feelings about their paid work. Also long-term use was associated with being divorced and not having children at home. All in all, the access to, experience of and meaning of paid work, children, partners and leisure were very influential in producing differential patterns of tranquillizer use.

Assessing Theoretical Adequacy

The two studies discussed can also be used to identify some of the criteria which could be used to assess theoretical adequacy in welfare research in the future.

Our discussion of Finch's work highlighted a number of such criteria. First, it suggests that the dynamic between agency and structure needs to acknowledge the welfare subjects as creative agents, acting upon, negotiating and developing their own strategies of welfare management. They are not passive receivers of policy enactment, instead they help reconstitute the outcomes of formal and informal policy provision. Secondly, the discussion has pointed to the need to understand both the welfare subject and the welfare provider as inhabiting multiple social categories (to which they may attach greater or lesser significance and imbue with different meanings at different times). Thirdly, whereas the most significant of these categories may be, arguably, those attached to dominant patterns of social power and inequality – around gender, class, race/ethnicity, age, disability and sexuality – other important dimensions within research on welfare are the social relations of power and the forms of identity attached to the provision and receipt of welfare, whether formal or informal.

Gabe and Thorogood's research paradigm meets a number of these dimensions of theoretical adequacy. They make a conscious shift away from using social categories as methodological variables, as in previous work in the area. In their study these categories are seen as, first, signifying subjective experience which is imbued with particular meanings, and, second, as being social positions shaped by the social relations of class, gender, race and ethnicity. These positions in turn find their structural expression through the institutions of the labour market, family, health services, culture and religion. In addition, they see these social positions not as discrete but as mutually interlocked and constitutive of subjective experience.

In terms of methods, in order to explore the meanings which women attach to their actions, they use a life history approach which enables them to allow, to a certain extent, for the meanings of support (or resources) and the relative salience of these, to emerge from the research subject herself, rather than as a response to a set of meanings presented by the interviewer. In addition, the institutions of family, health service, labour market and religion are investigated in terms of the meanings attached to them by the subjects. In this way, we begin to see more clearly how the negotiation and management of risks are influenced by differently available opportunities and resources. Thus, Caribbean women may attach particular negative meanings to a resource such as the health services in a way that white women do not, but their cultural experience and ethnic identity may better place them to view their work, family support and possible religious involvement more positively than some white women. This approach enables us to recognize both groups of women as creative agents operating within a system of risks and opportunities, complexly structured by economic, social and cultural dynamics, in which their welfare outcomes are negotiated through their access to, and management of, available resources.

Capacity for Action: Autonomy and Control

The two studies considered so far have stressed the importance of subjective experience, meanings and interpretation, in linking action and structure. Two further mediating concepts can be identified in research work on stress, social support and coping and these are the significance of personal control, or a degree of autonomy, in buffering the effects of stress. For example, Chapter 2 identified the work of Rosenfeld (1989), Ross and Mirowsky (1989) and Turner and Noh (1983) as examples of attempts to understand the relationship of social power (or lack of it) to emotional well-being (or lack or it).

The study by Turner and Noh (1983) attempts to link elements of subjective experience *and* agency in its conceptualization of personal control as being made up of three elements: first, the personal element derived from one's life history (we might call this subjective experience); second, one's conceptualization of the external world (whether one is influenced more by discourses of realism or fatalism); and third, one's attitude towards one's own competence or efficacy (we might call this one's perception of one's capacity for agency). In the study these are also related to an objective measure of social class. This work is particularly interesting because it begins to distinguish between different aspects of the individual experience and how these might connect to the social world. How-ever, the notion of social class, to which these elements are related, is objective and fixed, and there is no exploration of the dynamics between this variable and the elements of the personal. (For example, the research does not consider whether a subjective understanding of social class or gender influences the way one views one's capacity for agency). The studies by Ross and Mirowsky and Rosenfeld also highlight the significance for women of a sense of control over the demands of work and/or family, along with a sense of support, as important forms of protection against depression.

The constellation of meanings attributed to notions of autonomy and control and the related concept of independence is important in the study of coping strategies. To begin with, new right political discourses of welfare in Britain since the late 1970s were influential in counterpoising a culture of dependency generated by an over indulgent welfare state against a culture of the self-sufficient independent welfare consumer exercising their autonomy through choice in the welfare market-place. In these terms, being dependent upon state support is seen as morally bad, whereas independence and autonomy are approved of. Yet, at the same time, within this scheme, women's economic dependency on men was encouraged. Whether people themselves experience and understand dependency and autonomy in such dichotomized terms is something we need to know more about. The studies mentioned above by Ross and Mirowsky and Rosenfeld suggest that autonomy, control and independence are not fixed positions or conditions, but operate in tandem with the provision and receipt of formal and informal support. Thus, women appear to cope with stress by being able to juggle the configuration of these conditions in the way that suits them best at different times.

Furthermore, sociological literature on social change suggests that personal control and autonomy may have acquired greater significance in recent times, not because of the new right discourse of consumerism or acquisitive individu-alism, but because of the way in which more overriding social and economic changes have produced a culture of individualization. Ulrich Beck, for example, describes the process in this way:

> In the welfare states of the West, reflexive modernisation dissolves the traditional parameters of industrial society: class culture and consciousness, gender and family roles. It dissolves these forms of the conscience collective on which depend and to which refer the social and political organisations and institutions in industrial society. These de-traditionalisations happen in a *social surge of individualisation*. At the same time the *relations* of inequality remain stable. How is this possible? Against the background of a comparatively high material standard of living and advanced social security systems, the people have been removed from class commitments and have to refer to themselves in planning their individual labour market biographies (Beck 1992: 87).

In other words, the falling away of some of the fixed positions of class, family and kinship means that people are required increasingly to make their own way through social life without these firmer "identity hooks", although they do so in a situation of continuing forms of economic inequality and under the conditions of "collective fate" for example, mass unemployment and deskilling (ibid.: 88). Beck suggests that since forms of inequality no longer follow clear class lines, there is a tendency towards an individualization of social inequalities: "As a consequence, problems of the system are lessened politically and transformed into personal failure" (ibid.: 89). The process is also mirrored within the family, where women's aspirations for autonomy carry with them the risk of greater economic inequality (for women, divorce and single parenthood are as great an economic risk as unemployment or deskilling): "Families become the scene of continuous juggling of diverging multiple ambitions among occupational necessities, educational constraints, parental duties and the monotony of housework" (ibid.: 89). This process of individualization, Beck argues, puts individuals under greater pressure to attempt to direct or give meaning to their lives through their own actions or understanding. In this way it is possible to suggest that control and the goal of individual autonomy may have acquired greater significance in contemporary western societies.

In his book, *Modernity and Self-Identity* (1991), Giddens sees control as part of the reflexive project of the self, which in turn is a characterization of the period in which we live when:

> Mastery . . . substitutes for morality; to be able to control one's life circumstances, colonise the future with some degree of success and live within parameters of internally referential systems can, in many circumstances, allow the social and natural framework of things to seem a secure grounding for life's activities (Giddens 1991: 202).

Autonomy and control may thus be the spur and the means through which people exercise the capacity to act – their agency. At the same time, the possibility for autonomy and control seems to act as a buffer against stress. Analyses of social change suggest that it is only relatively recently that autonomy and control have acquired such a significance in people's lives. This suggests a further dimension of theoretical adequacy – that the ways in which individuals' agency is exercised are historically specific. That is to say, they are generated by, reflect and shape, social, economic and cultural dynamics.

Capacity for Action: Identity and Experience

Identity is a mediating concept which has surfaced as significant in recent research on the relationship between support and the family and between support and welfare provision. In her study of family obligations and social change, discussed earlier, Finch emphasizes the significance of social identity within the kin group as influencing the possibilities for support and the parameters of commitment (Finch 1989: 203–4). In other words, the way in which you are identified, and identify yourself as fitting in with your kin group, along with the reputation you and others build for yourself out of the readings of your previous behaviour, marks out the ways in which you provide and seek support. Finch gives the example of the mother, whose identity is constructed on her reputation as a constant source of help and consistent cheerfulness yet who is unable to negotiate support from her kin when she herself experiences marital problems and mental and emotional distress. "It is the social identity which individuals bring to each new stage of negotiations with relatives which will influence the course of the negotiations, because each person's reputation carried forward over time embodies a set of expectations about how they will act" (Finch 1989: 204). Finch's use of the term identity emphasizes its social construction, that is, how others place you. In the example above, the woman's subjective experiences are counterposed to the way others place her, within the discursive resources available to them about motherhood. Other literature offers a second conceptualization of identity – as a bridge which connects the self to experience.

This concept of identity, as part of the self, has emerged in theories of social change as marking the relationship between the individual and the social. In simple terms, identity signifies who you think you are and how you think you belong. Of course, these perceptions are not singular, unitary or fixed, nor can they be simply of our own making. On the other hand, neither are they simply imposed upon us (we do not become welfare consumers because the government tells us we are, nor do we travel easily from being train passengers to rail customers, or from patients to health care customers). Indeed, as Stuart Hall points out speaking about cultural identities: ". . . in late modern times [they are] increasingly fragmented and fractured; never singular but multiply constituted across different, often intersecting and antagonistic, discourses, practices and positions" (Hall 1996: 4). Hall goes on to define identity as the meeting point between, on the one hand, discourses and practices which place us as social subjects and, on the other, the processes which generate our subjectivities. In these terms "identities are thus points of temporary attachment to the subject positions which discursive practices construct for us" (Hall 1996: 6).

If we translate these abstract ideas into welfare research, then they enable us to link the personal to the social in two important ways. First, by highlighting the significance of subjectivities and, second, by linking these to an understanding of the way certain welfare discourses, and the practices which flow from them, construct identities for individuals (as old person, as disabled, as single mother, as poor, as consumer, as absent father). In other words, we can begin to ask: how far do these identities render subjective experiences meaningful and how far do these experiences render themselves to a process of identification? These questions suggest that we need not only understand what we mean by identity, but also what we mean by experience.

Our discussion so far has led us to two different meanings of identity: one that is derived from a social category (mother, woman, disabled person, lone mother, etc.), and one that is derived from the individual's attempts to bring coherence – a sense of self – from fragmented experiences of multiple positions. David Taylor has distinguished these two meanings as categorical identity and ontological identity. The first is based upon recognizing and identifying oneself or others as belonging to the *same* social category. The second focuses upon the uniqueness of the individual – how experiences mark out the individual as different (Taylor forthcoming).

A piece of research which aims to theorize the category of experience and link it to identity and axes of power is Gail Lewis's study of black women's experiences as social workers (Lewis 1996). She starts by suggesting that research which seeks to give voice to subjective experience often aims to use such experience in order to challenge existing knowledge. Thus, black women's experiences have been used to expose the partial knowledge which emerges from white women's experiences, and also to show that white women's experiences could not claim to represent all women. In this way, experience has established itself as a force with which to challenge dominant forms of knowledge. However, in this process, the experience of "othered" groups were assumed to belong to the collective rather than the individual. As we noted in Chapter 1, a parallel development has occurred in the acknowledgement of *agency* in structural theories of welfare: insofar as the concept of agency was recognized, it was in its collective form – in the power of the working class/women's movement/black community to make demands upon the welfare state.

A consequence of this tendency to emphasize a collective agency has been to downplay the possibility of individual agency by working class/women/black people. Similarly, Lewis argues that there has been a tendency in welfare research to ascribe a collective meaning of *individuality* or of *self*, to those constituting *others*. She quotes Nell Painter's observation (1995) that there is an implicit assumption that white people have psyches whereas black people have community (Lewis 1996: 25). Instead she proposes that in order to theorize experience we need to "concentrate on its historical specificity and excavate its embeddedness in webs of social, political and cultural relations which are themselves organised around axes of power and which act to constitute subjectivities and identities" (Lewis 1996: 27). In other words, experience is not self-evident, does not reveal truth. Rather, it is a way of understanding how its subject is positioned and how they understand and articulate their specific location (who and where they are, to whom they are speaking) and their multiple social positionings. They also bring to that experience a personal biography; this itself is a product of historical specificity.

Lewis's analysis of her interviews with black women social workers suggest that these women mobilize the significance of their experience as black women (experiences of struggling against and standing up to racism and poverty; collective memories of resistance; experiences of responsibilities for care across extended families) to locate themselves within the axes of class, race and gender and to assert the contribution and value they have as social workers *vis à vis* their black (and white) clients over whom they have organizational power. But they also employ these experiences to assert their value *vis à vis* other social workers (largely white, many of whom are women) in an occupational setting where they feel increasingly subordinated. In articulating these multiple identities they draw on both oppositional discourses of race and gender, and professional social work discourses of care, support and empowerment.

A further strand in the theoretical significance of the notion of identity takes us back to the issues of individualization, control and social change discussed in the previous section. An engagement with the understanding and structuring of self identity is, according to Giddens, a characteristic of contemporary social life: self-identity, is not a given but is something which individuals create and sustain through their own accounts (or narratives) of their life experiences. "In the post-traditional order of modernity, and against the backdrop of new forms of mediated experience, self-identity becomes a reflexively organised endeavour" (Giddens 1991: 5). In other words, our interest in the accounts people give of their experiences springs not only from a concern to register an individual voice within a collective chord, but from an acknowledgement that reflexivity may play a more significant part these days than in the past in shaping how individuals place themselves and therefore how they act. New circumstances, new risks, new identities (for example, created through divorce, the reorganization of social care, or unemployment) mean that people need to reassess the "proper thing to do" and one way they may do this is by recalling their experiences and reconstructing their identities.

Subjectivity, Identity and Social Welfare Movements

The work reviewed above suggests that in the context of rapid social, political and economic change the project of constructing one's own identity has become more significant as the traditional meanings attached to social identity derived from class, gender, nationality and so on, have become more fragmented and less reliable. What these parallel processes may mean, and where they may be important for understanding the strategies people adopt to protect and promote their own and others' welfare, is that new forms of social identity may emerge while old ones are resisted, or even become redundant. Furthermore, these new forms of identity may also create the basis for both individual and collective agency.

One clear example of a set of welfare discourses and practices which have been transformed in this way is in the area of disability. The notion of a disabled person was originally an administrative and medical construct designed to measure eligibility to benefits. The rise of the disability movement has taken hold of the concept of disability, shaken it free of the meanings inherent in its medical and administrative sense (passive, dependent, object of charity, set apart, de-gendered, asexual and so on) and transformed it into the basis for positive identification and action.

In Chapter 2 we noted the study of D'Ercole (1988) on stress, coping and support among single mothers in New York. She found that they were much more likely to draw their support from co-workers in the same situation rather than from family or neighbours. In this situation the terms of exchange of support were based upon mutuality and common experience rather than obligation. The identity constructed through welfare policy and practice and labour-market constraint – single parent – became the basis for identification and support. Similarly, identities created from medical and welfare discourses – such as "sexual deviants" – have been resisted and new positive ones claimed (for example, lesbian mothers). These too have become the basis for support and pressure for change. The significance of gay and lesbian friendship networks as sources of social support has also recently emerged in research (Nardi 1992a, Weeks et al. 1996) and the AIDS crisis has further served to highlight this. In many other areas, not all of them new, groups have reclaimed and rewrought welfare identities – users of psychiatric services, people with learning difficulties, carers, and so on.

The development of new social welfare movements based on the politics of identity has drawn attention to the particular, and often overlooked, needs of social groups and challenged the "false universalism" of welfare. However, such movements have occasionally found themselves caught in political cul-de-sacs. Campaigns which are based upon the collectivizing of an identity (for example, of disabled people) have been successful in countering negative and devaluing representations in dominant welfare discourses. However, they also run the risk of freezing or fixing people into single unitary identities, when in fact, their self-identities may be quite complexly and multiply constituted (in terms of class, race, ethnicity and so on). This means that the politics of domination may be challenged, but the effect of the dominant discourse in *totalizing* particular identities/categories left untouched (Williams 1996).

The problematic and complex nature of the welfare identities that service users create for themselves in particular situations is highlighted in a research report by John Baldock and Clare Ungerson *Becoming Consumers of Community Care* (Baldock & Ungerson 1994). In this study they interviewed 32 stroke patients and their carers in order to explore how they cope with their sudden and often unexpected change of circumstances within the parameters of the mixed economy of care provision resulting from the 1990 NHS and Community

Care Act. This legislation, among other things, instituted a move towards the encouragement of low-cost home care provided by the informal, voluntary and commercial sector, along with a right of users to assessment of their needs for care through a consultation process with a care manager. The implementation of the Act was couched firmly within the discourse of consumerism – that users will be able to articulate their needs and, with access to information, exercise choice within the mixed economy of care provision. Baldock and Ungerson found, however, that their respondents did not adapt in a straight-forward way to a consumer identity. One reason for this was that their respondents felt extreme uncertainty in the face of their new medical condition: "Organising social care, from the point of view of its users and consumers, is a largely unscripted process. That is to say that people have few ideas as to what *can* be done and at the same time and more importantly, they are very uncertain about *what* should be done" (1994: 44, original emphasis). In other words, to use a concept developed by Finch and discussed earlier in the chapter, there is little sense of "the proper thing to do".

A second factor underlying people's problematic relationship with a consumer identity was that respondents' past experiences and how they understood these experiences (as users of public services or consumers in the market) failed to provide them with clear guidelines as to how to act. The normative guidelines drawn from the discourse of consumerism in the market did not fit easily with the circumstances of requiring social care. Rather, whereas the role of service providers was to give people information in order to make choices, the researchers found that people did what they did, not on the basis of factual information, but on the basis of values and culture – as Finch's analysis would predict. Part of the immediate problem for stroke victims and their carers was adapting to a new condition of social dependency; it is this that was a key part of the unscripted process. Additionally, a consumer identity enabled people to think in terms of buying some things, say consumer durables, but not others, such as personal care.

Baldock and Ungerson argue that people brought to the situation a particular identity as a welfare user which, in terms we have outlined in this chapter, could be seen as the way in which experience and identity influence the capacity to act. They called the activities which flowed from this "habits of the heart" (from de Tocqueville) and placed these along two axes which distinguish between four types of "disposition toward the provision of care" (we might also call these "discourses of welfare"). The first of these is: *consumerism* – where, at its extreme, one expects nothing from the state and subscribes to a view of individual self sufficiency. Insofar as people drew on this discourse, they were those who, regardless sometimes of income, preferred the sense of control to be had from actively seeking and buying-in services through their own networks. In contrast, the second discourse, *privatism*, represented a different, more passive form of consumerism, in which people regarded dependency as a stigma, often refused offers of help and preferred to keep themselves to themselves, again valuing their autonomy. The third discourse was that of *welfarism* – people who drew on this "believe in the welfare state and their right to use it. This implies the active pursuit of one's entitlements" (1994: 52). Finally, the discourse of *clientalism* generated a traditional approach to the welfare state: "passive, accepting, patient and grateful". None of the respondents was constituted simply in terms of one discourse or another, but those who were able to participate more in the emerging topography of social care were those who saw themselves more actively as either consumerists or welfarists.

Though the concepts developed in this study are different from the other mediating concepts discussed so far in this chapter, substantively they serve a similar purpose. This research provides a good example of attempts to relate people's personal biographies, their experiences, values and identities to prevailing discourses of social care. It explores their capacities to act and their coping strategies within a context of normative structures and discursive practices (what these researchers refer to as "habits of the heart" and "dispositions towards the provision of care") and, to a lesser extent, existing social relations of power. In so doing it throws light on the way in which welfare subjects construct and position themselves in the attempt to meet their needs for welfare.

Discourses

The concept of *discourse* alongside that of *identity* has emerged prominently from the discussion so far in this chapter, as offering the potential to mediate between the individual and the structural and to help us understand the genesis of social action. Hall (1996), quoted on page 167, sees identity as the link between subject positions and discursive practices. Baldock and Ungerson investigate the discourse of consumerism and the identities people adopt within it. Other welfare research demonstrates a more explicit usage and linking of these concepts.

An investigation by Hartley Dean and Peter Taylor-Gooby, for example, into whether or not a dependency culture exists among social security claimants, explored the meaning of poverty discourses to those who, in administrative terms, may be described as poor (Dean & Taylor-Gooby 1992). They found that two-thirds of those interviewed denied they were poor, but that there were gender differences in this: men were more likely to resist the label of poor, whereas women (even women of the same households) were more willing to accept it. In a subsequent commentary, Dean suggests this response is related to the threat to identity men feel at the loss of their breadwinner role. For women, it is related to their greater responsibility for the day-to-day of making ends meet (Dean 1992).

Dean goes on to provide an understanding of this denial of poverty through the analysis of what forms of identity the discourse of poverty constitutes for poor people. He suggests eight senses of poverty operated for these claimants. The first is that the notion is outmoded and inappropriate to the modern world; the second, that you are only as poor as you feel, or that it is basically a state of mind. Third was the belief that to admit to poverty was self-pitying or self-indulgent; fourth, that it was to admit to an affliction; fifth, that it involved loss of dignity or ability to maintain standards of decency; sixth, that being poor was something one did not admit to but kept to oneself; seventh, that it was a category below the one that they might assign to themselves (i.e. working class, but not poor); and, finally, it was linked to a sense of grievance or personal injustice, in that they could not fulfil their aspirations or those of their children. In these terms, the discourse of poverty constitutes identities which poor people resist as negative and disempowering. Such identities also serve, in their eyes, to suggest that they are culturally separate from the rest of the population, when, in their own views, they share similar values, norms and aspirations as those who are not social security claimants. Furthermore, this discourse of poverty, like its neighbour, the discourse of underclass, obscures the specific experiences of different groups who are in poverty, such as women or minority ethnic groups. In political terms, Dean suggests that "those who would campaign against social inequality could begin to focus their own and their opponents' attention upon that process of subjection which 'poverty' constitutes but fails to describe" (Dean 1992: 87).

The usefulness of the concept of discourse is that it enables us to consider the structural and the ideological influences upon people's lives in one frame. But more than this, it also provides a way of understanding how people's needs for welfare are constructed in particular ways. The structural inequalities of the labour market in Britain generate significant material disadvantages for particular groups, including women. However, it is as much the meanings and interpretations of the discourses of work and family, which are embedded in the practices of the labour market and the policies and practices of income maintenance programmes, that create inequalities for women as it is the structure of the labour market *per se*. These discourses construct women's needs in particular ways such that challenges to women's inequalities in the labour market have involved challenging the interpretation of women's needs in welfare discourses.

Nancy Fraser has termed this process "the politics of needs–interpretation" (Fraser 1989). In her analysis of women and welfare in the US, she suggests that three dominant forms of welfare discourse exist. The first is *oppositional* discourse. An example of this in the UK context is the disability movement's reinterpretation of their needs in terms of rights to independent living and the breaking down of social and environmental barriers. Another example is the way the women's movement has challenged the definition of domestic violence as a criminal rather than domestic offence or private matter. The second major discourse is *expert* discourse; the discussion in Chapter 7 of professional/expert discourses of support (and the way they conflicted with clients' own perceptions of their needs) is an example of this. Another example is the introduction of mediation for divorcing couples with children where *expert* knowledge is brought to bear on a situation which was previously left to individual couples. The third discourse which is particularly, though not exclusively, pervasive in liberal welfare regimes is the *reprivatization* discourse where needs are delimited and returned to either the domestic sphere or contracted out to the private market sector.

In a similar way, Fiona Williams (1996) has analysed the implementation of the 1990 NHS and Community Care Act in Britain in terms of two competing dominant discourses and one oppositional one, each of which mobilizes concepts of difference and need in different ways. The first is a political discourse associated with neo-liberalism in which the 1990 Act represented the recognition of diversity being exercised through the individual consumer's choice – the right to choose care appropriate to his or her needs. The second is the managerialist discourse in which professional intervention is required to assess individual needs and managerialism is required to manage the diverse meeting of these differentiated needs within a mixed economy of care. The third discourse finds its roots in the new social welfare movements and in the practice of equal opportunities policies which stresses the articulation of needs through the empowering of groups representing users themselves.

In a somewhat different vein, Simon Duncan and Ros Edwards (1996) look at the relationship between policy discourses on lone mothers and the "underclass" in the context of lone mothers' own perceptions of their motivations and behaviours. They note that much neo-liberal social policy is informed by a universalist view of individuals as rational economic actors making decisions in terms of economic costs and benefits. In contrast, the decisions lone mothers take about paid work were found to be as much influenced by discourses, values and beliefs about motherhood and work as they were about perceptions of costs and benefits. Those lone mothers who chose not to work, far from falling into a deviant subculture which abhors self-reliance and social responsibility, did so on the basis of their perceptions of the "proper thing to do" as a mother. In fact, this group was likely to hold traditional ideas about the relationship between mothering and paid work. Furthermore, lone mothers' views about costs and benefits were not held "en bloc", they were mediated by class, race, ethnicity as well as geographical, regional, local and national labour market conditions and traditions.

Duncan and Edwards propose that women's choices are influenced by what they term "gendered moral rationalities". This concept is not dissimilar to Finch's "normative guidelines" and her notion of people's behaviour being governed by "the proper thing to do". The concept of gendered moral rationalities implies that single mothers do not make decisions about whether to take up paid work on the basis of rational economic cost-benefit calculations of the benefits of entering waged labour nor because of the existence of a policy framework (of, for example, child care) which allows them to calculate in these terms. Rather, complex and diverse understandings about their responsibilities towards their children as single mothers influence their decisions. Some groups of mothers prioritize "being there" for their children over the rewards of paid employment. Others prioritize financial betterment as the main part of their maternal responsibilities. These priorities are also influenced by, and constituted through, local and regional opportunities for paid work, as well as local and national discourses of both lone mothers and gender relations. These in turn influence the type of support (paid work, benefits, child care, training, etc.) provided to enable lone mothers to maintain themselves and their children.

In common with the work of Finch, and Gabe and Thorogood, mentioned earlier, this study attempts to spell out the conceptual links between structure, agency and identity, and to operationalize a dynamic conception of the relation-ship between policy-making and policy outcome. However, by extending our understanding of the context within which individuals take decisions about action to include the powerful shaping influence of multiple and often conflictual welfare discourses, it moves us beyond Finch's concept of normative guidelines. As we discuss below, it is similarly possible to extend the concept of resources further by linking it more concretely to the structural context of social welfare systems through the concept of risk.

Risks

The concept of risk has emerged in social scientific literature in at least two different ways. The first identifies risk (and uncertainty) as one of a number of key features of a more reflexive modernity (Beck 1992; Giddens 1991). That is to say, on the one hand, it is argued that we have moved away from the fixities of class, gender and ethnic and sexual identities, the security of steady jobs, steady marriages and of firm moral and national boundaries and into new areas of social and personal risk. On the other hand, globalization and industrializa-tion have generated risks outside of our individual, or even national collective control – pollution and other ecological crises. Part of the reflexive project, argued by these theorists, involves a calculation of the risks and opportunities involved. The concept of risk has also emerged in literature and policies on health and well-being. Here there has been a shift away from a primary focus on the treatment of illness to the identification of health risks which involve pre-ventative forms of intervention.

Both of these developments in thinking are subject to different interpreta-tions. On the one hand they could be read as highly individualistic. In the account of reflexive modernity, rational economic man could be argued to have been simply replaced by rational reflexive man calculating and negotiating his project of the self. Similarly the focus in health promotion programmes on the responsibility of individuals to examine, care for, protect and regulate their bodies could be seen to be a simple assertion of a new form of individualist, rational entrepreneurialism of the body. However, and on the other hand, both approaches, if placed within the context of the changing nature of risks, emphas-izing their continuing unequal distribution, offer the possibility of linking indi-vidual landscapes of risk and opportunities to the broader contours of inequal-ities in the distribution of risk and opportunity associated with, for example, poverty or health and illness. More importantly, it offers us a way of investigating how such risks have different meanings and consequences for different social groups. How do people perceive the risks that they face to their well-being? How do these perceptions relate to their life experiences, their self and social identities and their capacity for action? How do these relate to professional or expert discourses of risk? How far do lay people trust the often conflicting scientific evidence of the risks they face, and how do they deal with this?

A recent study of perceptions of risk amongst the population of a particularly disadvantaged inner city area in the Northwest of England was concerned to explore some of these issues empirically. Much of the limited work in this field is concerned to understand the structural origins of new social movements in the public health arena. In contrast, this study by Gareth Williams, Jennie Popay and Paul Bissell (1995) focused on why, in the face of significant hazards to health some communities, particularly those experiencing the traditional risks associated with poverty and material disadvantage, do not protest, organize or mobilize for change. In particular, they focused on the role of lay expert knowledge about risks in the development of new social movement.

Not surprisingly, perhaps, the respondents in this study were aware of the individualistic discourse around lifestyle and health but they were more likely to prioritize socio-economic factors as major influences on their own wellbeing and that of others living in the area. Many and diverse risks to health were endemic features of the lives they described – poor housing, a long legacy of industrial pollution, lack of stable employment, poor diet, a high prevalence of smoking, etc. The researchers argue that the respondents provided narrative accounts of an inter-relationship between the material circumstances in which people live and the way people feel about themselves and behave. They illustrate this with quotes from several respondents. One man, with a trade union history, accepted, for example, that levels of health damaging behaviour were high in the area but noted, "I put it down to one thing . . . there doesn't seem much point in trying to stop people smoking and what else. As long as the environment is going down the pan then people will go down with it" (Williams et al. 1995: 125).

The researchers suggest that there is a "silencing of doubt" or an "inability to express concern" evident in some of the narratives. Certainly some narratives foregrounded the practical constraints on people's opportunities to act to change things. For example, commenting on their response to a major chemical spillage in the area – one of 13 relatively major incidents in a 15 year period – a male respondent noted that he and his partner had initially worried about the impact on their unborn child but: ". . . we fairly quickly forgot about it . . . we have to live and work so . . .". In a similar vein another older man noted that: "You can't just sit around worrying about it can you?" Still others pointed to less obvious constraints on people's action: "A lot of these people can't step out of line. A lot of them are frightened of doing anything wrong in case they have to get out. They live in fear of eviction." The researchers also reported widespread distrust of the local service providers and those who had some power and potential influence over the respondents' lives – a distrust summed up succinctly by one respondent who noted that: "to me it is sheer bloody neglect by social services, the council, the police, everybody".

In their comments on the data Williams and colleagues argue that there was no lack of awareness of public health risks amongst their respondents. Rather they suggest that a more plausible explanation for the lack of action to change this would be that these respondents had made a realistic assessment that a connection between environmental risk and poor health would be difficult to make and that, in any event, whatever anxieties did exist, the difficulties of daily life crowded them out. They conclude that:

> against the background of the dominant values and ideology in society, both those that engage in protest over environmental and public health risks and those for whom the risks are so overwhelming that no protest seems worthwhile, can be defined as people whose perceptions are based on misapprehensions or ignorance. Revolt and apathy are both regarded as forms of anti-rationality. However the data presented here reveal a rather different picture. Our respondents clearly understood that certain things were making them ill. They also realised that their own behaviour, in interaction with the material environment, could play a part in the genera-tion of morbidity. They recognised the risks. . . . However, the men and women in our study were living in situations in which risk is widespread and persistent. There seemed to them to be little point in removing or reducing one or two risks . . . when the "odds" against them seem so overwhelming (Williams et al. 1995: 128).

The study by Williams and his colleagues raises a general concern about the generalizability of some of the current thinking and writing on "the risk soci-ety". Much of this literature is concerned to highlight the profound changes in the type of risks facing contemporary society. In a recent volume, for example, containing contributions from two of the most prominent writers in this field – Beck and Giddens – the editor, Jane Franklin, notes at the beginning of the book that, "Risk is not new. There has always been a contingent edge to life. What has changed is the nature of risk" (Franklin 1997: 2).

She goes on to suggest that every day "we have to decide whether to risk eating beef, risk drinking tap-water, risk going to our family butcher". What the work of Williams, Popay and Bissell highlights, however, is that for a significant proportion of the population of contemporary western societies the relevant questions may well be whether they can afford to eat at all. The concept of risk is useful then as long as we examine the unequal distribution of risks alongside the perceptions and meanings of risks.

In part, public policy in general and social welfare programmes in particular, may be seen as the political interpretation of the major risks facing the popula-tion and of how they might be shared and managed. In the Beveridge report of 1942 (Beveridge 1942) which introduced the post-war welfare programmes these risks were clearly identified as the five evils of squalor, disease, ignorance, idleness and want and, importantly, there was a widespread shared understanding within countries developing welfare states of the nature of these risks and appro-priate ways of responding to them. To a large extent these same risks are still relevant today, although in an important sense the existence of some of them, notably poverty, may be bitterly contested. Whatever the debate about the nature and extent of poverty in contemporary western societies, however, it is unques-tionably the case that new welfare risks have also emerged on the agenda, for example, violence, sexual abuse, stress, loss of autonomy – and most recently in the UK at least – social exclusion. Consensus has also evaporated. However, we have as yet little overall empirical knowledge of public perceptions of changing risks and of the relationship between these and professional, managerial and political interpretations of risk.

Mediating Concepts and Dimensions of Theoretical Adequacy: A Summary

This section has identified a number of concepts which we believe enable us to link the creative welfare subjects with the social structures in which they operate. These included the *normative guidelines and gendered moral rationalities* which suggest "the proper thing to do" in the circumstances and so influence the way people decide to act and the notion of *resources*, the structural properties that individuals draw on in their everyday lives which both enable and constrain their ability to act in chosen ways – their agency. We also explored some significant dimensions of *the* individual – particularly issues of *control and autonomy, identity and subjective experience*, and the ways these related to individual and collective *agency*. The growing significance given to these dimensions of the individual within theoretical work on social change, self-identity and individualization was also noted.

We have argued that these dimensions of the normative and the individual are engaged in a dynamic relationship with the *discourses* that constitute welfare needs: that people draw on particular, and sometimes multiple, discourses (medical, political, religious) to interpret and articulate their needs. At the same time, these discourses constitute people's identities and may position them in certain ways with certain assumptions of their behaviour (for example, deserving, undeserving, that they are able or unable to act for themselves). Finally, the notion of *risk* was brought in to provide a way of looking at the relationships between the broader contours of inequalities, professional and expert discourses of welfare risks and people's own perceptions of the balance of risks they face and opportunities available to them.

In the process of exploring these mediating concepts, we have also identified some tentative criteria against which we might assess theoretical adequacy within any new welfare research paradigm. First, we have suggested that welfare subjects should be conceptualized as creative and having agency, negotiating, developing their own strategies of welfare management, and in so doing, helping to reconstitute the forms of provision they use. Second, both the welfare user and the welfare provider can be seen as inhabiting multiple social categories and positionings to which they assign greater or lesser significance over time and place. Third, these social categories and positionings reflect both social roles and dominant forms of social relations of power (class, gender, race, ethnicity, sexuality, disability, age). Fourth, welfare users and welfare providers also operate within the social relations of power attached to provision and receipt of welfare, and these too change over time and place. Fifth, welfare subjects bring with them personal histories and experiences; the accounting of these helps construct identities of the self and social identities. These categories of belonging are in turn shaped by welfare discourses, but also generate alternative or oppositional discourses. Sixth, processes of articulation of experiences and identification in-fluence welfare subjects' individual and collective agency, including the coping strategies they adopt in relation to both informal and formal welfare provision. This may involve the acceptance of, resistance to, or rejection of particular welfare identities and the discourses that help form them. Finally, identities, subjectivities, social categories and social relations are all constructed in condi-tions of historical specificity.

A New Framework for Welfare Research

This final section returns to the problem posed at the beginning of Chapter 1: is it possible to generate a new paradigm for welfare research and practice which moves away from seeing people as the passive beneficiaries of state intervention and professional expertise, from seeing them as fixed, single categories of poor, old, single parent and so on, or simply in terms of one-dimensional, objective, socio-economic classifications? Throughout this book contributors have argued that to do this it is necessary to bridge and move beyond paradigms of research and practice which narrowly foreground either individuals or social structures as the major determinants of human welfare and action. In the early sections of this chapter we have identified some of the potential building blocks for the con-ceptual bridge that is required and some of the tests of adequacy that might be applied to a new, less dichotomous paradigm.

The following framework attempts to bring these elements together. It is presented on four analytical levels, each of which is connected to the other. At each level we identify different conceptual dimensions for analysis. These four levels of analysis are:

1   the welfare subject;
2   the social topography of enablement and constraint;
3   the institutional and discursive context of policy formation and implementation;
4   the contextual dynamics of social and economic change.

A diagrammatical representation of the discussion that follows is given in Figure 8.1. In this, these four levels of analysis are presented as four overlapping boxes, or transparencies, each of which superimposes itself on the other.

The first level of analysis is represented by the first box, which teases out four dimensions that make up the welfare subject. First, there is *subjectivity* – people's understanding and accounting of their own experiences; next, *identity* – their sense of being and belonging (both categorical and ontological); third, *social position* – the objective interpretation of a person's position in relation to wider forms of stratification and social relations of power, and, fourth, *agency* – their

ALL DIMENSIONS UNDERPINNED BY AND RECONSTITUTING SOCIAL RELATIONS OF POWER

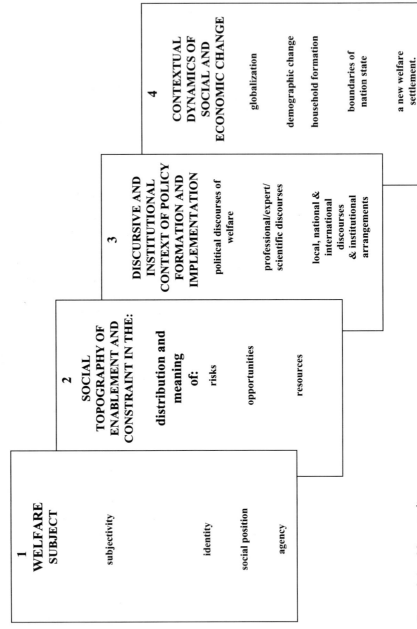

1
WELFARE SUBJECT

subjectivity

identity

social position

agency

2
SOCIAL TOPOGRAPHY OF ENABLEMENT AND CONSTRAINT IN THE:

distribution and meaning of:

risks

opportunities

resources

3
DISCURSIVE AND INSTITUTIONAL CONTEXT OF POLICY FORMATION AND IMPLEMENTATION

political discourses of welfare

professional/expert/ scientific discourses

local, national & international discourses & institutional arrangements

4
CONTEXTUAL DYNAMICS OF SOCIAL AND ECONOMIC CHANGE

globalization

demographic change

household formation

boundaries of nation state

a new welfare settlement.

Figure 8.1: New paradigm

capacity to act individually or collectively. Implicit in these four dimensions of the welfare subject is a shift away from seeing social group categories (class, gender, race, lone mothers, poor, etc.) as fixed, uniform or discrete. Instead, it is understood that the interrelatedness of these categories should be explored along with the temporal and spatial variability in their salience.

These dimensions of the welfare subject can then be related to dimensions identified in the second box. This depicts the social topography of welfare risks, opportunities and resources and how these are perceived, in order to help develop a more complex understanding of the landscapes of risk and opportunity that individuals inhabit in relation to conditions such as poverty and social exclusion. Quantitative studies can indicate the *distribution* of risks (for example the casualization of labour, forms of discrimination, homelessness, economic and welfare restructuring, including the marketization of welfare, as well as environmental hazards and crime and violence). In-depth qualitative research can explore people's own perceptions, or *meanings*, of the risks to which they are exposed, as well as the *opportunities* and *resources* available to them to protect themselves. By opportunities is meant the freedom to communicate needs, exercise rights, choices and autonomy. Resources refer not just to financial, but to personal resources, for example, coping strategies, networks, benefits, services, as defined earlier. The aim of this level of the analysis is to create a more dynamic understanding of people's own experiences and actions, and the place of benefits and services within these. This moves away from the assumption that people use, or respond to, benefits and services in uniform ways. It also points to possible flexible and diverse policy initiatives that might be developed to respond to the needs constituted by these landscapes.

The third box denotes a more dynamic approach to the notion of policy-making, policy-implementation and policy outcomes. Here, greater significance is given to the *discursive context* in which policies are made and implemented. The notion of discourses provides a way of understanding the dynamic between dimensions of the individual (their identity and subjectivity) and their capacity for and mode of action, on the one hand, and the existence and nature of policy provision, on the other. Welfare discourses and practices also interact with social and cultural values and affect the normative guidelines which influence how people act, as we saw in the studies discussed earlier. However, all these processes are subject to change. For example, changes in employment patterns may shift the way people behave, the resources available to them, the normative guidelines which shape their actions and the discursive context of welfare provision.

Discourses may operate at local, national or international level. International or global social policy discourses are also becoming increasingly important, both in terms of the development of European Union policy and in terms of international agencies such as WHO, UN, the IMF or World Bank (Deacon 1997). These different levels also involve different institutional arrangements for the formation, implementation and delivery of welfare services. These too influence the opportunities and resources available to individuals and groups within and across countries. For example, contemporary analysis of the EU places a great deal of emphasis upon the formation of social policy within a context of institutional complexity (Leibfried & Pierson 1995). This discursive and institutional context is, like the elements in the previous two boxes, both constituted through, and helps reconfigure, existing social relations of power. (In analyses of comparative social policy these social relations are conceptionalized as class/gender/race contracts or regimes (Esping-Andersen 1990; Ginsburg 1992.))

Finally, the fourth box in Figure 8.1 points to the need for welfare research to be informed by the wider dynamics of social and economic change. This would include, for example, the extent to which the intensified globalization of capitalism and technology has changed the nature and experience of work or the boundaries of the nation state in the West. It would include consideration of the extent to which women's claims for autonomy have contributed to the restructuring of household forms, or the effects of demographic change. These issues are connected to the question of identity, individualization and risk as well as to the question of how, within all these changes, welfare systems can develop policies of sufficient flexibility and comprehensiveness to insulate people from some risks and to provide them with the resources to control others.

A key dimension of the contextual dynamics of social and economic change which welfare research must address is the implications of the restructuring of state welfare provision. This is taking place in different yet parallel ways in most industrialized Western countries. In some places the process is being shaped by economic regionalization, such as the social and economic policies of the European Union. In other places, especially in Eastern Europe, international financial loan institutions, such as the International Monetary Fund and the World Bank, are having a profound influence on future social policies. Elsewhere, the national political discourses of neo-liberalism or new forms of centrism are shaping the priorities of needs. At the same time, as welfare provision is restructured, many factors already described are contributing to the constitution and distribution of old and new risks and social divisions. In many ways, these emerging divisions mirror older forms of inequality – especially around gender, race and class – but are reconstituted in new ways. In these changing conditions we need to understand the ways in which these risks are perceived by those whom they affect, what resources they use and need to act and cope, and how they articulate their welfare claims and challenge dominant welfare discourses.

Concluding Comments

The analytical framework illustrated in Figure 8.1 – dimensions of the individual welfare subject; the social topography of risks and opportunities; the discursive context for policy formulation and implementation; and the wider dynamics of social and economic change – provides the basis for a less dichotomized approach to the study of welfare needs and provision. This does not mean that it is necessary for welfare research to engage equally with all four domains to be theoretically adequate. However, we would argue that theoretical adequacy does demand that research begins to take account of the influences operating at all four levels while perhaps focusing the analytical lens on smaller parts of the wider landscape.

In relation to research methodology, all four domains can utilize both qualitative and quantitative methods. However, as this book has shown, we need to question the historical dominance that some methods hold in particular areas – qualitative in some, quantitative in others. The methodological challenge is to use a more appropriate mix of methods. We need to develop methods which, for example, uncover subjectivities and meanings around need and risk, or help us evaluate welfare interventions in a more systematic way. This will require a greater use of established methods – be they qualitative approaches or Randomized Control Trials – as well as the development of new methods and new ways of combining methods. These sorts of theoretical and methodological developments will also require conceptual innovations, of the kind we have drawn out in this chapter, which enable us to link the domains together.

Much is changing in individuals' lives but many old inequalities are also intensifying in new ways. It is not only appropriate but also urgent that we begin to investigate new ways of researching these issues, new ways of breaking down the separation of the individual from the social, new ways of understanding the relationship between human behaviour and social policy, and between social policy, social inequality and social change. This book is a contribution to that investigation.

References

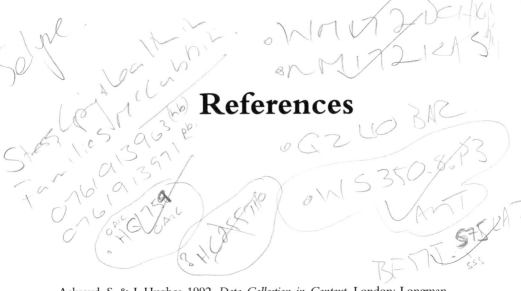

Ackroyd, S. & J. Hughes 1992. *Data Collection in Context*. London: Longman.

Ahmad, W. & K. Atkin (eds) 1996. *Race and Community Care*. Buckingham: Open University Press.

Alderson, P. 1996. Boots that don't fit. *The Guardian*, 24 April 1996.

Alexander, S. & B. Taylor 1980. In defence of "patriarch". *New Statesman* **99**, 661.

Alexander, F., M. M. Roberts, A. Higgins & B. Muir 1988. Use of risk factors to allocate schedules for breast cancer screening. *Journal of Epidemiology and Community Health* **42**, 193–9.

Allan, G. A. 1979. *A Sociology of Friendship and Kinship*. London: Allen and Unwin.

Allan, G. A. 1989. *Friendship: Developing a Sociological Perspective*. Hemel Hempstead: Harvester Wheatsheaf.

Anderson, J. M., C. Blue & A. Lau 1991. Women's perspectives on chronic illness: Ethnicity, ideology and restructuring of life. *Social Science and Medicine* **33**(2), 101–13.

Anderson, R. 1992. *The Aftermath of Stroke: The Experience of Patients and Their Families*. Cambridge: Cambridge University Press.

Aneshensel, C. S., R. R. Ferichs & V. A. Clark 1981. Family roles and sex differences in depression. *Journal of Health and Social Behaviour* **22**, 379–93.

Aneshensel, C. S., C. Rutter & P. Lachenbruch 1991. Social structure, stress and mental health: Competing conceptual and analytic models. *American Sociological Review* **56** (April), 166–78.

Antonovsky, A. 1974. Conceptual and methodological problems in the study of resistance resources and stressful life events. In *Stressful Life Events: Their Nature and Effects*, B. S. Dohrenwend & B. P. Dohrenwend (eds), 245–58. New York: John Wiley.

Antonucci, T. C. & H. Akiyama 1987. An examination of sex differences in social support among older men and women. *Sex Roles* **17**(11/12), 737–49.

Arber, S. & J. Ginn 1991. *Gender and Later Life: A Sociological Analysis of Resources and Constraints*. London: Sage.

Atkeson, B. M., K. S. Calhoun, P. A. Resick & E. Ellis 1982. Victims of rape: Repeated assessment of depressive symptoms. *Journal of Consulting and Clinical Psychology* **50**, 96–102.

Atkinson, D. 1986. Engaging competent others; A study of the support networks of people with mental handicap. *British Journal of Social Work*: Supplement 16.

Audit Commission 1992. *Community Care: Managing the Cascade of Change*. London: HMSO.

Avison, W. R. & R. J. Turner 1988. Stressful life events and depressive symptoms: Disaggregating the effects of acute stressors and chronic strains. *Journal of Health and Social Behaviour* **29**, 253–64.

Bailey, J. B. & R. B. Bhagat 1987. Meaning and measurement of stressors in the work environment: An evaluation. In *Stress and Health: Issues in Research Methodology*, S.V. Kasl & C. L. Cooper (eds). Chichester: John Wiley.

Balbo, L. 1987. Crazy quilts. In *Women and the state*, A. S. Sassoon (ed.). London: Hutchinson.

Baldock, J. & C. Ungerson 1994. *Becoming Consumers of Community Care.* York: Joseph Rowntree Foundation.

Barker, D. 1994. *Mothers, Babies and Disease in Later Life.* London, BMJ Publications.

Barnardo's 1990. *Missing the Target.* London: Barnardo's.

Barnes, M. & G. Wistow (eds) 1992. *Researching User Involvement.* Leeds University: Nuffield Institute Seminars.

Barnett, R., L. Biener & G. Baruch (eds) 1987. *Gender and Stress.* New York: Free Press.

Barrett, M. 1980. *Women's Oppression Today.* London: Verso.

Bartley, M. 1990. Do we need a strong programme in medical sociology? *Sociology of Health and Illness* **12**, 371–90.

Baruch, G. K., L. Beiner & R. C. Barnett 1987. Women and gender in research on work and family stress. *American Psychologist* **42**(2), 130–35.

BASW (British Association of Social Work). The Social Work Task. Birmingham: BASW.

Batta, I. D. & R. I. Mawby 1981. Children in local authority care: A monitoring of racial difference in Bradford. *Policy and Practice* **9**, 137–50.

Baum, A. & N. Grunberg 1990. Gender, stress and health. *Health Psychology* **10**(2), 80–85.

Baxter, C., L. Ward, K. Pooina & Z. Nadirshaw 1990. *Double Discrimination; Issues and Services for People with Difficulties from Black and Ethnic Minority Communities.* London: King's Fund Centre/Commission for Racial Equality.

Beaglehole, R., C. E. Salmond, A. Hooper, J. Huntsman, M. Stanhope, J. C. Cassel & A. M. Prior 1977. Blood pressure and social interaction in Tokelauan migrants in New Zealand. *Journal of Chronic Disability* **30**, 803–12.

Bebbington, P., C. Tennant & J. Hurry 1991. Adversity in groups with an increased risk of minor or affective disorder. *British Journal of Psychiatry* **158**, 33–40.

Beck, U. 1992. *The Risk Society: Towards a New Modernity.* London: Sage.

Beck, U. & E. Beck-Gernsheim 1995. *The Normal Chaos of Love.* Cambridge: Polity Press.

Becker, S. & S. MacPherson (eds) 1988. *Public Issues and Private Pain.* London: Insight.

Beckford 1984. *A Child in Trust, the Report of the Commission of Inquiry into the Circumstances Surrounding the Death of Jasmine Beckford.* London: Borough of Brent.

Beech, B. A. 1985 *Consumer View of Randomised Trials of Chorionic Villus Sampling.* Lancet **i**, 1157.

Bell, C. & H. Newby 1971. *Community Studies.* London: Allen and Unwin.

Beloff, H. (ed.) 1986. *Coping with Life.* London: Methuen.

Ben-Porath, Y. S. 1987. *Issues in the Psychosocial Adjustment of Refugees.* (Contract No. 278-85-0024 CH). Prepared for the National Institute of Mental Health Refugee Assistance Program, Mental Health/Technical Assistance Centre, Minneapolis: University of Minnesota.

Beresford, B. 1992. *Coping with Childhood Epilepsy; An Examination into Factors Mediating Adjustment in Children with Epilepsy.* Unpublished PhD thesis, Department of Psychology, University of Exeter.

Beresford, B. 1994. *Positively Parents. Caring for a Severely Disabled Child.* London: HMSO.

185

Berkman, L. F. 1984. Assessing the physical health effects of social networks and social support. *American Review of Public Health*, 413–32.

Berkman, L. F. 1985. The relationship of social networks and social support to morbidity and mortality. In *Social Support and Health*, S. Cohen & S. L. Syme (eds). London: Academic Press.

Bettelheim, B. 1943. Individual and mass behaviour in extreme situations. *Journal of Abnormal Social Psychiatry* **38**, 417–52.

Beuret, K. & L. Makings 1986. *Love in a Cold Climate: Women, Class and Courtship in a Recession*. Paper at British Sociological Association Annual Conference, Loughborough University, Mimeo: North Staffs. Polytechnic.

Beutler, L. E., P. P. Machado & S. A. Neufeldt 1995. Therapist variables. In *Handbook of Psychotherapy and Behaviour Change*, A. E. Bergin & S. L. Garfield (eds). New York: John Wiley.

Beveridge, W. 1942. Report on Social Insurance and Allied Services, Cmd 6404, HMSO.

Bhalla, A. L. & K. Blakemore 1981. Elders of the ethnic minority groups. *AFFOR – All Faiths For One Race*. Birmingham: Roman Publishers.

Biestek, F. 1961. *The Casework Relationship*. London: Allen & Unwin.

Billings, A. G. & R. H. Moos 1984. Coping, stress and social resources among adults with unipolar depression. *Journal of Personality and Social Psychology* **46**, 877–91.

Binney, V., G. Harkell & J. Nixon 1981. *Leaving Violent Men*, London: National Women's Aid Federation: England.

Blakemore, K. & M. Boneham 1993. *Age, Race and Ethnicity: A Comparative Approach*. Buckingham: Open University Press.

Blazer, D. G. 1982. Social support and mortality in an elderly community population. *American Journal of Epidemiology* **115**, 686–94.

Bograd, M. 1988. Feminist perspectives on wife abuse: an introduction. In *Feminist Perspectives on Wife Abuse*, K. Yllö & M. Bograd (eds). Beverly Hills, California: Sage.

Bolton, P. 1984. Management of compulsorily admitted patients to a high security unit. *International Social Psychiatry* **30**, 77–84.

Booth, T. A. 1978. From normal baby to handicapped child. *Sociology* **12**, 203–21.

Borchorst, A. & B. Siim 1987. Women and the advanced welfare state – A new kind of patriarchal power. In *Women and the State*, A. S. Sassoon (ed.). London: Hutchinson.

Bowlby, J. 1961. Processes of mourning. *International Journal of Psycho-Analysis* **44**, 317.

Bowling, A., B. Jacobson & L. Southgate 1993. Health service priorities: Explorations in consultation of the public and health professionals on priority setting in an inner London health district. *Social Science and Medicine* **87**(7), 851–8.

Boyce, W. T., M. Kay & C. Uitti 1988. The taxonomy of social support: Ethnographic analysis among adolescent mothers. *Social Science and Medicine* **26**(11), 1079–85.

Bradshaw, J. & H. Holmes 1989. *Living On The Edge: A Study of the Living Standards of Families on Benefit in Tyne and Wear*. London: Tyneside Action Group.

Brannen, J. (ed.) 1992. *Mixing Methods. Qualitative and Quantitative Research*. Aldershot: Avebury.

Brannen, J. & G. Wilson 1987. *Give and Take in Families*. London: Allen and Unwin.

Bransfield, F. 1990. *Disability and the concept of self*. Unpublished MA thesis, Department of Sociology, University of York.

Brewer, C. & J. J. Lait 1980. *Can Social Work Survive?* London: Temple Smith.

Breznitz, S. & L. Goldberger 1982. Stress research at a crossroads. In *Handbook of Stress: Theoretical and Clinical Aspects*, L. Goldberger & S. Breznitz (eds), 3–6. New York: The Free Press.

Bristol Broadsides 1981. *Tears and Joy (by parents of mentally handicapped children)*. Bristol: Bristol Broadsides.

Bristol, M. M. & J. Gallagher 1986. Research on fathers of young handicapped children. Evolution, review, and some future directions. In *Families of Handicapped Persons: Research, Progress and Policy Issues*, I. J. Gallagher & P. M. Vietze (eds), 81–100. Baltimore, Maryland: Paul H. Brooks Publishing Co.

Broadhead, W. E., B. H. Kaplan, S. A. James, E. H. Wagner, V. J. Shroenbach, R. Grimson, S. Heydon, G. Tibblin & S. H. Grehlbach 1983. The epidemiological evidence for a relationship between social support and health. *American Journal of Epidemiology* **117**, 521–37.

Broverman, I. K., D. Broverman, F. Clarkeson, P. Rosenkranz & S. Vogels 1970. Sex role stereotypes and clinical judgements of mental health. In *Women and Mental Health*, E. Howell & M. Bayes (eds), 86–97. New York: Basic Books.

Brown, C. 1981. Mothers, fathers and children: From private to public patriarchy. In *Women and Revolution. The Unhappy Marriage of Marxism and Feminism*, L. Sargent (ed.), 239–67. New York: Maple; London: Pluto.

Brown, D. R. & L. E. Gary 1987. Stressful life events, social support networks and the physical and mental health of urban black adults. *Journal of Human Stress* **13**, pp. 165–174, Winter.

Brown, G. W. (ed.) 1989. *Life Events and Illness*. London: Unwin Hyman.

Brown, G. W. & T. Harris 1978. *Social Origins of Depression: A Study of Psychiatric Disorder in Women*. London: Tavistock.

Brown, G. W. & T. Harris 1989. *Life Events and Illness*. New York: Guilford Press.

Brown, G. W., A. Bifulco, T. Harris & L. Bridge 1986. Life stress, chronic sub-clinical symptoms and vulnerability to clinical depression. *Journal of Affective Disorder* **11**, 1–19.

Brown, P. & E. J. Mikkelsen 1990. *No Safe Place: Toxic Waste, Leukaemia and Community*. Berkeley, California: University of California Press.

Bryant, C. 1995. *Practical Sociology, Post-Empiricism and the Reconstruction of Theory and Application*. Cambridge: Polity Press.

Bryer, J. B., B. A. Nelson, J. B. Miller & P. A. Krol 1987. Childhood sexual and physical abuse as factors in adult psychiatric illness. *American Journal of Psychology* **141**, 1426–30.

Bryman, A. 1988. *Quantity and Quality in Social Research*. London: Unwin Hyman.

Bryman, A. & R. Burgess (eds) 1994. *Analysing Qualitative Data*. London: Routledge.

Bull, R. & I. Shaw 1992. Constructing causal accounts in social work. *Sociology* **126**, 635–49.

Bulmer, M. 1987. *The Social Basis of Community Care*. London: Unwin Hyman.

Burghes, L. 1980. *Living From Hand to Mouth: A Study of Sixty-five Families Living on Supplementary Benefit*. London: Child Poverty Action Group.

Burnam, M. A., R. L. Hough, R. Escobar, M. Karno, D. M. Timbers, C. A. Telles & B. Z. Locke 1987. Six-month prevalence of specific psychiatric disorders among Mexican Americans and non-Hispanic Whites in Los Angeles. *Archives of General Psychiatry* **44**, 687–94.

Burr, M. L. & P. M. Sweetnam 1980. Family size and paternal unemployment in relation to myocardial infarction. *Journal of Epidemiology and Community Health* **34**(2), 93–5.

Burrows, R. & B. Loader (eds) 1994. *Towards a Post-Fordist Welfare State?* London: Routledge.

Burstyn, V. 1983. Masculine dominance and the state. In *Socialist Register*, R. Miliband & J. Savile (eds), 45–89. London: Merlin.

Burton, C. 1985. *Subordination*. Sydney: Allen and Unwin.

Bury, M. 1982. Chronic illness as biographical disruption. *Sociology of Health and Illness* **4**, 167–82.

Buss, T. F. & F. S. Redburn 1983. *Mass Unemployment: Plant Closings and Community*. Beverly Hills, California: Sage.

Button, H. 1991. Vulnerability: A concept reconsidered. *Educational Administration Quarterly* **27**(3), 378–91.

Campbell, B. 1993. *Goliath; Britain's Dangerous Places*. London: Methuen.

Campbell, D. T. & J. C. Stanley 1973. *Experimental and Quasi-experimental Designs for Research*. Chicago, Illinois: Rand McNally.

Carlisle 1986. *A Child in Mind: The Report of the Commission of Inquiry into the Circumstances Surrounding the Death of Kimberley Carlisle*. London: Borough of Greenwich.

Carr-Hill, R. A. & K. I. Macdonald 1973. Problems in the analysis of life-histories. *Sociological Review Monograph* **35**, 57–95.

Cartwright, A. 1979. *The Dignity of Labour?* London: Tavistock.

Carver, C. S., M. F. Scheier & J. K. Weintraub 1989. Assessing coping strategies: A theoretically based approach. *Journal of Personality and Social Psychology* **54**, 267–83.

Cassel, J. C. 1975. Studies of hypertension in migrants. In *Epidemiology and Control of Hypertension*, O. Paul (ed.), 41–62. Miami, Florida: Symposia Specialists.

Chalmers, I. 1986. Minimising harm and maximising benefit during innovation in health care: Controlled or uncontrolled experimentation? *Birth* **13**(3), 155–164.

Charmaz, K. 1995. Grounded theory. In *Rethinking Methods in Psychology*, J. A. Smith, R. Harre & L. V. Langenhove (eds). London: Sage.

Chave, S., J. Morris & S. Moss 1978. Vigorous exercise in leisure time and the death rate: A study of male civil servants. *Journal of Epidemiology and Community Health* **32**(4), 239–43.

Cheal, D. 1988. *The Gift Economy*. London: Routledge.

Chodorow, N. 1978. *The Reproduction of Mothering: Psychoanalysis and the Sociology of Gender*. Berkeley, California: University of California Press.

Clarke, C. L. with S. Asquith 1985. *Social Work and Social Philosophy. A Guide for Practice*. London: Routledge and Kegan Paul.

Clegg, F. 1988. Disasters: Can psychologists help the survivors? *The Psychologist* **1**(4), 134–35.

Cleveland Report 1987. *Report of the Inquiry into Child Abuse in Cleveland*. London: HMSO.

Cobb, S. 1976. Social support as a moderator of life stress. *Psychosomatic Medicine* **38**, 300–14.

Cobb, S. & S. V. Kasl 1977. *Termination: The Consequences of Job Loss*. NIOSH Publication No. 77–224. Cincinnati, Ohio: US Department of Health, Education and Welfare.

Cochrane Collaboration. 1997. *Cochrane Colloquium Report*. Oxford.

Cohen, F. 1979. Personality, stress, and the development of physical illness. In *Health Psychology*, G. C. Stone, F. Cohen & N. E. Adler (eds). San Francisco, California: Jossey-Bass.

Cohen, P. & H. S. Bains 1988. *Multi-Racial Britain*. Basingstoke: Macmillan.

Cohen, S. & L. S. Syme (eds) 1985. *Social Support and Health*. Orlando, Florida: Academic.

Collinson, D. L. & J. Hearn 1994. Naming men as men: Implications for work, organization and management. *Gender, Work and Organization* **1**(1), 2–22.

Colmen, R. & S. Sadiq 1991. *Just About Surviving – Life on Income Support*. Family Service Unit Reports.

Connell, R. W. 1985. Theorising gender. *Sociology* **19**, 260–72.

Connell, R. W. 1987. *Gender and Power*. Cambridge: Polity Press.

Connell, R. W. 1990. The state, gender and sexual politics. *Theory & Society* **19**, 507–44.

Connelly, N. 1988. *Care in the Multiracial Community*. London: Policy Study Institute, Discussion Paper 20.

Corby, B. 1992. Alternative theory bases in child abuse. In *Child Abuse and Neglect: Facing the Challenge*, W. Stainton Rogers, D. Hevey, J. Roche & E. Ash (eds). London: Batsford/OUP 2nd edition.

Corden, A. & P. Craig 1991. *Perceptions of Family Credit*. London: HMSO.

Cornwell, J. 1984. *Hard Earned Lives: Accounts of Health and Illness From East London*. London: Tavistock.

Coyne, J. & D. Smith 1991. Couples coping with a myocardial infarction: A contextual perspective on wives' distress. *Journal of Personality and Social Psychology* **61**(3), 404–12.

Coyne, J. C. & G. Downey 1991. Social factors and psychopathology: Stress, social support and coping process. *Annual Review of Psychology* **42**, 401–25.

Creighton, S. 1985. Fatal child abuse: How preventable is it? *Child Abuse Review* **4**, 318b–328.

Curtis, P. 1991. *Midwives in Hospital*. Unpublished PhD. thesis, Department of Sociology, University of Manchester.

Curtis, S. 1987. Self-reported morbidity in London and Manchester. *Social Indicators Research* **19**, 255–72.

Dale, J. & P. Foster 1986. *Feminists and State Welfare*. London: Routledge and Kegan Paul.

Dalla Costa, M. & S. James 1973. *The Power of Women and the Subversion of the Community*. Bristol: Falling Wall Press.

Dalley, G. 1988. *Ideologies of Caring: Rethinking Community and Collectivism*. London: Macmillan.

Davidson, J. R. T., D. Hughes, D. Blazer & L. K. George 1991. Post-traumatic stress disorder in the community: An epidemiological study. *Psychological Medicine* **21**, 713–21.

Davies, C. & S. Roche 1980. The place of methodology: A critique of Brown and Harris. *Sociological Review* **28**(3), 641–56.

Day, R., J. A. Nielsen, A. Korten, G. Ernberg, C. Dube & J. Gebhart 1987. Stressful life events preceding the acute onset of schizophrenia: a cross-national study from the World Health Organization. *Culture, Medicine and Psychiatry* **11**, 123–205.

Deacon, B. 1997. *Global Social Policy*. London: Sage.

Dean, H. 1992. Poverty discourse and the disempowerment of the poor. *Critical Social Policy* **35**, 79–88.

Dean, H. & J. Taylor-Gooby 1992. *Dependency Culture: the Explosion of a Myth*. Hemel Hempstead: Harvester Wheatsheaf.

Dean, K. 1986. Social support and health: Pathways of influence. *Health Promotion* **1**(2), 133–50.

Dean, K., E. Holst, S. Kreiner, C. Schoenborn & R. Wilson 1994. Measurement issues in research on social support and health. *Journal of Epidemiology and Community Health* **48**(2), 201–6.

Dean, K. (ed.) 1993 *Population Health Research: Linking Theory and Methods*. London: Sage.

Deitch, C. 1984. Collective action and unemployment: Responses to job loss by workers and community groups. *International Journal of Mental Health* **13**, 139–53.

Delphy, C. 1984. *Close To Home: A Material Analysis of Women's Oppression*. London: Hutchinson.

Delphy, C. & D. Leonard 1977. *The Main Enemy. A Materialist Analysis of Women's Oppression*. London: W.R.R.C. (First published in French, 1970).

Delphy, C. & D. Leonard 1992. *Familiar Exploitation: A New Analysis of Marriage in Contemporary Western Societies.* Cambridge: Polity Press.

Dennis, N. E., F. Henriques & C. Slaughter 1956. *Coal Is Our Life.* London: Eyre and Spottiswood.

Department of Health 1989a. *Working for Patients.* London: HMSO.

Department of Health 1989b. *Caring for People.* London: HMSO.

Department of Health, 1997. *The New NHS: Modern, Dependable.* London: HMSO.

Depner, C. E., E. Wethington & B. E. Ingersoll-Dayton 1984. Social support: methodological issues in design and measurement. *Journal of Social Issues* **40**(4), 37–54.

D'Ercole, A. 1988. Single mothers: Stress, coping and social support. *Journal of Community Psychology* **16**, Jan 1988.

Dew, M. A., E. J. Bromet & H. C. Schulberg 1987. A comparative analysis of two community stressors' long-term mental health effects. *American Journal of Community Psychology* **15**, 167–84.

Dex, S. 1985. *The Sexual Divisions Of Work.* Brighton: Wheatsheaf.

Dhooge, Y. & J. Popay 1988. The social construction of unemployment: Defining a social work role. In *Public Issues and Private Pain*, S. Becker & S. MacPherson (eds). London: Insight.

Dhooper, S. S. 1984. Social networks and support during the crisis of heart attack. *Health and Social Work* **9**, 294–303.

Dobash, R. E. & R. Dobash 1979. *Violence Against Wives.* London: Open Books.

Dobash, R. E. & R. P. Dobash 1988. Research as social action: The struggle for battered women. In *Feminist Perspectives on Wife Abuse*, K. Yllö & M. Bograd (eds). Beverly Hills, California: Sage.

Dobash, R. E. & R. Dobash 1992. *Women, Violence and Social Change.* London: Routledge.

Dobash, R. E., R. Dobash, M. Wilson & M. Daly 1992. The myth of sexual symmetry in marital violence. *Social Problems* **39**, 71–91.

Dominelli, L. 1996. *Sociology of Social Work.* Basingstoke: Macmillan.

Donaldson, L. J. & D. G. Clayton 1984. Occurrence of cancer in Asians and non-Asians. *Journal of Epidemiology and Community Health* **38**(3), 203–7.

Dowding, V. M. & C. G. Barry 1990. Cerebral palsy: Social class differences in prevalence in relation to birthweight and severity of disability. *Journal of Epidemiology and Community Health* **44**, 191–5.

Duck, S. (ed.) 1990. *Personal Relationships and Social Support.* London: Sage.

Duck, S. E. (ed.) 1984. *Personal Relationships 5: Repairing Personal Relationships.* London: Academic Press.

Duncan, S. & R. Edwards 1996. Lone mothers and paid work: neighbourhoods, local labour markets and welfare state regimes. *Social Politics, International Studies in Gender, State and Society* **13**(2/31), 95–222.

Duncan, S. & R. Edwards 1997. *Single Mothers in an International Context: Mothers or Workers?* London: UCL Press.

Dworkin, A. 1974. *Woman Hating.* New York: Dutton.

Edgell, S., S. Walklate & G. Williams 1995. *Debating the Future of the Public Sphere.* Avebury, Aldershot.

Edwards, J. 1995. Parenting skills: Views of community health and social service providers about the needs of their "clients". *Journal of Social Policy* **24**(2), 237–59.

Edwards, J. 1998. Screening out men: has mum changed the washing powder? In *Men, Gender Divisions and Welfare*, J. Popay, J. Hearn & J. Edwards (eds). London: Routledge.

Edwards, J. & J. Popay 1994. Contradiction of support and self-help: Views from providers of community health and social services to families with young children. *Health and Social Care* **2**, 31–40.

Edwards, J. R. & C. L. Cooper 1988. Editorial – Research in stress, coping and health: theoretical and methodological issues. *Psychological Medicine* **18**, 15–20.

Ehrenreich, B. 1983. *The Hearts of Men: American Dreams and the Flight from Commitment.* London: Pluto.

Eisenstein, Z. R. 1981. *The Radical Future of Liberal Feminism.* Boston, Massachusetts: Northeastern University Press.

Endicott, J. & R. L. Spitzer 1978. A diagnostic interview: the schedule for affective disorders and schizophrenia. *Archives of General Psychology* **35**, 837–44.

Endler, N. S. & J. D. A. Parker 1990. Multidimensional assessment of coping: A critical evaluation. *Journal of Personality and Social Psychology* **58**(5), 844–54.

Engel, B. T. 1985. Stress is a noun! No, a verb! No, an adjective! In *Stress and Coping*, T. M. Field, P. M. McCabe & N. Schneiderman (eds), 3–12. Hillsdale, New Jersey: Erlbaum.

England, H. 1986. *Social Work as Art: Making Sense for Good Practice.* London: Allen and Unwin.

Ernst, S & L. Goodison 1981. *In Our Own Hands.* London: The Women's Press.

Esping-Andersen, G. 1990. *The Three Worlds of Welfare Capitalism.* Cambridge: Polity Press.

Evers, H. 1984. Old women's perceptions of dependency and some implications for service provision. *Journal of Epidemiology and Community Health* **38**(4), 306–19.

Everson, E. 1982. *Hidden Violence: A Study of Battered Women in Northern Ireland.* Belfast: Farset Co-operative Press.

Eysenck, H. J. 1983. Stress, disease and personality: The "innoculation" effect. In *Stress Research: Issues for the 80s*, C. L. Cooper (ed.), 121–46. Chichester, England: John Wiley.

Farber, E. A. & B. Egeland 1987. Invulnerability among abused and neglected children. In *The Invulnerable Child*, E. J. Anthony & B. J. Cohler (eds), 253–88. New York: Guildford Press.

Felton, B. J., T. A. Revenson & G. A. Hinrichsen 1984. Stress and coping in the explanation of psychological adjustment among chronically ill adults. *Social Science and Medicine* **18**(10), 889–98.

Field, F. (1997) Re-inventing welfare: A response to Lawrence Mead. In *From Welfare to Work: Lessons from America*, A. Deacon (ed.). London: I.E.A. Health & Welfare Unit.

Finch, J. 1989. *Family Obligations and Social Change.* Cambridge: Polity Press.

Finch, J. & D. Groves (eds) 1983. *A Labour of Love.* London: Routledge and Kegan Paul.

Finch, J. & J. Mason 1993. *Negotiating Family Responsibilities.* London: Routledge.

Fink, A. & L. McCloskey 1990. Moving child abuse and neglect prevention programs forward: Improving program evaluation. *Child Abuse and Neglect* **14**, 187–206.

Finkelhor, D., R. J. Gelles, G. T. Hotaling & M. A. Straus (eds) 1983. *The Dark Side of Families: Current Family Violence Research.* London: Sage.

Fisher, M., C. Newton & E. Sainsbury 1984. *Mental Health Social Work Observed.* London: George Allen and Unwin.

Flaherty, J. & J. Richman 1988. Gender differences in the perception and utilization of social support: Theoretical perspectives and an empirical test. *Social Science and Medicine* **2**, pp. 1221–8.

Fletcher, B. & R. Payne 1980. *Stress and Work: A Review and Theoretical Framework, Part 1.* Chichester, England: John Wiley.

Folkman, S. & R. S. Lazarus 1980. An analysis of coping in a middle-aged community sample. *Journal of Health and Social Behaviour* **21**, 219–39.

191

Folkman, S., R. S. Lazarus, C. Dunkel-Schetter, A. DeLongis & R. Gruen 1986. The dynamics of a stressful encounter: cognitive appraisal, coping and encounter outcomes. *Journal of Personality and Social Psychology* **50**, 992–1003.

Forsythe, C. J. & B. Compas 1987. Interaction of cognitive appraisals of stressful events and coping: Testing the goodness-of-fit hypothesis. *Cognitive Therapy and Research* **11**(4), 473–85.

Fox, J. 1988. Social networks interaction: New jargon in health inequalities. *British Medical Journal* **297**: 373–4.

Frankenberg, R. 1966. *Communities in Britain.* Harmondsworth: Penguin.

Frankenberg, R. 1976. In the production of their lives; Sex and gender in British community studies. In *Sexual Divisions and Society: Process and Change*, D. L. Leonard & S. Allen (eds), 25–31. London: Tavistock.

Franklin, J. (ed.) 1997. *The Politics of Risk Society.* Cambridge: Polity Press.

Fraser, N. 1989. *Unruly Practices: Power, Discourse and Gender in Contemporary Social Theory.* Cambridge: Polity Press.

Freud, S. 1930/1961. *Civilisation and Its Discontents.* Translated by J. Strachey. New York: W. W. Norton.

Friedman, S. B., P. Chodoff, J. W. Mason & D. A. Hamburg 1963. Behavioural observations on parents anticipating the death of a child. *Pediatrics* **32**, 610–25.

Fryer, D. 1992. Introduction to Marienthal and beyond. *Journal of Occupational and Organizational Psychology* **65,** 269–75.

Funch, D. P. & J. M. Marshall 1984. Measuring life stress: Factors affecting fall-off in the reporting of life events. *Journal of Health and Social Behaviour* **25**, 453–64.

Gabe, J. & N. Thorogood 1986. Tranquillisers as a resource. In *Tranquillisers: Social, Psychological and Clinical Perspectives*, J. Gabe & P. Williams (eds). London: Tavistock.

Gadzella, B. M., D. W. Ginther, M. Tomcala & G. Bryant 1990. Stress as perceived by professionals. *Psychological Reports* **67**, 979–83.

Gallers, J., D. W. Foy, C. P. Donahoe & J. Goldfarb 1988. Post-traumatic stress disorder in Vietnam combat veterans: Effects of traumatic violence exposure and military adjustment. *Journal of Traumatic Stress* **1**, 181–91.

Game, A. 1991. *Undoing the Social: Towards a Deconstructive Sociology.* Milton Keynes: Open University Press.

Garcia, J. 1982. Women's views of antenatal care. In *Effectiveness and Satisfaction in Antenatal Care*, M. Enkin & I. Chalmers (eds). London: William Heinemann Medical Books.

Garcia, J., R. Kilpatrick, M. Richards 1988 (eds). *The Politics of Maternity Care.* Oxford: Oxford University Press.

Gamarnikow, E., D. H. J. Morgan, J. Purvis & D. Taylorson (eds) 1983. *The Public and the Private.* London: Heinemann.

Garmezy, N. 1985. Stress-resistant children: The search for protective factors. In *Recent Research in Developmental Psychopathology*, J. E. Stevenson (ed.), 213–33. Oxford: Pergamon.

Gelles, R. J. 1974. *The Violent Home: A Study of Physical Aggression Between Husbands and Wives.* Los Angeles, California: Sage.

Gelles, R. J. 1987. *Family Violence.* Los Angeles, California: Sage.

Geyer, S. 1991. Life events prior to manifestation of breast cancer: A limited prospective study covering eight years before diagnosis. *Journal of Psychosomatic Research* **35**(2/3), 355–63.

Giddens, A. 1979. *Central Problems in Social Theory.* London: Macmillan.

Giddens, A. 1991. *Modernity and Self-identity; Self and Society in the Late Modern Age.* Cambridge: Polity Press.

Gilligan, C. 1982. *In a Different Voice: Psychological Theory and Women's Development*. Cambridge, Massachusetts: Harvard University Press.

Ginsburg, N. 1992. *Divisions of Welfare: A Critical Introduction to Comparative Social Policy*. London: Sage.

Glendinning, C. 1983. *Unshared Care: Parents and Their Disabled Children*. London: Routledge and Kegan Paul.

Glendinning, C. 1985. *A Single Door*. London: Allen and Unwin.

Glendinning, C. & J. Millar 1992. *Women and Poverty in Britain*. (2nd edition). Hemel Hempstead: Harvester Wheatsheaf.

Glennerster. H. M., P. Matsagonis, P. Owens & S. Hancock 1994. *Implementing GP Fundholding. Wild Card or Winning Hand?* Buckingham: Open University Press.

Goffman, E. 1961. *Asylums*. New York: Anchor.

Goplerud, E. & R. A. Depue 1985. Behavioural response to naturally occurring stress in clothymia and dysthymia. *Journal of Abnormal Psychology* **94**, 128–39.

Gordon, L. (ed.) 1990. *Women, The State and Welfare*. Madison, Wisconsin: University of Wisconsin Press.

Gore, S. 1978. The effect of social support in moderating the health consequences of unemployment. *Journal of Health and Social Behaviour* **19**, 15–65.

Gore, S. L. & T. W. Mangione 1983. Social roles, sex roles and psychological distress: Additive and interactive models of sex differences. *Journal of Health and Social Behaviour* **24**, 300–12.

Gottlieb, B. H. (ed.) 1981. *Social Networks and Social Support*. Beverly Hills, California: Sage.

Gottlieb, B. H. (ed.) 1988. *Marshalling Social Support*. Beverly Hills, California: Sage.

Gottlieb, B. H. & F. Wagner 1991. Stress and support processes in close relationships. In *The Social Context of Coping*, J. Eckenrode (ed.). New York: Plenum.

Gough, I. 1979. *The Political Economy of the Welfare State*. London: Macmillan.

Gove, W. R. & J. F. Tudor 1973. Adult sex roles and mental illness. *American Journal of Sociology* **78**, 812–35.

Graham, H. 1982. Coping: Or how mothers are seen and not heard. In *On the Problem of Men*, S. Friedman & E. Sarah (eds), 101–16. London: The Women's Press.

Graham, H. 1983a. Caring – A labour of love. In *A Labour of Love: Women, Work and Caring*, J. Finch & D. Groves (eds). London: Routledge and Kegan Paul.

Graham, H. 1983b. Do her answers fit his questions? Women and the survey method. In *The Public and the Private*, E. Gamarnikow, D. H. J. Morgan, J. Purvis & D. Taylorson (eds). London: Heinemann.

Graham, H. 1984. *Women, Health and the Family*. Brighton: Harvester Wheatsheaf.

Graham, H. 1991a. The concept of caring in feminist research: The case of domestic service. *Sociology* **25**, 61–78.

Graham, H. 1991b. Personal communication.

Graham, H. 1993. *Hardship and Health in Women's Lives*. London: Harvester Wheatsheaf.

Graham, H. & A. Oakley 1981. Competing ideologies of reproduction: Medical and maternal perspectives on pregnancy. In *Women, Health and Reproduction*, H. Roberts (ed.). London: Routledge.

Greve, J. 1971. *Homeless in London*. Edinburgh: Scottish Academic Press.

Gurin, G., J. Veroff & S. Field 1960. *Americans View Their Mental Health*. New York: Basic Books.

Haines, V. A. 1988. Social networks analysis, structuration theory and the holism – individualism debate. *Social Networks* **10**(2), 157–82.

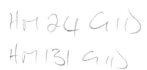

Hall, S. 1996. "Who Needs 'Identity'?". In *Questions of Cultural Identity*, S. Hall & P. du Gay (eds). London: Sage.

Hallett, C. (ed.) 1996. *Women and Social Policy: An Introduction*. Hemel Hempstead: Harvester Wheatsheaf.

Hamilton, S. & B. J. Fagot 1988. Chronic stress and coping styles: a comparison of male and female undergraduates. *Journal of Personality and Social Psychology* 55, 819–23.

Hammen, C. 1988. Self cognitions, stressful events and the prediction of depression in children of depressed mothers. *Journal of Abnormal Child Psychology* 16, 347–60.

Handy, J. A. 1991. The social context of occupational stress in a caring profession. *Social Science and Medicine* 32(7), 819–30.

Hanmer, J. 1978. *Violence and the Social Control of Women*. In *Power and the State*, G. Littlejohn, B. Smart, J. Wakeford & N. Yuval-Davis (eds). London: Croom Helm.

Hanmer, J. 1993. *Violence, Abuse and the Stress-coping Process*. Project 1. End of award report to the ESRC. Bradford: Violence, Abuse and Gender Relations Research Unit, University of Bradford.

Hanmer, J. 1995. *Patterns of Agency Contact with Women who have experienced violence from known men*. Bradford: Violence, Abuse and Gender Relations Research Unit, University of Bradford. University of Bradford. Research paper No. 12.

Hanmer, J. 1996. Women and violence: Commonalities and diversities. In *Violence and Gender Relations: Theories and Interventions*, B. Fawcett, B. Featherstone, J. Hearn & C. Toft (eds), 1–21. London: Sage.

Hanmer, J. 1998. Out of control: Men, violence and family life. In *Men, Gender Divisions and Welfare*, J. Popay, J. Hearn & J. Edwards (eds). London: Routledge.

Hanmer, J. & S. Saunders 1984. *Well-founded Fear: A Community Study of Violence to Women*. London: Hutchinson.

Hanmer, J. & S. Saunders 1993. *Women, Violence and Crime Prevention*. Aldershot: Avebury.

Harding, S. 1990. Feminism, science and the anti-enlightenment critiques. In *Feminism and Postmodernism*, L. Nicholson (ed.). London: Routledge.

Harrison, J. 1983. Women and ageing: Experience and implications. *Ageing and Society* 3(2), 209–35.

Hartmann, H. 1979. The unhappy marriage of Marxism and feminism. *Capital and Class* 8, 1–33.

Hartsock, N. C. M. 1983. *Money, Sex and Power: Towards a Feminist Historical Materialism*. Longman: New York.

Hartsock, N. C. M. 1989. Post-modernism and political change: Issues for feminist theory. *Cultural Critique* 14, 15–33.

Haynes, S. G., M. Feinleib & W. B. Kannel 1980. The relationship of psychosocial factors to coronary heart disease in the Framingham study; III. Eight-year incidence of coronary heart disease. *American Journal of Epidemiology* 3, 37–58.

Hearn, J. 1982. Notes on patriarchy, professionalisation and the semi-professions. *Sociology* 16, 184–202.

Hearn, J. 1983. *Birth and Afterbirth. A Materialist Account*. London: Achilles Heel.

Hearn, J. 1987. *The Gender of Oppression: Men, Masculinity and the Critique of Marxism*. Brighton: Wheatsheaf.

Hearn, J. 1992. *Men in the Public Eye*. London: Routledge.

Hearn, J. 1993. *Violence, Abuse and the Stress-coping Process, Project 2*. End of award report to the ESRC. Bradford: University of Bradford.

Hearn, J. 1994. The organization(s) of violence: men, gender relations, organizations and violences. *Human Relations* 47(b): 731–54.

Hearn, J. 1995a. *"It Just Happened" – A Research and Policy Report on Men's Violence to Known Women*. Bradford: Violence, Abuse and Gender Relations Research Unit, University of Bradford. Research Paper No. 6.

Hearn, J. 1995b. *Patterns of Agency Contacts With Men Who Have Been Violent To Known Women*. Bradford: Violence, Abuse and Gender Relations Research Unit, University of Bradford Research Paper No. 13.

Hearn, J. 1996. Men's violence to known women: Men's accounts and men's policy development. In *Violence and Gender Relations: Theories and Interventions*, B. Fawcett, B. Featherstone, J. Hearn & C. Toft (eds), 99–114. London: Sage.

Hearn, J. 1997. *The Violences of Men*. London: Sage.

Hearn, J. 1998. Men will be men: The ambiguity of men's support for men who have been violent to known women. See Popay, Hearn, Edwards (1998).

Hearn, J. & D. Collinson 1994. Theorizing unities and differences between men and between masculinities. In *Theorizing Masculinities*, H. Brod & M. Kaufman (eds), 97–118. Thousand Oaks, California: Sage.

Hearn, J. & W. Parkin 1993. Organisations, multiple oppressions and postmodernism. In *Postmodernism and Organisations*, J. Hassard & M. Parker (eds), 148–62. London: Sage.

Heather, N. 1976. *Radical Perspectives in Psychology*. London: Methuen.

Hedges, A. 1985. Group interviewing. In *Applied Quantitative Analysis*, A. Walker (ed.). Aldershot: Gower.

Heifetz, L. J. 1977. Professional preciousness and the evolution of parent training strategies. In *Research and Practice in Mental Retardation – Care and Prevention*, P. Mittler (ed.). Manchester: Manchester University Press.

Henwood, K. L. & N. F. Pidgeon 1992. Qualitative research and psychological theorizing. *British Journal of Psychology* **83**, 97–111.

Herbert, T. B., R. C. Silver & J. H. Ellard 1991. Coping with an abusive relationship: How and why do women stay? *Journal of Marriage and the Family* **53**, 311–25.

Hernes, H. M. 1987. *Welfare State and Woman Power*. Oslo: Norwegian University Press.

Hernes, H. M. 1988. The welfare state citizenship of Scandinavian women. In *The Political Interests of Gender, Developing Theory and Research with a Feminist Face*, K. B. Jones & A. G. Jonsdottir (eds), 187–213. London: Sage.

Higginbottom, T., M. Shipley & G. Rose 1982. Cigarettes, lung cancer and coronary heart disease: The effects of inhalation and tar yield. *Journal of Epidemiology and Community Health* **36**(2), 113–17.

Hill, S., U. Harries & J. Popay 1996. Is the Short Form 36 (SF-36) suitable for routine health outcomes assessment in health care for older people? Evidence from preliminary work in community based health services in England. *Journal of Epidemiology and Community Health* **50**: 94–8.

Ho, S., S. Donnan & A. Sham 1988. Psychosomatic symptoms, social support and self worth among the elderly in Hong Kong. *Journal of Epidemiology and Community Health* **42**, 377–82.

Hochschild, A. 1983. *The Managed Heart. The Commercialization of Human Feeling*. Berkeley, California: University of California Press.

Hollis, F. 1964. *Casework: A Psychosocial Therapy*. New York: Random House.

Holmes, T. H. & R. H. Rahe 1967. Social readjustment rating scales. *Journal of Psychosomatic Research* **11**, 213–18.

Holroyd, K. A. & R. S. Lazarus 1982. Stress, coping and somatic adaptation. In *Handbook of Stress*, L. Goldberger & S. Breznitz (eds). New York: Free Press.

Holter, H. (ed.) 1984. *Patriarchy in a Welfare Society*. Oslo: Universitetsforlaget.

REFERENCES

Homer, M., A. Leonard & P. Taylor 1984. *Private Violence: Public Shame*. Cleveland, Ohio: Cleveland Refuge and Aid for Women and Children.

Hornung, C. 1977. Social status, status inconsistency and psychological stress. *American Sociological Review* **42**, 213–18.

House, J. S., C. Robbins & H. L. Metzner 1982. The association of social relationships and activities with mortality: Prospective evidence from the Tecumseh County health study. *American Journal of Epidemiology* **116**, 123–40.

Howe, D. 1986. *Social Workers and their Practice in Welfare Bureaucracies*, Aldershot, England: Gower.

Hugman, R. 1991. *Power in Caring Professions*. Basingstoke: Macmillan.

Hunt, P. 1980. *Gender and Class Consciousness*. London: Macmillan.

Hutton, W. 1995. *The State We're In*. Jonathan Cape: London.

Jackson, B. & D. Marsden 1962. *Education and the Working Class*. London: Routledge and Kegan Paul.

Jackson, E. H. 1967. Status consistency and symptoms of stress. *American Sociological Review* **27**, 469–80.

Jacobson, D. 1989. Context and the sociological study of stress: An invited response to Pearlin. *Journal of Health and Social Behaviour* **30**, 257–60.

Jahoda, A., I. Markova, M. Cattermole 1988. Stigma and self-concept of people with a mild mental handicap. *Journal of Mental Deficiency Research* **32**, 103–13.

Jahoda, M. 1987. Unemployed men at work. In *Unemployed People: Social and Psychological Perspectives*, D. Fryer & P. Ullah (eds). Milton Keynes: Open University Press.

Johnson, B. K. & M. B. Kenkel 1991. Stress, coping and adjustment in female adolescent incest victims. *Child Abuse and Neglect* **15**, 293–305.

Jones, D. 1986. *Mortality Following Bereavement: Some Results from the OPCS Longitudinal Study*. Postgraduate Journal.

Jones, H. & J. Millar (eds) 1996. *Politics of the Family*. Aldershot: Avebury.

Jones, S. 1985a. *Depth interviewing*. See Walker (1985).

Jones, S. 1985b. *The analysis of depth interviews*. See Walker (1985).

Jordan, B. & N. Parton (eds) 1983. *The Political Dimensions of Social Work*. Oxford: Basil Blackwell.

Joshi, H. (ed.) 1989. *Changing Population in Britain*. Oxford: Blackwell.

Journal of Social Issues, 1988. (Special issue on the psychology of unemployment – individual and community responses) **44**, 4.

Kahn, R. L. 1973. Conflict, ambiguity and overload: Three elements in job stress. *Occupational Mental Health* **3**, 2–9.

Kahneman, D. P., A. Slovic & A. Tversky (eds) 1982. *Judgement Under Uncertainty: Heuristics and Biases*. Cambridge: Cambridge University Press.

Kanner, A. D., J. C. Coyne, C. Schaefer & R. S. Lazarus 1981. Comparison of two modes of stress measurement: daily hassles and uplifts versus major life events. *Journal of Behavioural Medicine* **4**(1), 1–39.

Kaplan, B. H., J. C. Cassel & S. Gore 1977. Social support and health. *Medical Care* **15**(5), 47–58.

Karasek, R. A., T. G. T. Theorell, J. Schwartz, C. Pieper & L. Alfredsson 1982. Job, psychological factors and coronary heart disease. In *Psychological Problems Before and After Myocardial Infarction*, H. Denolin (ed.). Basel: Karger.

Karno, M., R. L. Hough, M. A. Burnam, J. I. Escobar, D. M. Timbers, F. Santana & J. H. Boyd 1987. Lifetime prevalence of specific psychiatric disorders among Mexican Americans and non-hispanic whites in Los Angeles. *Archives of General Psychiatry* **44**, 695–701.

Karp, D. 1996. *Speaking of Sadness: Depression, Disconnection and the Meanings of Illness.* Oxford: Oxford University Press.

Kasl, S. V. 1987. Methodologies in stress and health: Past difficulties, present dilemmas, future directions. See Kasl and Cooper (1987).

Kasl, S.V. & C. L. Cooper (eds) 1987. Research Methods in Stress and Health Psychiatry. Chichester: John Wiley.

Katz, J. L., H. Weiner, T. G. Gallagher & L. Hellman 1970. Stress, distress and ego defenses. *Archives of General Psychiatry* **23**, 131–42.

Kelly, L. 1988. *Surviving Sexual Violence.* Cambridge: Polity Press.

Kessler, R. C. 1979. A strategy for studying differential vulnerability to the psychological consequences of stress. *Journal of Health and Social Behaviour* **20**, 100–8.

Kessler, R. C., J. B. Turner & J. S. House 1989. Unemployment, re-employment and emotional functioning in a community sample. *American Sociological Review* **54**, 648–57.

Kessler, R. C., R. H. Price & C. B. Wortman 1985. Social factors in psychopathology: Stress, social support, and coping processes. *Annual Review of Psychology* **36**, 531–72.

Kitzinger, C. 1987. *The Social Construction of Lesbianism.* London: Sage Publications.

Knuttila, M. 1987. *State Theories.* Toronto: Garamond.

Koeske, G. S. & R. D. Koeske 1990. Buffering aspects of social support on social stress. *American Journal of Ortho-Psychiatry* **60**(July), 440–51.

Krippendorf, K. 1980. *Content Analysis.* Beverly Hills, California: Sage.

Krueger, R. A. 1994. *Focus Groups.* Beverly Hills, California: Sage.

Lamb, M. E. 1983. Fathers of exceptional children. In *The Family and the Handicapped Child: Understanding and Treatment*, M. Seligman (ed.), 125–46. New York: Grune and Stratton.

Land, H. 1976. Women: Supporters or supported? In *Sexual Divisions and Society: Process and Change*, D. L. Barker & S. Allen (eds), 108–132. London: Tavistock.

Land, H. 1990. Time to care. In *Women's Issues in Social Policy*, M. Maclean & D. Groves (eds). London: Routledge.

Langan, M. & L. Day 1992. *Women, Oppression and Social Work: Issues in Antidiscriminatory Practice.* London: Routledge.

Lazarus, R. S. 1966. *Psychological Stress and the Coping Process.* New York: McGraw-Hill.

Lazarus, R. S. & S. Folkman 1984. Coping and adaptation. In *Handbook of Behavioural Medicine*, W. D. Gentry (ed.), 282–325. New York: The Guildford Press.

Leaf, P. J., M. M. Weissman, J. K. Myers, G. L. Tischler & C. E. Holzer 1984. Social factors related to psychiatric disorder: the Yale epidemiologic catchment area study. *Social Psychology* **19**, 53–61.

Lefcourt, H. M. 1973. The function of the illusions of control and freedom. *American Psychologist* **28**, 417–25.

Lefcourt, H. M. 1976. Locus of control and the response to aversive events. *Canadian Psychological Review* **17**, 202–9.

Leibfried, S. & P. Pierson 1995. *European Social Policy: Between Fragmentation and Integration.* Washington DC: Brookings Institute.

Lennon, M. C., J. L. Martin & L. Dean 1990. The influence of social support on AIDS-related grief reaction among gay men. *Social Science and Medicine* **31**(4), 477–84.

Leonard, P. 1997. *Postmodern Welfare.* London: Sage.

Levi, L. 1965. The urinary output of adrenalin and noradrenalin during pleasant and unpleasant emotional states. *Psychosomatic Medicine* **27**, 80–5.

Lewis, G. 1996. Black women's experience and social work. *Feminist Review* **53**, 24–56.

197

Lewis, J. 1992. Gender and the development of welfare regimes. *Journal of European Social Policy* **2**(3), 159–73.

Lewis, J. & B. Meredith 1988. *Daughters Who Care: Daughters Caring for Mothers at Home*. London: Routledge.

Lister, R. 1990. Women, economic dependency and citizenship. *Journal of Social Policy* **19**, 445–67.

Lister, R. 1992. *Women, Economic Dependency and Social Security*. Manchester: Equal Opportunities Commission.

Lonsdale, S. 1990. *Women and Disability: The Experience of Physical Disability Among Women*. London: Macmillan.

Lord, V., D. Gray & S. Pond 1991. The police stress inventory: Does it measure stress? *Journal of Criminal Justice* **19**, 139–49.

Lorde, A. 1984. *Sister Outsider*. New York: Crossing Press.

Loscocco, K. A. & G. Spitz 1990. Working conditions, social support and the well-being of male and female factory workers. *Journal of Health and Social Behaviour* **31**, 324–31.

Lynch, K. 1989. Solidarity labour: Its nature and marginalisation. *Sociological Review* **37**, 1–14.

Macdonald, G. & K. I. Macdonald 1995. Ethical issues in social work research. In *Ethical Issues in Social Work*, D. Smith & R. Hugman (eds). London: Routledge.

Macdonald, G., B. Sheldon & J. Gillespie (1992). Contemporary studies of the effectiveness of social work. *British Journal of Social Work* **22**, 615–42.

Macdonald, K. I. 1995. Comparative homicide and the proper aims of social work: A sceptical note. *British Journal of Social Work* **25**, 489–97.

MacKinnon, C. A. 1982. Feminism, Marxism, method and the state: An agenda of theory. *Signs* **7**, 515–44.

MacKinnon, C. A. 1983. Feminism, Marxism, method and the state: Towards feminist jurisprudence. *Signs* **8**, 635–58.

MacKinnon, C. A. 1987. *Feminism Unmodified. Discourses on Life and Law*. Cambridge, Massachusetts and London: Harvard University Press.

MacKinnon, C. A. 1989. *Towards a Feminist Theory of the State*. Cambridge, Massachusetts and London: Harvard University Press.

Madge, N. 1993. *Families at Risk*. London: Heinemann.

Malson, M. 1983. The social support system of black families. *Marriage and Family Review* **32**, 30–48.

Mama, A. 1989a. Violence sgainst black women: gender, race and state responses. *Feminist Review* **32**, 30–48.

Mama, A. 1989b. *The Hidden Struggle: Statutory and Voluntary Sector Responses to Violence against Black Women in the Home*. London: London Race and Housing Research Unit.

Marmot, M. G. & N. Madge 1987. An epidemiological perspective on stress and health. See Kasl & Cooper (1987).

Marmot, M. G., M. J. Shipley & G. Rose 1984. Inequalities in death – specific explanations of a general pattern?. *Lancet* **I**, 1003.

Marsh, P. & J. Triseliotis 1996. *Ready to Practise? Social Workers and Probation Officers: Their Training and First Year in Work*. Aldershot: Avebury.

Martin, D. 1976. *Battered Wives*. San Francisco, California: Glide Publications.

Mason, J. 1989. Reconstructing the public and the private: The home and marriage in later life. In *Home and Family: Creating the Domestic Sphere*, G. Allan & G. Crow (eds). London: Macmillan.

Mason, J. 1994. Linking qualitative and quantitative data. In *Analysing Qualitative Data*, A. Bryman & R. Burgess (eds). London: Routledge.

Mason, J. W., J. T. Maher, L. H. Hartley, E. Mougey, M. J. Perlow & L. G. Jones 1976. Selectivity of corticosteroid and catecholamine response to various natural stimuli. In *Psychopathology of Human Adaptation*, G. Serban (ed.). New York: Plenum.

Mayall, B. 1986. *Keeping Children Healthy*. London: Allen and Unwin.

Mays, N., N. Goodwin, G. Malbon, B. Leese, A. Mahon & S. Wyke 1998. *What were the achievements of Total Purchasing Pilots in their first year and how they can be explained*. Kings' Fund: London.

McCord, J. 1978. A thirty year follow up of treatment effects. *American Psychologist* **33**, 284–88.

McCord, J. 1981. Consideration of some effects of a counselling program. In *New Directions in the Rehabilitation of Criminal Offenders*, S. E. Martin, L. B. Sechrest & R. Redner (eds). Washington: National Academy Press.

McCrae, R. R. 1984. Situational determinants of coping responses: Loss, threat and challenge. *Journal of Personality and Social Psychology* **46**, 919–28.

McCubbin, H., C. B. Joy, A. E. Cauble, J. K. Comeau, J. M. Patterson & R. H. Needle 1980. Family stress and coping: A decade review. *Journal of Marriage and the Family*, November, 855–71.

McGuffin, P. & P. Bebbington 1988. The Camberwell collaborative depression study. III. Depression and adversity in the relatives of depressed patients. *British Journal of Psychology* **152**, 775–82.

McIntosh, M. 1978. The State and the oppression of women. In *Feminism and Materialism: Women and Modes of Production*, A. Kuhn & A. M. Wolpe (eds), 254–89. London: Routledge and Kegan Paul.

McKee, L. & C. Bell 1985. Marital and family relations in times of male unemployment. In *New Approaches to Economic Life*, B. Roberts, R. Finnegan & D. Gallie (eds), 387–99. Manchester: Manchester University Press.

McKee, L. & C. Bell 1986. His unemployment: Her problem. The domestic and marital consequences of male unemployment. In *The Experience of Unemployment*, S. Allen, K. Purcell, A. Watson & S. Wood (eds), 134–49. London: Macmillan.

McKee, L. & M. O'Brien 1983. Interviewing men: Taking gender seriously. In *The Public and the Private*, E. Gamarnikow, D. H. J. Morgan, J. Purvis & D. Taylorson (eds). London: Heinemann.

McLeod, J. D. & R. C. Kessler 1990. Socioeconomic status differences in vulnerability to undesirable life events. *Journal of Health and Social Behaviour* **31**(6), 162–72.

Meeks, S., L. L. Cartensen, B. Tamsky, T. Wright & D. Pellegrini 1989. Age differences in coping: Does less mean worse? *International Journal of Aging and Human Development* **28**(2), 127–40.

Merikangas, K. R. 1982. Assortative mating for psychiatric disorders and psychological traits. *Archives of General Psychiatry* **39**, 1173–80.

Millar, J. & C. Glendinning 1989. Gender and poverty. *Journal of Social Policy* **18**, 363–81.

Miller, J. B. 1976. *Toward a New Psychology of Women*. Boston, Massachusetts: Beacon Books.

Miller, S. 1983. *Men and Friendship*. London: Gateway.

Miller, W. B. 1962. The impact of a total community delinquency control project. *Social Problems* **Fall**, 168–91.

Millett, K. 1971. *Sexual Politics*. London: Sphere.

Mirza, H. 1992. *Young Female and Black*. London: Routledge.

199

Mitchell, R. E. & C. A. Hodson 1983. Coping with domestic violence: Social support and psychological health among battered women. *American Journal of Community Psychology* **11**(6), 629–54.

Monat, A. & R. S. Lazarus (eds) 1977. *Stress and Coping: An Anthology*. New York: Columbia University Press.

Moore, G. 1990. Stuctural determinants of men's and women's personal networks. *American Sociological Review* **October**, 726–35.

Morgan, M., D. Patrick & J. Charlton 1984. Social networks and psychological support among disabled people. *Social Science and Medicine* **19**(5), 489–97.

Morris, J. (ed.) 1989. *Able Lives: Women's Experiences of Paralysis*. London: The Women's Press.

Morris, J. 1991. *Pride Against Prejudice: Transforming Attitudes to Disability*. London: The Women's Press.

Morris, J. 1992. "Us" and "them"? Feminist research. In *Community Care: A Reader*, J. Bornat, C. Pereira, D. Pilgrim & F. Williams (eds). London: Macmillan.

Morris, J. 1993. *Independent Lives? Community Care and Disabled People*. London: Macmillan.

Morris, L. 1990. *The Workings of the Household*. Cambridge: Polity Press.

Morris, L. D. 1985. Renegotiation of the domestic division of labour in the context of male redundancy. In *New Approaches to Economic Life*, B. Roberts, R. Finnegan & D. Gallie (eds), 400–16. Manchester: Manchester University Press.

Moser, K. A., A. J. Fox, D. R. Jones & P. O. Goldblatt 1986. Unemployment and mortality: Further evidence from the OPCS Longitudinal Study 1979–81. *Lancet* **I**, 365–6.

Murgatroyd, S. & R. Woolfe 1982. *Coping with Crisis: Understanding and Helping People in Need*. London: Harper and Row.

Murphy, M. 1991. Pressure points. *Social Work Today* 13.6.91, 12–13.

Murray, C. 1990. *The Emerging British Underclass*. London: IEA Health and Welfare Unit.

Myers, J. K., M. M. Weissman, G. L. Tischler, C. E. Ilozer, P. J. Leaf, H. Oveschel, J. C. Anthory, J. H. Boyd, J. D. Burke Jr, M. Kramer & R. Stolzman 1984. Six month prevalence of psychiatric disorders in three communities. *Archives of General Psychiatry* **41**, 959–67.

NACRO 1991. *Race and Criminal Justice*, NACRO briefing. London: National Association for the Care and Resettlement of Offenders.

Nardi, P. L. 1992a. That's what friends are for: Friends as family in the lesbian and gay community. In *Modern Homosexualities: Fragments of Lesbian and Gay Experience*, K. Plummer (ed.). London: Routledge.

Nardi, P. L. (ed.) 1992b. *Men's Friendships*. Newbury Park, California: Sage.

Nasir, S. 1996. Race, gender and social policy. In *Women and Social Policy: An Introduction*, C. Hallett (ed.). Hemel Hempstead: Harvester Wheatsheaf.

Newmann, J. P. 1986. Gender, life strains and depression. *Journal of Health and Social Behaviour* **27**, 161–78.

NHS Executive 1992. *Local Voices: The Views of Local People on Purchasing for Health*. London: Department of Health.

Nichols, K. A. 1984. *Psychological Care in Physical Illness*. London: Croom Helm.

Nolen-Hoeksema, S. 1987. Sex differences in unipolar depression: Evidence and theory. *Psychology Bulletin* **10**(2), 259–82.

Nuckolls, K. B., J. Cassel & B. H. Kaplan 1972. Psychosocial assets, life crisis and the prognosis of pregnancy. *American Journal of Epidemiology* **95**, 431–41.

O'Brien, M. 1981. *The Politics of Reproduction*. London: Routledge and Kegan Paul.

Oakley, A. 1988a. Experimentation in social science: The case of health promotion. *Social Sciences in Health* **4**(2), 73–89.

Oakley, A. 1998b. Science, gender and women's liberation: an argument against post-modernism. *Women's Studies International Forum* **21**(2), 133–46.

Oakley, A. (forthcoming). Gender, methodology and people's ways of knowing: some problems with feminism and the paradigm debate in social science. *Sociology*.

Oakley, A. 1974. *Housewife*. London: Penguin.

Oakley, A. 1980. *Women Confined: Towards a Sociology of Childbirth*. Oxford: Martin Robertson.

Oakley, A. 1981. Interviewing women: A contradiction in terms. In *Doing Feminist Research*, H. Roberts (ed.). London: Routledge and Kegan Paul.

Oakley, A. 1982. *Subject Women*. London: Fontana.

Oakley, A. 1985. *Sex, Gender and Society*. Aldershot: Gower.

Oakley, A., 1989. Who's afraid of the randomised controlled trial? Some dilemmas of the scientific method and good research practice. *Women and Health* **15**, 25–59.

Oakley, A. 1992a. *Social Support and Motherhood: The Natural History of a Research Project*. Oxford: Basil Blackwell.

Oakley, A. 1992b. Social support in pregnancy: methodology and findings of a 1 year follow-up study. *Journal of Reproductive and Infant Psychology*. **10**: 219–31.

Oakley, A. & J. Ashton 1997 (eds). *The Gift Relationship Revisited*. Harmondsworth: Penguin.

Oakley, A. & D. Fullerton 1996. The lamp-post of research: Support or illumination? In *Evaluating Social Interventions*, A. Oakley and H. Roberts (eds). Essex: Barnado's.

Oakley, A. & L. Rajan 1990. Obstetric technology and maternal emotional wellbeing: A further research note. *Journal of Reproductive and Infant Psychology*. **8**: 45–55.

Oakley, A. & L. Rajan 1991. Social class and social support: The same or different? *Sociology* **25**(1), 31–59.

Oakley, A. & H. Roberts (eds) 1996. *Evaluating Social Interventions*. Essex: Barnado's.

Oakley, A., D. Hickey & L. Rajan 1996. Social support in pregnancy: Does it have long-term effects? *Journal of Reproductive and Infant Psychology*. **14**: 7–22.

Oakley, A., L. Rajan & A. Grant 1990. Social support and pregnancy outcome: Report of a randomized trial. *British Journal of Obstetrics and Gynaecology* **97**, 155–62.

Oakley, A., A. Rigby & D. Hickey 1993. Women and children last? Class, health and the role of the maternal and child health services. *European Journal of Public Health* **3**(4).

Oakley, A., M. Mauthner, L. Rajan & H. Turner 1994. *An Evaluation of NEWPIN*. London: Social Science Research Unit.

Oates, R. K. & D. C. Bross 1995. What have we learned from treating physical abuse? *Child Abuse and Neglect* **19**, 463–73.

Oliver, M. 1990. *The Politics of Disablement: Critical Texts in Social Work and the Welfare State*. London: Macmillan.

Oliver, M. (ed.) 1991. *Social Work – Disabled People and Disabling Environments*. London: Jessica Kingsley.

Oliver, M. 1996. *Understanding Disability*. London: Jessica Kingsley.

Oliver, S. 1995. How can health service users contribute to the NHS research and development programme? *British Medical Journal* **310**: 1318–20.

Olsen, O., L. Iverson & S. Sabroe 1991. Age and the operationalisation of social support. *Social Science and Medicine* **32**(7), 767–71.

Oppenheim, C. 1990. *Poverty: The Facts*. London: Child Poverty Action Group.

Oremland, E. K. 1988. Work dynamics in family care of haemophilic children. *Social Science and Medicine* **26**(4), 467–75.

Orens, L. 1979. The welfare of labouring women, 1860–1950. *Feminist Studies* **5**, Spring.

Orlinsky, D. E., K. Grawe & B. K. Parkes 1995. Process and outcome in psychotherapy. In *Handbook of Psychotherapy and Behaviour Change*, A. E. Bergin & S. L. Garfield (eds). New York: John Wiley.

Osmond, C., D. J. P. Barker & J. M. Slattery 1990. Risk of death from cardiovascular disease and chronic bronchitis determined by place of birth in England and Wales. *Journal of Epidemiology and Community Health* **44**, 139–41.

Pagel, M. D., W. W. Erdly & J. Becker 1987. Social networks: We get by with (and in spite of) a little help from our friends. *Journal of Personality and Social Psychology* **53**, 793–804.

Pahl, J. 1980. Patterns of money management. *Journal of Social Policy* **9**, 313–35.

Painter, N. 1995. *Soul Murder: African-American Slave Families*. Paper presented to the xviiith Congress of Historical Studies, Montreal.

Paley, J. 1990. *Training Manual for Child Abuse Consultants*. London: NSPCC.

Palmer, A. 1993. Guilty when proved innocent. *The Spectator*, August, 9–10.

Parker, G. 1989. *A Study of Non-Elderly Spouse Carers: Final Report*. York: Social Policy Research Unit.

Parker, G. 1990. *With Due Care and Attention: A Review of Research on Informal Care*. London: Family Policy Studies Centre.

Parker, G. 1992. *With This Body: Caring and Disability in Marriage*. Buckingham: Open University Press.

Parker, G. & J. Seymour 1998. Male carers in marriage: re-examining the feminist analysis of informal care. In *Men, Gender Divisions and Welfare*, J. Popay, J. Hearn & J. Edwards (eds). London: Routledge.

Parker, R. 1986. Fathers, families and support systems. Their role in the development of at-risk and retarded infants and children. In *Families of Handicapped Persons: Research, Programs and Policy Issues*, J. J. Gallagher & P. M. Vietze (eds), 101–13. Baltimore, Maryland: Paul H. Brooks Publications.

Parry, G. 1986. Paid employment, life events, social support and mental health in working-class mothers. *Journal of Health and Social Behaviour* **27**, 193–208.

Pascall, G. 1986. *Social Policy: A Feminist Analysis*. London: Tavistock.

Patton, M. Q. 1990. 2nd Edition. *Qualitative Evaluation and Research Methods*. London: Sage.

Paykel, E. S. 1983. Methodological aspects of life events research. *Journal of Psychosomatic Research* **27**, 341–52.

Payne, R. & J. Firth 1987. *Stress in Health Professionals*. Chichester: John Wiley.

Payne, S. 1991. *Women, Health and Poverty*. London: Harvester Wheatsheaf.

Peace, S. 1990 (ed.). *Social Gerontology: The Research Process*. London: Sage.

Pearlin, L. I. 1982. The social contexts of stress. In *Handbook of Stress – Theoretical and Clinical Aspects*, L. Goldberger & S. Breznitz (eds), 367–79. New York: The Free Press.

Pearlin, L. I. 1983. Role strains and personal stress. In *Psychosocial Stress: Trends in Theory and Research*, H. B. Kaplan (ed.), 3–32. New York: Academic Press.

Pearlin, L. I. 1989. The sociological study of stress. *Journal of Health and Social Behaviour* **30**, 241–56.

Pearlin, L. & C. Aneshensel 1986. Coping and social supports: Their functions and applications. In *Applications of Social Science to Clinical Medicine and Health*, L. H. Aiken & D. Mechanic (eds). New Brunswick, New Jersey: Rutgers University Press.

Pearlin, L. & M. A. Lieberman 1978. Social sources of emotional distress. *Research in Community and Mental Health* **1**, 217–48, R. Simmons (ed.). Greenwich Connecticut: JA1.

Pearlin, L. I. & Schooler, C. 1978. The structure of coping. *Journal of Health and Social Behaviour* **19**, 2–21.

Pearlin, L. I. & H. Turner 1987. The family as a context of the stress process. In *Research Issues in Stress and Health Psychiatry*, S. V. Kasl & C. L. Cooper (eds). 143–65. Chichester: John Wiley.

Pearlin, L. I., M. A. Lieberman, E. G. Menaghan & J. T. Mullan 1981. The stress process. *Journal of Health and Social Behaviour* **December**, 337–35.

Pearson, G. 1989. Women and men without work: The political economy is personal. In *The Haunt of Misery: Critical Essays*, C. Rojek, G. Pearson & S. Collins (eds). London: Routledge.

Pearson, M., C. Dawson, H. Moore & S. Spencer 1993. Health on borrowed time? Prioritizing and meeting needs in low-income households. *Health and Social Care in the Community* **1**, 45–54.

Perlman, H. 1957. *Casework: A Problem-Solving Approach*. Chicago, Illinois: University of Chicago Press.

Phoenix, A. 1991. *Young Mothers*. Cambridge: Polity Press.

Piper, C. 1995. *Marketing the Children Act 1989: The Invisibility of Mothers and Fathers*. Paper presented to the Social Policy Association Annual Conference (18 July), Sheffield Hallam University.

Plachta, J. 1992. Talking the same language. In *The Guardian*, 11 February.

Popay, J. & G. Williams (eds) 1994. *Researching the People's Health*. London: Routledge.

Popay, J., J. Hearn & J. Edwards (eds) 1998. *Men, Gender Divisions and Welfare*. London: Routledge.

Post, R. M., D. R. Rubinow & J. C. Bellenger 1986. Condemning and sensitization in the longitudinal course of affective illness. *British Journal of Psychology* **149**, 191–201.

Pouchaud, F. 1977. *Approaches to the Khmer Mentality*. Washington, DC: Published through Pastoral Care of Migrants and Refugees.

Ptacek, J. 1988. Why do men batter their wives? In *Feminist Perspectives on Wife Abuse*, K. Yllö & M. Bograd (eds). Beverly Hills, California: Sage.

Quinton, D. & M. Rutter 1988. *Parenting Breakdown*. Aldershot: Avebury.

Quittner, A. L., R. L. Gluekauf & D. N. Jackson 1990. Chronic parenting stress: Moderating versus mediating effects of social support. *Journal of Personality and Social Psychology* **59**(6), 1266–78.

Qureshi, H. 1990. The concept and measurement of social support. In S. Peace (ed.) *Social Gerontology: The Research Process*. London: Sage.

Rachman, S. J. & G. T. Wilson 1980. *The Effects of Psychological Therapy*. Oxford: Pergamon Press.

Ramazanoglu, C. 1988. *Feminism and the Contradictions of Oppression*. London: Routledge.

Raymond, J. 1986. *A Passion for Friends: Towards a Philosophy of Female Affection*. Boston, Massachusetts: Beacon Press.

Reiner, B. S. & I. Kaufmann 1969. *Character Disorders in Parents of Delinquents*. New York: Family Service Association of America.

Renne, K. S. 1974. Measurement of social health in a general population survey. *Social Science Research* **3**, 25–44.

Richards, L. & T. Richards 1994. From filing cabinet to computer. In *Analysing Qualitative Data*, A. Bryman & R. Burgess. London: Unwin Hyman.

Riessman, C. K. 1989. Life events, meaning and narrative: The case of infidelity and divorce. *Social Science and Medicine* **29**(6), 743–51.

Riessman, C. K. 1990. *Divorce Talk*. New Brunswick, New Jersey: Rutgers University Press.

Ritchie, J. & L. Spencer 1994. Qualitative data analysis for applied policy research. See Bryman & Burgess, 1994.

Roberts, H. (ed.) 1981. *Women, Health and Reproduction*. London: Routledge and Kegan Paul.

Roberts, H. 1979. Book review. In *Women's Studies International Quarterly* 2, 129–30.

Robinson, R. & J. Le Grand (eds) 1994. *Evaluating the NHS Reforms*. Hermitage: Policy Journals.

Rogers, A. & H. Elliott 1997. *Primary Care: Understanding Health Need and Demand*. London: Radcliffe Press.

Rogers, C. R. 1951. *Client-centred Therapy: Its Current Practice, Implications and Theory*. Boston, Massachusetts: Houghton, Mifflin.

Rojek, C., G. Peacock & S. Collins (eds) 1988. *Social Work and Received Ideas*. London: Routledge.

Rosario, M., M. Shin, H. Morch & C. B. Huckabee 1988. Gender differences in coping and social supports; Testing socialization and role constraint theories. *Journal of Community Psychology* (Special Issue, Women in the Community) 16(1), 55–69.

Rose, H. 1983. Hand, brain and heart: A feminist epistemology for the natural sciences. *Signs* 9, 73–90.

Rosenfeld, S. 1989. The effects of women's employment: Personal control and sex differences in mental health. *Journal of Health and Social Behaviour* 30, 77–91.

Ross, C. E. & J. Mirowsky 1989. Explaining the social patterns of depression; Control and problem-solving – or support and talking? *Journal of Health and Social Behaviour* 30(June), 206–19.

Rowbotham, S. 1979. The trouble with patriarchy. *New Statesman 98*. **December** 970–1.

Roys, P. 1988. Social services. In *Britain's Black Population*, A. Bhat, R. Carr-Hill & S. Ohri (eds). (Second edn). Aldershot: Gower.

Rutter, M. 1987. Psychosocial resilience and protective mechanisms. *American Journal of Orthopsychiatry* 57, 316–31.

Sainsbury, D. 1994. *Gendering Welfare States*. London: Sage.

Schaefer, C., J. C. Coyne & R. S. Lazarus 1981. The health-related functions of social support. *Journal of Behavioural Medicine* 5(4), 381–405.

Scheff, T. 1966. *Being Mentally Ill*. Chicago: Aldine.

Scott, J. 1986. Gender: A Useful Category of Historical Analysis. *American Historical Review* 91(5), 1053–75.

Scott, R. 1970. *The Making of a Blind Man*. Basic Books, New York.

Scott-Samuel, A. 1980. Why don't they want our health services? *Lancet*, 23 February, 412–3.

Segal, J. 1988. Utilization of stress and coping research: Issues of public education and public policy. In *Stress, coping and development in children*, N. Garmezy & M. Rutter (eds), 303–34. Baltimore: The John Hopkins University Press.

Seligman, M. E. P. 1975. *Helplessness: On Development and Death*. San Francisco: W. H. Freeman.

Selye, H. 1976. *The Stress of Life*. (Rev. edn). New York: McGraw-Hill.

Selye, H. 1982. History and present status of the stress concept. In *Handbook of Stress: Theoretical and Clinical Aspects*, L. Goldberger & S. Breznitz (eds), 7–17. New York: The Free Press.

Seymour, J. 1994. *The Negotiation of Coping: Disablement, Caring and Marriage*. End-of-Award Report to the Economic and Social Research Council, May 1994.

Seymour, J., G. Dix & T. Eardley 1996. *Joint Accounts: Methodology and Practice in Research Interviews with Couples.* York: Social Policy Research Unit Report no. 4.

Seymour, J. (forthcoming). Using gendered discourses in negociations: couples and the onset of disablement in marriage. In *Gender, Power and the Household*, L. Mekie, L. S. Bowlby & S. Gregory (eds). London: Macmillan.

Shakespeare, T., K. Gillespie-Sells & D. Davies 1996. *The Sexual Politics of Disability.* London: Cassell.

Sharpe, S. 1984. *Double Identity: The Lives of Working Mothers.* London: Penguin.

Sheldon, B. 1978. Theory and practice in social work: A re-examination of a tenuous relationship. *British Journal of Social Work* **8**, 1–22.

Showalter, E. 1987. *The Female Malady: Women, Madness and English Culture, 1830–1980.* London: Virago.

Shrout, P. E., B. G. Link, B. P. Dohrenwend, A. E. Skodol, A. Stuerve & J. Mirotznik 1989. Chronic life events as risk factors for depression: The role of fateful events. *Journal of Abnormal Psychology* **98**(4), 460–467.

Silverman, D. 1993. *Interpreting Qualitative Data.* London: Sage.

Skrabanek, P. 1990. Why is preventive medicine exempted from ethical constraints? *Journal of Medical Ethics* **16**: 187–90.

Slavin, L. A. & K. L. Rainer, M. L. McCreary & K. K. Gowda 1991. Towards a multicultural model of the stress process. *Journal of Counselling and Development* **70**, Sept./Oct, 156–63.

Smart, C. 1991. The legal and moral ordering of child custody. *Journal of Law and Society*, **18**(4): 485–500.

Smith, D. 1987. The limits of positivism in social work research. *British Journal of Social Work.*

Smith, J. A. 1995. Semi-structured interviewing and qualitative analysis. See Smith et al. 1995.

Smith, J. A. 1995b. Repertory grids: an interactive case study perspective. See Smith et al. 1995.

Smith, J. A., R. Harre & L. V. Langenhove (eds) 1995. *Rethinking Methods in Psychology.* London: Sage.

Snyder, D. K. & S. Scheer 1981. Predicting adjustment following brief residence at a shelter for battered women. *American Journal of Community Psychology* **9**, 559–66.

Social Care and Research Seminar 1986. *On Researching the Topic of "Care".* Studies in Sexual Politics 11. University of Manchester: Department of Sociology.

Social Work Today 13.6.91: 12–7.

Southall Black Sisters 1990. *Against the Grain. Southall Black Sisters 1919–1989.* London: Southall Black Sisters.

Stacey, M. 1982. *Masculine or Feminine Powers? Action in the Public Domain.* Paper presented to International Sociological Association Annual Conference, Mexico. August. University of Warwick: Mimeo.

Stanley, L. 1984. Should "sex" really be "gender" – or "gender" really be "sex"? In *Applied Sociological Perspectives*, R. J. Anderson & W. W. Sharrock (eds), 1–19. London: Allen and Unwin.

Stern, J. 1981. *Unemployment and Its Impact on Morbidity and Mortality.* Discussion Paper No. 93, Centre for Labour Economics, London School of Economics.

Stetz, K. M., F. M. Lewis & J. Primomo 1986. Family coping strategies and chronic illness in the mother. *Family Relations* **35**, 515–22.

Stewart, M. J. 1989. Social support: Diverse theoretical perspectives. *Social Science and Medicine* **28**(12), 1275–82.

Stoltenberg, J. 1990. *Refusing to be a Man: Essays on Sex and Justice*. New York: Meridian/ Penguin.

Stone, A. A., R. C. Kessler & J. A. Haythornthwaite 1991. Measuring daily events and experiences: Decisions for the researcher. *Journal of Personality* **59**(3), 575–607.

Straus, M. A. 1978. A sociological perspective on the prevention and treatment of wife-beating. In *Battered Women: A Psychosociological Study of Domestic Violence*, M. Roy (ed.). New York: Van Nostrand Reinhold.

Straus, M. A. & G. Hotaling (eds) 1980. *The Social Causes of Husband-Wife Violence*. Minneapolis, Minnesota: University of Minnesota Press.

Strauss, A. 1987. *Qualitative Analysis for Social Scientists*. Cambridge: Cambridge University Press.

Straw, P. & S. Kendrick 1988. The subtlety of strategies: Towards an understanding of the meaning of family life stories. *Life Stories* **4**, 36–47.

Taylor, D. (forthcoming). Social identity and social policy: Engagements with postmodern theory. *Journal of Social Policy*.

Taylor, J. T., L. M. Chatters, M. B. Tucker & E. Lewis 1990. Developments in research on black families: A decade review. *Journal of Marriage and the Family* **52**, 993–1014.

Taylor, R & G. Ford 1983. Inequalities in old age: An examination of age, sex and class differences in a sample of community elderly. *Ageing and Society* **3**(2), 183–208.

The Observer, 1995. Sick pay price as doctors put faith in hunches. 5/2/98.

Thoits, P. A. 1983. Dimensions of life events that influence psychological distress: An evaluation and synthesis of the literature. In *Psychological Stress: Trends in Theory and Research*, H. B. Kaplan (ed.), 33–103. New York: Academic Press.

Thoits, P. A. 1994. Stressors and problem solving: The individual as psychological activist. *Journal of Health and Social Behaviour* **35**, 143–59.

Thoits, P. A. 1995. Stress, coping and social support processes: Where are we? what next? *Journal of Health and Social Behaviour*, 53–79.

Thomas, W. I. & F. Znaniecki 1958. *The Polish Peasant in Europe and America*. (Second edn). New York: 6.

Thompson, E. P. 1963. *The Making of the English Working Class*. Harmondsworth: Penguin.

Thomson, E. P. 1971. Harold Wilson: *The Labour Government, 1964–70*: A review, *New Society*, 29 July.

Titmuss, R. 1971. *The Gift Relationship*. London: Allen and Unwin.

Titterton, M. 1989. *The Management of Personal Welfare*. University of Glasgow: Department of Social Administration and Social Work.

Titterton, M. 1992. Managing threats to welfare: The search for a new paradigm. *Journal of Social Policy* **21**(1), 1–23.

Titterton, M. 1996. Personal communication.

Torkington, N. P. K. 1991. *Black Health – A Political Issue; The Health and Race Project*. Liverpool: Liverpool Institute of Higher Education and Catholic Association for Racial Justice.

Townsend, P. 1962. *The Last Refuge*. London: Routledge and Kegan Paul.

Townsend, P. 1981. The structured dependency of the elderly: A creation of social policy in the twentieth century. *Ageing and Society* **1**, 5–28.

Tudor-Hart, J. 1971. The inverse care law. *Lancet*. 27 February, 405–12.

Turner, R. J. 1983. Direct, indirect and moderating effects of social support on psychological distress and associated conditions. In *Psychological Stress: Trends in Theory and Research*, H. B. Kaplan (ed.), 105–55. New York: Academic Press.

Turner, R. J. & W. R. Avison 1992. Innovations in the measurement of life stress: Crisis theory and the significance of event resolution. *Journal of Health and Social Behaviour* **33**: 36–50.

Turner, R. Z. & S. Noh 1983. Class and psychological vulnerability among women: The significance of social support and personal control. *Journal of Health and Social Behaviour* **24**, 2–15.

Twigg, J. & K. Atkin 1991. *Evaluating Support to Informal Carers (Part 2)*: Final Report. University of York: Social Policy Research Unit.

Twigg, J., K. Atkin & C. Perring 1990. *Evaluating Support to Informal Carers (Part 1)*: Final Report. University of York: Social Policy Research Unit.

Uehava, E. 1990. Dual exchange theory, social networks and informal social support. *American Journal of Sociology* **96**(3), November, 521–57.

Ulbrich, P. M., G. J. Warheit & R. S. Zimmerman 1989. Race, socioeconomic status, and psychological distress: An examination of differential vulnerability. *Journal of Health and Social Behaviour* **30**, 131–46.

Ullah, P. 1987. Unemployed black youths in a northern city. In *Unemployed People: Social and Psychological Perspectives*. D. Fryer & P. Ullah 1987 (eds). Milton Keynes: Open University Press.

Ungerson, C. 1987. *Policy is Personal; Sex, Gender and Informal Care*. London: Tavistock.

Ungerson, C. (ed.) 1990. *Gender and Caring*. Brighton, Sussex: Harvester, Wheatsheaf.

Ursel, J. 1986. The state and the maintenance of patriarchy: a case study of the family, labour and welfare legislation in Canada. In *Family, Economy and the State*, J. Dickinson & B. Russel (eds). London: Croom Helm.

Ussher, J. 1991. *Women's Madness: Misogyny or Mental Illness?* Hemel Hempstead: Harvester Wheatsheaf.

Ussher, J. 1996. Putting the pleasure back into sex. *New Scientist* **2015**, 41.

Ventura, J., K. H. Nuechterlein, D. Lukoff & J. P. Hardesty 1989. A prospective study of stressful life events and schizophrenic relapse. *Journal of Abnormal Psychology* **4**, 407–11.

Vingerhoets, A. J. & G. L. Van Heck 1990. Gender, coping and psychosomatic symptoms. *Psychological Medicine* **20**(1), 125–35.

Vogler, C. 1989. *Labour Market Change and Patterns of Financial Allocation Within Households*. Nuffield College, Oxford: ESRC/SCELI working paper 12.

Voysey, M. 1975. *A Constant Burden: The Reconstitution of Family Life*. London: Routledge and Kegan Paul.

Walby, S. 1986. *Patriarchy at Work*. Cambridge: Polity Press.

Walby, S. 1988. Gender politics and social theory. *Sociology* **22**, 25–32.

Walby, S. 1990. *Theorising Patriarchy*. Oxford: Blackwell.

Walker, A. (ed.) 1985. *Applied Qualitative Analysis*. Aldershot: Gower.

Walker, L. E. 1979. *The Battered Woman*. New York: Harper & Row.

Walters, V. 1993. Stress, anxiety and depression: women's accounts of their mental health problems. *Social Science and Medicine* **36**(4), 393–402.

Waltz, M., B. Badura, H. Pfaff & T. Schott 1988. Marriage and the psychological consequences of a heart attack: A longitudinal study of adaptation to chronic illness after three years. *Social Science and Medicine* **27**(2), 149–58.

Wamboldt, F., P. Steinglass & A. Kaplan de Nour 1991. Coping within couples: Adjustment two years after forced geographic relocation. *Family Press* **30**, 347–61.

Wan, T. T. H. 1982. *Stressful Life-Events, Social-Support Networks and Gerontological Health*. Lexington, Mass.: D C Heath & Co.

Warr, P. B., M. Banks & P. Ullah 1985. The experience of unemployment among black and white urban teenagers. *British Journal of Psychology* **76**, 75–87.

Webster, C. 1994. Conservatives and Consensus: The politics of the National Health Service, 1951–1964. In *The Politics of the Welfare State*, A. Oakley & S. Williams (eds), 54–74. London: UCL Press.

Weeks, J., C. Donovan & B. Heaphy 1996. *Families of Choice: Patterns of Non-Heterosexual Relationships. A Literature Review.* London: South Bank University School of Education Politics and Social Science, Research Paper.

Wenger, G. C. 1984. *The Supportive Network: Coping with Old Age*, 305–26. London: Allen and Unwin.

Werner, E. E. 1989. High-risk children in young adulthood: A longitudinal study from birth to 32 years. *American Journal of Orthopsychiatry* **59**, 72–81.

West, P. 1981. From bad to worse: People's experience and stereotypes of epilepsy. In *Perspectives on Epilepsy*, S. McGovern (ed.). Crowthorne: British Epilepsy Association.

West, P. 1990. The status and validity of accounts obtained at interview: A contrast of two studies of families with a disabled child. *Social Science and Medicine* **30**(11), 1229–39.

West, R. R. & D. A. Evans 1986. Lifestyle change in long term survivors of acute myocardial infarction. *Journal of Epidemiology and Community Health* **40**(2), 103–9.

Wheaton, B. 1983. Stress, personal coping resources and psychiatric symptoms: An investigation of interactive models. *Journal of Health and Social Behaviour* **24**, 208–29.

White, M. 1997. Harman tussle with sidekick, *The Guardian*, 20 November, p. 12.

Wilkinson, G. 1991. Stress – another chimera. *British Medical Journal* **302**, 6770, 191–2.

Wilkinson, R. 1996. *Unhealthy Societies: "The Afflictions of Inequality"*. London: Routledge.

Wilkinson, S. & C. Kitzinger 1993 (eds). *Hetero Sexuality*. London: Sage.

Williams, F. 1989. *Social Policy: A Critical Introduction, Issues of Race, Gender and Class*. Cambridge: Polity Press.

Williams, F. 1992a. Somewhere Over the Rainbow: Universality and diversity in social policy. In *Social Policy Review*, N. Manning & R. Page (eds). Social Policy and Administration.

Williams, F. 1992b. Women with learning difficulties are women too. In *Women Oppression and Social Work*, M. Langan & L. Day (eds). London: Routledge.

Williams, F. 1995. Race/ethnicity, gender and class in welfare states: A framework for comparative analysis. *Social Politics: International Studies in Gender, State and Society* **2**(2), 127–59.

Williams, F. 1996. Postmodernism, feminism, and the question of difference. In *Social Theory, Social Change and Social Work*, N. Parton (ed.). London: Routledge.

Williams, F. 1998. Troubled masculinities in social policy discourses: Fatherhood. In *Men, Gender Divisions and Welfare*, J. Popay, J. Hearn & J. Edwards (eds). London: Routledge.

Williams, G. & J. Popay 1994. Lay knowledge and the privilege of experience. In *Challenging Medicine*, J. Gabe, D. Kelleher & G. Williams (eds). London: Routledge.

Williams, G. H., J. Popay & P. Bissell 1995. Public health risks in a material world: barriers to social movements in health. In *Medicine, Health and Risk*, J. Gabe (ed.) Oxford: Blackwell, 67–90.

Williams, G. H. 1984. The genesis of chronic illness: Narrative reconstruction. *Sociology of Health and Illness* **6**, 175–200.

Willmott, P. 1986. *Social Networks and Informal Care and Public Policy*. London: Policy Studies Institute.

Willmott, P. 1987. *Friendship Networks and Social Support*. London: Policy Studies Institute.

Willmott, P. & M. Young 1960. *Family and Class in a London Suburb*. London: Routledge and Kegan Paul.

Wilson, E. 1978. *Women and the Welfare State*. London: Tavistock.

Wilson, H. S. 1989. Family care-giving for a relative with Alzheimer's dementia: Coping with negative choices. *Nursing Research* **38**(2), 94–104.

Wootton, B. 1959. *Social Science and Social Pathology*. London: Allen & Unwin.

Yllö, K. 1988. Political and methodological debates in wife abuse research. In *Feminist Perspectives on Wife Abuse*, K. Yllö & M. Bograd (eds). Beverly Hills, California: Sage.

Yllö, K. & M. Bograd (eds) 1988. *Feminist Perspectives on Wife Abuse*. Beverly Hills, California: Sage.

Young, A. 1980. The discourse on stress and the reproduction of conventional knowledge. *Social Science and Medicine* **14**, 133–46.

Young, M. & P. Willmott 1957. *Family and Kinship in East London*. London: Routledge & Kegan Paul.

Zvonkovic, A. M., T. Guss & L. Ladd 1988. Making the most of job loss: Individual and marital features of underemployment. *Family Relations* **37**, 56–61.

Index